Advanced Integrated Approaches to Environmental Economics and Policy:

Emerging Research and Opportunities

Sebastiano Patti
University of Catania, Italy

Giampiero Trizzino
Regional Council of Environment and Territory, Italy

A volume in the Advances
in Finance, Accounting, and
Economics (AFAE) Book Series

IGI Global
DISSEMINATOR OF KNOWLEDGE

Published in the United States of America by
IGI Global
Business Science Reference (an imprint of IGI Global)
701 E. Chocolate Avenue
Hershey PA, USA 17033
Tel: 717-533-8845
Fax: 717-533-8661
E-mail: cust@igi-global.com
Web site: http://www.igi-global.com

Library of Congress Cataloging-in-Publication Data

Names: Patti, Sebastiano, 1967- editor. | Trizzino, Giampiero, 1977- editor.
Title: Advanced integrated approaches to environmental economics and policy : emerging research and opportunities / Sebastiano Patti and Giampiero Trizzino, editors.
Description: Hershey, PA : Business Science Reference, [2019] | Summary: "This book examines environmental economics and policy and the strategic role of environmental issues on the global economy"-- Provided by publisher.
Identifiers: LCCN 2019003637 | ISBN 9781522595625 (hardcover) | ISBN 9781522595649 (ebook) | ISBN 9781522595632 (softcover)
Subjects: LCSH: Environmental economics. | Economic policy. | Consumer behavior.
Classification: LCC HC79.E5 A347 2019 | DDC 333.7--dc23
LC record available at https://lccn.loc.gov/2019003637

This book is published in the IGI Global book series Advances in Finance, Accounting, and Economics (AFAE) (ISSN: 2327-5677; eISSN: 2327-5685)

British Cataloguing in Publication Data
A Cataloguing in Publication record for this book is available from the British Library.

Advances in Finance, Accounting, and Economics (AFAE) Book Series

ISSN:2327-5677
EISSN:2327-5685

Editor-in-Chief: Ahmed Driouchi, Al Akhawayn University, Morocco

MISSION

In our changing economic and business environment, it is important to consider the financial changes occurring internationally as well as within individual organizations and business environments. Understanding these changes as well as the factors that influence them is crucial in preparing for our financial future and ensuring economic sustainability and growth.

The **Advances in Finance, Accounting, and Economics (AFAE)** book series aims to publish comprehensive and informative titles in all areas of economics and economic theory, finance, and accounting to assist in advancing the available knowledge and providing for further research development in these dynamic fields.

COVERAGE

- Fiscal Policy
- Finance
- Economics of Innovation and Knowledge
- Development Economics
- Stock Market
- Economics Geography
- Economics of Migration and Spatial Mobility
- E-Accounting
- Applied Finance
- Borrowing and Lending

IGI Global is currently accepting manuscripts for publication within this series. To submit a proposal for a volume in this series, please contact our Acquisition Editors at Acquisitions@igi-global.com or visit: http://www.igi-global.com/publish/.

The Advances in Finance, Accounting, and Economics (AFAE) Book Series (ISSN 2327-5677) is published by IGI Global, 701 E. Chocolate Avenue, Hershey, PA 17033-1240, USA, www.igi-global.com. This series is composed of titles available for purchase individually; each title is edited to be contextually exclusive from any other title within the series. For pricing and ordering information please visit http://www.igi-global.com/book-series/advances-finance-accounting-economics/73685. Postmaster: Send all address changes to above address.

Titles in this Series

For a list of additional titles in this series, please visit:
https://www.igi-global.com/book-series/advances-finance-accounting-economics/73685

Financial Technology and Disruptive Innovation in ASEAN
Muhammad Anshari (Universiti Brunei Darussalam, Brunei) Mohammad Nabil Almunawar (Universiti Brunei Darussalam, Brunei) and Masairol Masri (Universiti Brunei Darussalam, Brunei)
Business Science Reference • © 2020 • 331pp • H/C (ISBN: 9781522591832) • US $195.00 (our price)

International Trade Policies in the Era of Globalization
Ahu Coşkun Özer (Marmara University, Turkey)
Business Science Reference • © 2020 • 363pp • H/C (ISBN: 9781522595663) • US $205.00 (our price)

Management Accounting Standards for Sustainable Business Practices
Ionica Oncioiu (Titu Maiorescu University, Romania) Gary Cokins (Analytics-Based Performance Management LLC, USA) Sorinel Căpuşneanu (Titu Maiorescu University, Romania) and Dan Ioan Topor (1 Decembrie 1918 University, Romania)
Business Science Reference • © 2020 • 360pp • H/C (ISBN: 9781799801788) • US $215.00 (our price)

Handbook of Research on Economic and Political Implications of Green Trading and Energy Use
Ramesh Chandra Das (Vidyasagar University, India)
Business Science Reference • © 2019 • 421pp • H/C (ISBN: 9781522585473) • US $225.00 (our price)

Emerging Research on Monetary Policy, Banking, and Financial Markets
Cristi Spulbar (University of Craiova, Romania) and Ramona Birau (Constantin Brâncuşi University of Targu Jiu, Romania)
Business Science Reference • © 2019 • 322pp • H/C (ISBN: 9781522592693) • US $195.00 (our price)

For an entire list of titles in this series, please visit:
https://www.igi-global.com/book-series/advances-finance-accounting-economics/73685

IGI Global
DISSEMINATOR OF KNOWLEDGE

701 East Chocolate Avenue, Hershey, PA 17033, USA
Tel: 717-533-8845 x100 • Fax: 717-533-8661
E-Mail: cust@igi-global.com • www.igi-global.com

Editorial Advisory Board

Table of Contents

Preface

During the last 50 years, the environment has been considered as a conditioning element of well-being by the population. The most critical issues, however, are determined by the difficulties of defining the environmental assets and the inclusion of the latter in the market.

The compromise between man and environment exists, because man has realized over the centuries that, if the environment is irreparably degraded, the safety of the humans will be in danger.

The modern economy of well-being has led man to the conviction that knowing and valuing the environment is certainly an indispensable factor to determine economic growth, technological innovation, ethics as well as process and product quality.

The relationship between humans and environment increased during the last one century. Resources are continuously taken from nature and transformed to be used, to be finally returned in the form of waste. Besides, economic development can take place in harmony with the preservation of the natural environment.

It is necessary, thus, an integrated approach to better understand the relationship specified above. An approach able to take into consideration different themes of environmental economics and policy. Therefore, it will be useful to foster proper concepts coming from economics of natural resources, environmental economics, environmental policy, geology and natural science.

The theme of environment, moreover, involve many different private and public institutions, civil and religious. In other words, it concerns all of us and future generations, particularly.

Environmental economics and policy might to promote solutions of optimality and sustainability. Hence, it must take a long-term view. The short-term time horizon, in which economic decisions are made, is prevalent with respect to that of the long and medium term, especially in contemporary economies, characterized by finance processes.

This book focuses on the value of environment and natural resources. It purposes an advanced integrated approach to the environmental concerns and provides a set of multidisciplinary works. A key aim of the book is the provision of multiple perspectives on environment. The chapters found in this publication highlight different views in order to provide an opportunity to reflect about environmental issues, waste management, climate change, low carbon and circular economy.

The book consists of three sections: the first focuses on the linkage between environment and sustainability, the second takes into account issues as integral ecology, climate change, waste and circular tourism and third discusses about environment, consumer behaviour and urban governance.

The first chapter explores the relationship between green economy approach and sustainable development, emphasizing the contribution the former provides to the latter.

The second chapter highlights the knowledge created on bio-economy to develop a conceptual and theoretical framework based on the transdisciplinary study of biology and socioeconomy to be used in further research.

The third chapter describes the non-use ecosystem resources with a value for the production process through Reflective Analysis, systems theory and feed-in indicators. This would enable the sustainability of organisms in the ecological system with their interwoven functions intact.

The fourth chapter regards the role of an integral ecology and the relevance of educational policies, discussing how educational challenge might play an important role to protect environment against degradation and human negligence.

The fifth chapter takes into consideration the public's risk perception towards an operating incineration plant by using word-frequency-based decision-making to provide insight into risk mitigation while enhancing public acceptance.

The sixth chapter focuses on the linkage between climate change and profit loss, discussing a case history of rice farmers due to salinity intrusion in the Vietnamese Mekong Delta.

The seventh chapter discusses about the environmental challenge for tourism, showing the passage from linear to circular tourism. Environment and tourism relate each other providing both positive and negative externalities.

The eighth chapter analyzes a model of the behavior of the ecological consumer in order to know the motivations that influence the decision to purchase organic products in the municipality of Guadalajara.

The ninth chapter analyzes the implications of democratic or political and administrative or fiscal decentralization in the downward accountability, participatory and deliberative democracy to shape the urban governance of natural resources, facilities, infrastructure.

The book provides a platform for masters' students as well as environmental professionals stakeholders to discuss relevant ideas and knwoledge related to environmental economics and policy.

The authors showed a passion for understanding environment issues in an integrated approach and global context.

The book editors are very thankful to the editorial team and the staff of IGI Global for their interest, encouragement and support throughout the entire preparation of this book.

We editors wish all readers a pleasant and entertaining, insightful and inspiring lesson from the contributions of this IGI Global book. Indeed, we strongly hope that this book values IGI Global as a premium publisher in environmental economics and policy that strongly promotes the much needed intellectual advances and their contribution to humanity across the planet.

Sebastiano Patti
University of Catania, Italy

Giampiero Trizzino
Regional Council of Environment and Territory, Italy

Acknowledgment

The editors would like to acknowledge the help of all the people involved in this project.

The editors would like to thank the chapters' authors for their commitment.

Secondly, the editors wish to acknowledge the contributions of all the reviewers, which helped to improve quality as well as content presentation of chapters. The editors would like to thank each one of the authors who served as referees.

This book is the result of the contribution of all of them.

Sebastiano Patti
University of Catania, Italy

Giampiero Trizzino
Regional Council of Environment and Territory, Italy

Section 1
Environment and Sustainability

Chapter 1
Achieving Sustainable Development Through a Green Economy Approach

Seda Yıldırım
Tekirdag Namık Kemal University, Turkey

Durmuş Çağrı Yıldırım
Tekirdag Namık Kemal University, Turkey

ABSTRACT

Sustainable development aims to create a balance between economic, social, and environmental elements for continuity between humanity and the natural environment. Current economic systems and production or consumption models prevent achieving sustainable development in the long term, and the green economy approach seems to be the best option for sustainable development. This chapter investigates the relationship between green economy and sustainable development. Accordingly, the study presents a brief view of the green economy approach and sustainable development goals. As a result, the study discusses the contribution of green economy for achieving sustainable development goals.

INTRODUCTION

The term of sustainability has been shining in every kinds of area in human life. Recently, sustainable development takes part in every countries (Strowbridge, 2012) as a main issue because of the truth that the survival is related with sustainable and green civilization in the long term (Meadows et.al., 1972; WCED, 1987; Beatley

DOI: 10.4018/978-1-5225-9562-5.ch001

and Manning, 1998; Berke & Conroy, 2000; OECD, 2008; Puppim de Olivera, 2012; Bostancı &Albayrak, 2017; Yıldırım, Yıldırım & Gedikli,2016). The need of sustainable development came to the literature by study of Meadows, Meadows and Randers (1972) which was called as "The limits to grow" and determined that there should be balance between economic growth and earth's resources (Meadows et.al., 1972). Essentially, sustainable development was determined as a significant and important issue by United Nations Conference on the Human Environment in 1972 (UNEP, 1972) and then Brundtland Commission which was known as World Commission on Environment and Development published a report as "Our Common Future" in 1987 (WCED, 1987). According to WCED's report (1987), development should meet the needs of present with protecting the future ones. In 1992, the term of sustainability from sustainable development came to sustainable economy with United Nations Conference on Sustainable Development by United Nations (Puppim de Olivera, 2012).

Green economy aims to economic growth and improve economic life conditions as well as reducing environmental harm (UNEP, 2011). Understanding the implications of green economy is so crucial for sustainable development that measure is another crucial topic for determining the degree of being sustainable for economies. Hart (1999) suggested sustainable measure and some sustainability indicators for the world and the links between economy, environment and society were found as so important indicator for sustainable community. In addition, sustainable development can be successful when economic, social and environmental responsibilities are carried out coordinately (Munasinghe, 2002). In general, it can be said that sustainable economy is much more related with environmental responsibilities and economic growth. Although, governments try to keep green economy for sustainable development and they develop new strategies and plans through green economy, the indicators of being green economy can't provide sufficient results for governments. Maybe governments can't understand being green or being green and green economy can't reach to citizens or business practically (Puppim de Olivera, 2012).

This chapter explains how green economy helps and support sustainable development. In this context, the chapter investigates the relationship between green economy and sustainable development goals. Without achieving sustainable development goals, sustainable development can't be achieved. Today, 2030 Sustainable Development Goals is the last accepted goals by the world and every kinds of economy try to achieve these goals to reach sustainable development.

A VIEW OF GREEN ECONOMY CONCEPT IN THE CONTEXT OF SUSTAINABLE DEVELOPMENT

Sustainable economy which is known as green economy generally, is a vital part of sustainable development that governments have changed their traditional economic plans into green ones since the awareness of sustainability arose. After the formal notice of sustainable development in 1992 by Rio+20, the UN General Assembly keeps having sustainability and in 2012 there were two basic issue as "Green Economy in the Context of Sustainable Development and Poverty Eradication" and "International Framework for Sustainable Development" in Rio de Janeiro (UNEP, 2011). This shows that the UN is so consistent to keep sustainability and spread it to the world. Green economy was found as a term at first in "Blueprint for a Green Economy" by David Pearce, Anil Markandya, and Ed Barbie in 1989. Accordingly, it can be said that Pearce et.al. (1989) gave a life to green economy in the literature. Although there were always ideas about green economy, the formal life of green economy began in 2012. So it can be said that sustainable economy is a complex and universal issue that the policy of green economy influences every states and this new term should be introduced so carefully. In fact, there were so many evidences that showing sustainable development is the key of survival in the long term and the need of green economy should be discussed immediately. As seen in table 1, sustainable economy entered the literature almost 40 years ago and probably it was always in human life and economic life as an idea (Chappells & Trentmann, 2015). With The Rio Declaration (2012), we see the reality of green economy and after this Rio Conference, the UNEP and other organizations and states carry out the sustainable economy implementation and discuss the policy of sustainable development.

Pearce (1992) determined that three factors as "constraining human greed, sustainability and decoupling" for sustainable economy. The duty of sustainable economy is not limiting human's needs or welfare (Pearce, 1992). Green economy makes sustainable development with improving human life via providing human needs during reducing environmental risks (UNEP, 2011). Green economy includes green production and business activities that providing efficient usage of natural resources and being less harmful for the environment (UNCTAD, 2012). As practical approach, green economy has three basic goals for sustainable development such as "reducing carbon emission and pollution; enhancing energy and resource efficiency; preventing the loss of biodiversity and ecosystem services" (United Nations, 2011:31). In addition, green economy has lots of implementation and policies for sustainable production and consumption that the Rio Declaration published some principles to understand green economy and measure it. In general idea, green economy supports sustainable development with "promoting inclusiveness, efficiency and

Table 1. A brief history for green economy

Development Levels	Year	Topic	By
Idea of sustainable-green economy	1972	Limits to Grow: A Report for the Club of Rome's Project on the predicament of mankind	Meadows, Meadows, Randers and Behrens III., 1972
Report for environmental economy	1972	Conference on Human Environment	United Nations conference in Stockholm, 1972
Coming soon related with sustainable development	1987	Our common Future	Brundtland Report
Birth as a term	1989	Blueprint for a Green Economy	Pearce, Markandya and Barbier, 1989
Introduction level	1992	The Rio Declaration: Earth Summit and Agenda 21	Rio Conference: UNCED in Rio 1992
Being a policy	2008, 2009, 2010	Policy development	UNEP discuss green economy as a term (2008), UNEP launched Green economy Initiative (2008), Global Green New Deal (2009,April) and UN Climate Change Conference (2009,June), Ministers and Heads of Delegation of the UNEP Global Ministerial Environment Forum (2010)
The life begins formally	2012	Green Economy in the Context of Sustainable Development and Poverty Eradication", and "International Framework for Sustainable Development	United Nations Conference on Sustainable Development Rio +20 (2012)

Source: by authors

decarbonisation". Green economy includes goals of having sustainable food and agriculture, providing social equality and ending high numbers of unemployment. Also green economy is responsible for providing new innovative technologies and projects to save natural resources and usage of resources efficiently. Lastly, sustainable economy tries to provide sustainable energy (UNDESA, 2012). Ocampo (2012) explains macroeconomic dimensions of green economy with four issues. As Ocampo's determination, inter-temporal welfare, environmental protection, sustainable production-consumption and finance of new innovative green technology and implementation are analyzed in the concept of green economy (Ocampo, 2012).

Global Sustainability Panel (2011) summarized some characteristics for green economy such as below (UNDESA, 2012:10):

- Green economy is a power source for sustainable development that it transforms economic growth into sustainable development.
- Green economy keeps long-term perspective.
- Green economy measures development beyond GDP.
- Green economy encourage green employment areas and jobs.
- Green economy features "technology, innovation, cooperation and organization" together.
- Green economy manage price system through social and environmental cost
- Green economy supports green energy systems
- Green economy manage natural resources in the context of productivity and sustainability.
- Green economy support cooperation between organization, people and countries.

Green economy is a universal issue that universal organizations should help and support states to understand and transit into sustainable economy. In this point, five basic organizations as "the United Nations Environment Programme (UNEP), the International Labour Organization (ILO), the United Nations Development Programme (UNDP), the United Nations Industrial Development Organization (UNIDO) and the United Nations Institute for Training and Research (UNITAR)" tries to help states to get green economy (UNEP, 2016). Nowadays, both of developed and developing countries try to transform their usual economic strategy into green economic strategy. For example, The European Environment Agency (EEA) carries out green economy program as a part of the European Union and EEA helps the EU members to transform green economy with having 33 members today (EEA, 2016). The EPA (Environmental Protection Agency) of United States also tries to protect human health and the environmental life in the US (EPA, 2015). AECEN(Asian Environmental Compliance and Enforcement Network) was established in 2005 by 13 Asian countries to promote environmental implementations in Asia with several agencies (Cambodia, India, Indonesia, Japan, Korea, People's Republic of China, Lao PDR, Malaysia, the Maldives, Mongolia, Myanmar, Nepal, Pakistan, Philippines, Singapore, Sri Lanka, Thailand, and Vietnam) (AECEN, 2015).

Most of developed and developing states have their long-termed green policies and strategies for green economy that they want to reach their goals for almost next 30 or 50 years at the future. But there are lots of challenges to have green economy for countries in the short and mid-term (OECD, 2001). According to World Economic and Social Survey 2013, the challenges of sustainable development can be explained in three basic parts as "economic, social and environmental" that these challenges should be analyzed and solved in their own categories (UNEP, 2013). If these challenges can be overcome, sustainable development can be achieved.

On the other side, there have been countries that transformed their economy into green economy to reach sustainable development. For example, African countries have transformed its many policies for green economy. Also African governments encourage green economy for economic development in the long term (United Nations Economic Commission for Africa, 2012). According to UNEP (2010)'s study, the role of green economy for sustainable economy I so important and for some countries, there have already been positive outputs. For Uganda, green economy approach provided "Organic Agriculture" and organic agriculture supported economic growth. Bangladesh began to use "Solar PV" for energy; Brazil has encouraged sustainable cities through sustainable planning initiatives (Stone, 2010).

ACHIEVING SUSTAINABLE DEVELOPMENT GOALS THROUGH GREEN ECONOMY APPROACH

The World Green Economy Organization determines that green economy includes elements as "*low carbon, climate-resilient, resource-efficient and socially-inclusive* (WGEO, 2018:9)". In this point, it can be said that Green Economy Approach is mostly linked with sustainable development that the success of sustainable development goals almost depends on implementations of green economy. Nowadays, sustainable development goals have become the most important goals for the world. To reach sustainable development goals in the long term, the collaboration of economy side is so important. Because the main elements of sustainable development contains "environmental, social and economic" issues (Emas, 2015) and it can be said that sustainable development goals needs the balance between these three issues. United Nations Conference on Environment and Development (UNCED) which is the first conference for sustainable development in 1992, pointed out environmental, social and economic problems. In 2002 Earth Summit (Rio+10) set important goals for sustainable development. These goals were the first that was called as the Millennium Development Goals. The Millennium Development Goals included: "ending extreme poverty and hunger, achieving primary education universally, promoting gender equity, reducing child death, improving health, reducing crucial diseases such as HIV/AIDS, malaria etc., ensuring environmental sustainability, making partnership for sustainable development" (Kanianska, 2017:13). In 2012, Rio+20 set Sustainable Development Goals and set green economy guidelines (Sustainable Development Goals Knowledge Platform, n.d.). By 2015, the world meets 2030 Sustainable Development Goals (SDGs). 2030 Sustainable Development Goals (SDGs) can be called as the future goals because it is the last accepted goals to be achieved by the world. 2030 Sustainable Development Goals (SDGs) has 17 main goals that are summarized as below:

- ***Goal 1: No Poverty:*** It is the first goal that poverty should be reduced by 2030. By 2030, all men and women, especially poor and vulnerable, should be provided with equal access to economic resources and basic services. By 2030, it is also important to reduce the vulnerability and vulnerability of the poor and vulnerable to economic, social and environmental shocks and disasters. The programs and policies required to end poverty in all its dimensions need to be implemented in cooperation between both developed and developing countries (Sustainable Development Goals - Goal 1, n.d.).
- ***Goal 2: Zero Hunger***: Until 2030, vulnerable people should be provided with safe, nutritious and adequate food supply throughout the year, especially for the poor and the infants. It is important to educate the nursing mothers and pregnant women. By 2030, it is aimed to strengthen agriculture, to support family farmers and fishermen, and to establish sustainable food production systems. In order to adapt to climate change, it is important to switch to flexible agricultural practices for the continuation of land and soil quality. By 2020, established and diversified seed and plant banks were established at national, regional and international levels; it is also an important goal to ensure that these seeds are fairly accessible to everyone. In addition, it is aimed to share the internationally accepted genetic resources and traditional information freely (Sustainable Development Goals - Goal 2, n.d.).
- ***Goal 3: Good Health and Well-Being***: By 2030, it was aimed to reduce infant mortality by decreasing globally, especially by reducing preventable deaths in newborns and infants under 5 years of age. By 2030, it is an important goal to terminate the outbreaks of AIDS, tuberculosis, malaria and other neglected tropical diseases and to combat hepatitis, waterborne diseases and other communicable diseases. It is aimed to reduce an early death rate of one third by protection and treatment from non-communicable diseases, addiction (drug, alcohol etc.) and to increase mental health. Including family planning, knowledge and education and reproductive health in national strategies and programs by 2030; Ensuring universal access to sexual and reproductive health services and ensuring access to health services in a safe, effective and high quality manner are important elements (Sustainable Development Goals - Goal 3, n.d.).
- ***Goal 4: Quality Education***: By 2030, it is necessary to ensure that all girls and boys complete their primary and secondary education in a free, equal and quality manner. In this context, it is necessary to ensure that early childhood development of girls and boys in all over the world is provided to care and pre-primary education. In addition, it is important to facilitate the access of all girls and boys to the necessary vocational and higher education after secondary education and to have equal access to these opportunities.

By 2030, the number of young people and adults with relevant skills, including technical and professional skills for employment, decent work and entrepreneurship, is expected to increase significantly. By 2030, all students need to undertake and implement the necessary training plans to adopt a culture without sustainable development and sustainable lifestyles, human rights, gender equality, peace culture and violence. Until 2030, the provision of adequate and adequate teacher supply in developing countries, underdeveloped countries and underdeveloped islands is an important goal (Sustainable Development Goals - Goal 4, n.d.).

- ***Goal 5: Gender Equality***: It is necessary to end all kinds of discrimination against women and girls everywhere. All violence against women and girls in all public and private areas, including human trafficking, sexual and other forms of exploitation, must end. In connection with violence, the elimination of all harmful practices such as child, early and forced marriage and female genital mutilation are also important targets. On the other hand, to ensure full and effective participation of women in leadership in political, economic and public life; providing equal economic rights to women and encouraging entrepreneurship, empowering women to make full use of information and communication technologies are important steps towards gender equality. Ensuring universal access to sexual and reproductive health and rights, which are accepted in accordance with the International Population and Development Conference Action Plan and the Beijing Action Platform and the final reports of the review conferences, is also an important sub-goal (Sustainable Development Goals - Goal 5, n.d.).
- ***Goal 6: Clean Water and Sanitation:*** Until 2030; providing universal and fair access to safe and affordable drinking water for all; providing a healthy environment to meet the needs of women, girls and other vulnerable people; reducing waste, ensuring disposal of waste; By minimizing the release of hazardous chemicals and materials, reducing the rate of untreated wastewater by half and greatly increasing recycling, and ensuring the worldwide availability of reusable safe water supply, ensuring efficiency in water resources used in all sectors and increasing sustainability are important sub-targets. Until 2020, protection and improvement of mountains, forests, wetlands and other water-related ecosystems are important; Increasing the support of collaborations and local communities in preventing water pollution is also an important sub-objective (Sustainable Development Goals - Goal 6, n.d.).
- ***Goal 7: Affordable and Clean Energy:*** By 2030, providing universal access to economic, reliable and modern energy services; to significantly increase the share of renewable energy in the global energy mix; to double the

global recovery rate in energy efficiency; develop and invest in international cooperation to facilitate access to clean energy research and technology, including renewable energy, energy efficiency, advanced and clean fossil fuel technology; Supporting developing and underdeveloped countries in energy investments and sustainable energy issues are important sub-targets (Sustainable Development Goals - Goal 7, n.d.).

- ***Goal 8: Decent Work and Economic Growth***: Important sub-objectives; sustain economic growth per capita in line with national conditions and, in particular, at least 7 per cent per annum in least developed countries; to achieve higher levels of economic efficiency through diversification, technological improvement and innovation by focusing on high value-added and labor-intensive sectors; to promote policies supporting entrepreneurship, creativity and innovation, and to promote the formalization and growth of micro, small and medium-sized enterprises, including access to financial services. Equal pay, equal and efficient employment and decent work opportunities for all men and women, including young people and persons with disabilities ; By 2020, it is important to da significantly reduce the proportion of young people who are not employed and who are not in education. As in other objectives, it is important to establish and implement cooperation between countries in the context of this target (Sustainable Development Goals - Goal 8, n.d.).
- ***Goal 9: Industry, Innovation and Infrastructure***: It is important to develop quality, reliable, sustainable and flexible infrastructure facilities, including regional and cross-border infrastructure, to support economic development and human well-being. In To promote inclusive and sustainable industrialization, to significantly increase the employment and gross domestic product of the industry according to national conditions; to support entrepreneurship in underdeveloped and developing countries; In order to make the infrastructure and improvement industries sustainable, increasing the efficiency of resource utilization and ensuring that all countries take action in line with their own capabilities by adopting environmentally friendly technologies and industrial processes are among the important sub-targets. Within the context of these issues, improvement in especially underdeveloped countries is among both expectations and targets (Sustainable Development Goals - Goal 9, n.d.).
- ***Goal 10: Reduced Inequalities***: By 2030, improving the income level of 40 percent of the population; ell strengthen and support everyone's social, economic and political participation, regardless of age, gender, disability, race, ethnic origin, origin, religion or economic or other circumstances; Eliminating discriminatory laws, policies and practices and ensuring equality of opportunity, including promoting appropriate legislation, policies and actions are important sub-objectives. The establishment of inter-country

cooperation and the support of the less developed countries on these issues are also important targets (Sustainable Development Goals - Goal 10, n.d.).

- ***Goal 11: Sustainable Cities and Communities***: Until 2030; Have enough, safe and affordable housing for everyone; and ensuring that everyone can access basic services. Improvement of shanty settlements; reach safe, affordable, accessible and sustainable transport systems for all, improving road safety, particularly by expanding public transport, paying particular attention to the needs of vulnerable persons, women, children with disabilities and the elderly; developing inclusive and sustainable urbanization and capacity for participatory, integrated and sustainable human settlement planning and management in all countries; To strengthen the efforts to protect the world's cultural and natural heritage; significantly reduce the number of deaths and the number of affected people and significantly reduce the direct economic losses related to global gross domestic product caused by catastrophes, including water-related disasters, focusing on the protection of the poor and vulnerable people; to reduce the environmental negative impacts of cities on the one hand, including special attention to air quality and municipal and other waste management; providing universal access to safe, inclusive and accessible, green and public spaces, especially for women and children, the elderly and the disabled; Supporting positive economic, social and environmental links between urban, urban and rural areas by strengthening national and regional development planning as are important sub-objectives. Also by 2020; In accordance with the Sendai Disaster Risk Framework, the adoption and implementation of integrated policies and plans for adoption and implementation of integrated policies and plans, climate efficiency, mitigation and adaptation to climate change, resistance to disasters, development and implementation are increasing significantly. In 2015-2030, creating holistic disaster risk management at all levels is an important sub-goal. It is also expected that underdeveloped countries should be encouraged to build and cooperate in building (Sustainable Development Goals - Goal 11, n.d.).
- ***Goal 12: Responsible Consumption and Production***: Taking into account the 10-year framework of sustainable consumption and production programs and the development and capacities of developing countries, it is necessary to ensure that all countries act together with developing countries. To ensure the adaptation of environmentally sensitive chemicals and all wastes to the environment in an environmentally friendly manner by 2020; In order to minimize the negative impacts on human health and the environment, it is necessary to considerably reduce the emission to air, water and soil. By 2030, significantly reduce waste generation through recycling and reuse; It is important to create and spread the awareness of sustainable development that

brings harmony between man and nature. Activities and collaborations are also important for the adoption of sustainable consumption culture and for increasing environmental awareness (Sustainable Development Goals - Goal 12, n.d.).

- ***Goal 13: Climate Action***: It is important to reduce the negative conditions that cause climate change and to raise awareness. To meet the needs of developing countries from each source until 2020, the United Nations Climate Change Convention needs to be adjusted to a budget of $100 billion per year, and ensure that the Green Climate Fund has a common capital as soon as possible (Sustainable Development Goals - Goal 13, n.d.).
- ***Goal 14: Life Below Water:*** Until 2025, it is necessary to prevent and significantly reduce all types of marine pollution, especially on land activities, including marine litter and food pollution. By 2020, it was aimed to sustain and manage marine and coastal ecosystems in a sustainable way to take action for their restorations to avoid significant negative impacts, including strengthening their durability, and to obtain healthy and productive oceans. Until 2020, there were bans that contributed to overcapacity and overfishing, eliminating subsidies contributing to illegal, unreported and unregulated fishing. The World Trade Organization should be an integral part of the negotiations for fisheries subsidies. Issues such as the protection of the oceans, the efficient use of water resources and the sustainability of fishing are addressed in this context (Sustainable Development Goals - Goal 14, n.d.).
- ***Goal 15: Life on land:*** By 2030, for sustainable development, ensure the protection of mountain ecosystems, including biodiversity; reduce degradation in natural habitats; stop loss of biodiversity; Taking necessary measures to prevent the destruction of threatened species is one of the important objectives (Sustainable Development Goals - Goal 15, n.d.).
- ***Goal 16: Peace, Justice and Strong Institutions:*** Reducing violence and mortality rates everywhere; introducing the rules of law to everyone in national and international environments and ensuring equal access to justice; prevention of child abuse; preventing illegal arms sales; preventing all kinds of corruption; the legal identity of citizens all over the world and the promotion of strategies and policies for sustainable development are important targets (Sustainable Development Goals - Goal 16, n.d.).
- ***Goal 17: Partnerships for the goals:*** The sub-goals in this target are handled according to specific titles. These are: finance, technology, capacity, trade, systematic substances ". According to the finance category; financial support for developing and underdeveloped countries is a very important goal. It is important to develop a global partnership for sustainable development,

> complemented by multi-stakeholder partnerships that mobilize and share knowledge, expertise, technology and financial resources to support the realization of sustainable development goals in all countries, especially developing countries (Sustainable Development Goals - Goal 17, n.d.).

Green economy approach aims to support sustainable development goals in fact. As presented in table 2, main themes of sustainable development such as poverty, hunger, equality, environmental pollution are mostly related with green economy approach. In addition, the need of green economy can be summarized as Table 3:

The University of Cambridge Institute for Sustainability Leadership examined six basic outcomes for 2030 Sustainable Development Goals through green economy. As seen in table 3, economy is related with every SDGs and it can have a positive/ negative impact on sustainable development in the long term. If countries keep green economy approach today, they can achieve most of sustainable development goals until 2030. Although there have been still arguments about effectiveness of green economy, nobody can ignore green economy in the long term. For example, Bina (2013) argued usability of green economy in the current market system and she determined that there was a discrepancy between scarcity and development. That's why current economy can't work with sustainable development goals. The current economic approaches as conventional economy decrease the possibility of achieving sustainable development goals in the long term. So, there need to be green economy approach to keep sustainable development goals. The balance between economy, social and environment will provide sustainable development in the long term that green economy approach tries to provide this balance for countries.

It is a fact that economic development will always continue for countries. Green economy accepts this fact and also it refers to use natural resources efficiently and being less harmful for the environment for next generation and future (WGEO, 2018). When green economy approach is employed, there will be new business areas, sectors and job opportunities. WGEO (2018) determined the business as the most important motive element for green economy. Green Economy needs green business and green business will contribute sustainable development.

In Table 4, sixty biggest market/industry opportunities are showed. According to WGEO (2018), four basic industry areas as "Food and Agriculture , City-Public services, Energy and Materials, Health and Well-Being" will rise through green enterprise. These new businesses will new winners and losers. The transitions to green economy will determine new world in the future. So, countries who keeps new technologies such as Industry 4.0 and innovations and green agriculture or green energy, will be winner in the green economy (WGEO, 2018).

Table 2. The relationship between 2030 sustainable development goals and green economy

2030 SDGs*		The Need of Green Economy
1.No Poverty:	People who living less than 1.90 $ in a day, are regarded as poor in anywhere that by 2030, the number of these poor people should be reduced.	The first goal has a direct relation with green economy. Because current economic models which uses conventional economic approaches, are not interested in society's welfare. That's why there are huge gaps between rich and poor people in the world. To provide more equal life standards for everybody, green economy approach must be implemented in the long term. The success of this goal mostly depends on green economy's adaptation.
2.Zero Hunger:	SDG 2 has two main issues such as hunger and food security. The rate of undernourished and poor nurtured people should be reduced. Also, agricultural biodiversity should be protected and sustained.	Green economy aims to provide welfare for everybody that hunger shouldn't be a problem in the long term. If poverty brings hunger, maybe more equal life standards can improve the rate of hungry people.
3.Good Health and Well-Being:	The rate of maternal mortality and newborns death should be reduced. Every kinds of illnesses and deaths from traffic accidents, environmental pollution should be reduced and *AIDS, tuberculosis, malaria and neglected tropical diseases and combat hepatitis* should be ended.	Green economy supports sustainable development that providing good health and well-being life for everybody is important purpose in the long term. Setting a balance between economy and society is a main goal for green economy.
4.Quality Education:	Without gender discrimination, primary and secondary education should be given to every child freely. University education should be more accessible by 2030. Also it is important to learn and adopt culture of sustainable life.	For better life standards, better education should be given to people. With quality education, people can be more qualified. Green economy's approach can success this goal in the long term.
5.Gender Equality:	By 2030, every kinds of discrimination should be ended. Women's employment should be supported and equal opportunities should be given to women. Also every kinds of harassment to women should be ended.	Gender equality is related with most of other 2030 SDGs such as SDG 4 and SDG 8. Green economy's approach can prevent discrimination in every kinds of social or economic life.
6.Clean Water and Sanitation:	Safe, clean and affordable drinking water should be accessible for everybody in the world by 2030. For getting quality and clean water, reduce pollution. Also local governments should take responsibility and improve sanitation management.	Firstly, Green Economy Approach forces businesses to get sustainable production, marketing etc. Because businesses transform their current production technologies into sustainable production systems to save environmental life.
7.Affordable and Clean Energy:	By 2030, renewable energy systems should be expanded.	To reach sustainable development, green energy and its technology should be more expanded. In this context, green economy approach forces governments and businesses to work by alternative and eco-friendly energy sources.
8.Decent Work and Economic Growth:	By 2030, provide full employment and work situation for everybody, protect labor rights. Sustainable economic growth is so important, especially least developed countries should be supported for economic growth. Supporting SMEs(small and medium sized enterprises) is important.	Green Economy Approach aims to balance between economic, social and environment life. So, work for everybody and equal work rights should be provided.

continued on following page

Table 2. Continued

2030 SDGs*		The Need of Green Economy
9.Industry, Innovation and Infrastructure:	For economic growth, sustainable regional and transborder infrastructure should be provided. Universal information and communication technology should be provided.	Transition to green economy needs new technology and innovative production methods that green economy provides SDG 9 more easily.
10.Reduced Inequalities:	Every kinds of inequality situations between countries should be reduced.	Green economy tries to reduce inequalities. So, this goal is coherent with green economy's purposes.
11.Sustainable Cities and Communities:	Sustainable urbanization should be expanded. Municipal and other local governments should support sustainable lifestyle and its culture in the city.	When countries keep green economy, the goal of sustainable cities can be realized more easily.
12.Responsible Consumption and Production:	World's population is getting higher year to year and natural resources can't be enough to meet everybody's need If sustainability is ignored. So, sustainable production methods should be expanded and sustainable consumption behavior should be adopted widely.	Sustainable production and sustainable consumption are both related with green economy that this goal has a same approach with green economy's implementations.
13.Climate Action:	The climate change is a serious threat for next generation's sustainability. So, the most important step is to acknowledge the United Nations Framework Convention on Climate Change.	With the help of green economy, countries can struggle with the factors that influencing climate negatively.
14.Life Below Water:	Reducing marine pollution and ending overfishing are important to save waters and coastal ecosystems. Also countries which are small ısland, should be supported economically.	Thinking about sustainability of sea biodiversity will prevent overfishing. Accordingly, green economy approach can reduce profit-drive fishing methods. Universally, developed countries can support small ısland's people.
15.Life on land:	Areas of forests and biodiversity should be protected.	For sustainability, countries should think about ecological life as much as economic life that green economy can provide this goal.
16.Peace, Justice and Strong Institutions:	For sustainable development, non-discriminatory laws and policies should be promoted.	Green economy approach aims to get balance between economy, social welfare and ecological life. So, countries should provide laws and policies to get the balance social welfare and economic life together.
17.Partnerships for the goals:	To reach 2030 sustainable development goals, countries should keep partnerships between each other and help least developed countries to catch them.	After economic barriers disappear, partnerships will increase and countries can help or support each other more easily. Green economy's aim can gather up countries for universal future.

*The information was taken from United Nation's web site (Sustainable Development Goals, n.d.)
Source: by authors

CONCLUSION

The reality of climate change should be accepted by all over the world. Then every kind of economic, social or politic implementations should be planned according to this reality. Economic and social challenges are related with human life but environmental challenges are not related with human life as much as others that improvements and protection of environmental life is seen so difficult in the long term. In this point, green economy and sustainable consumption should be work

Table 3. Six outcomes for 2030 sustainable development goals

Outcomes *	Green Economy's Responsibility for:	2030 SDGs
Basic Needs	Food, water, energy, shelter, sanitation, communications, transport, credit, health	SDG 1, SDG 2, SDG 3, SDG 6, SDG 7, SDG 13
Decent Work	Secure, socially inclusive jobs and working conditions for all	SDG 3, SDG 10, SDG 8
Well-Being	Enhanced health, education, justice and equality of opportunity for all	SDG 3, SDG 4, SDG 5, SDG 10, SDG 11, SDG 15
Healthy Ecosystems	Maintain ecologically sound landscapes and seas for nature and people	SDG 14, SDG 15
Climate stability	Limit GHG levels to stabilize global temperature rise to well below 2^0 C	SDG 7, SDG 10
Resource Security	Preserve stocks of natural resources through efficient and circular use	SDG 12

*These outcomes are originally belonged to The University of Cambridge Institute for Sustainability Leadership.

Source: WGEO, 2018:9

together. Because natural resources can't be renewable forever to meet unlimited human needs and wants. When there is less conventional economic approach or less consumption madness, meeting society's needs and keeping environmental sustainability can be carried out more successfully. For example, Developing or emerging countries should be more careful about sustainable development because these countries need to grow and develop to reach better life standards or economic level in the world. In this point, their usage of natural resources or energy consumption will be higher than developed or less developed countries (European Commission, 2006). On the other side, some studies show that higher educated women can get higher life standards and job opportunities in developing or emerging countries (Yıldırım, Yıldırım & Coltu, 2019). Equal work, equal life standards and equal education rights are all sustainable development goals and green economy approach can improve the current economy in the long term.

Sustainable development is the main issue for every economy. Although sustainable development is accepted by the most of developed and developing countries, reaching sustainable development point needs long-term strategic planning. These log-term planning includes some sustainable development goals (SDGs) that we can evaluate the degree of sustainable development according to fulfillment of SDGs. Sustainable

Table 4. Biggest green business areas for sustainable development

Food and Agriculture	Cities	Energy and Materials	Health and Well-Being
Reducing food waste in value chain	Affordable housing	Circular models-automotive	Risk pooling
Forest ecosystem services	Energy efficiency-buildings	Expansion of renewables	Remote patient monitoring
Low-income food markets	Electric and hybrid vehicles	Circular models appliances	Telehealth
Reducing consumer food waste	Public transport in urban areas	Circular models-electronics	Advances genomics
Product reformulation	Car sharing	Energy efficiency-non-energy intensive industries	Activity services
Technology in large-scale farms	Road safety equipment	Energy storage systems	Detection of counterfeit drugs
Dietary switch	Autonomous vehicles	Resource recovery	Tobacco control
Sustainable aquaculture	ICE vehicle fuel efficiency	End-use steel efficiency	Weight management programs
Technology in smallholder farms	Building resilient cities	Energy-efficiency-energy intensive industries	Better disease management
Micro-irrigation	Municipal water leakage	Carbon capture and storage	Electronic medical records
Restoring degraded land	Cultural tourism	Energy access	Better maternal and child health
Reducing packaging waste	Smart metering	Green chemicals	Healthcare training
Cattle intensification	Water and sanitation infrastructure	Additive manufacturing	
	Office sharing	Local content in extractives	
Urban agriculture	Timber buildings	Shared infrastructure	Lo-cost surgery
	Durable and modular buildings	Mine rehabilitation	
		Grid interconnection	

Source: WGEO, 2018:17

development can't be thought without sustainable development goals (SDGs) and SDGs can't be succeed without green economy. The term of green economy can't substitute sustainable development but reaching sustainable development is almost based on green economy (United Nations, 2011). As a result, it can be said that green economy approach supports sustainable development goals and in the long way of reaching sustainable development point, green economy approach can't be ignored.

ACKNOWLEDGMENT

This study is derived from a paper that was presented in International Congress of Islamic Economy, Finance and Ethics 2018-Autumn, 3-4 November 2018, Istanbul, Turkey.

REFERENCES

AECEN. (2015). *AECEN Executive Committee Meeting*. Retrieved May 10, 2019, from https://www.aecen.org/sites/default/files/final_meeting_summary_for_aecen_executive_commmitee_meeting_2015.pdf

Beatley, T., & Manning, K. (1998). *The Ecology Of Place: Planning For Environment, Economy And Community*. Washington, DC: Island Press.

Berke, P. R., & Conroy, M. M. (2000). Are We Planning for Sustainable Development? An Evaluation of 30 Comprehensive Plans. *Journal of the American Planning Association*, *66*(1), 21–33. doi:10.1080/01944360008976081

Bina, O. (2013). The green economy and sustainable development: An uneasy balance? *Environment and Planning. C, Government & Policy*, *31*(6), 1023–1047. doi:10.1068/c1310j

Bostanci, S. H., & Albayrak, A. N. (2017). The role of eco-municipalities in climate change for a sustainable future. In W. Ganpat & W. A. Isaac (Eds.), *Environmental Sustainability and Change Adaptation Strategies* (pp. 213–231). IGI Global. doi:10.4018/978-1-5225-1607-1.ch008

Chappells, H., & Trentmann, F. (2015). Sustainable consumption in history: Ideas, resources and practices. In L. A. Reisch & J. Thøgersen (Eds.), *Handbook of research on sustainable consumption* (pp. 51–70). Cheltenham, UK: Edward Elgar. doi:10.4337/9781783471270.00011

EEA. (2016). *Sustainability transitions: Now for the long term*. Retrieved May 10, 2019 from file:///C:/Users/hp/Downloads/Sustainability%20transitions%20Now%20for%20the%20long%20term.pdf

EEA. (2018). *Who we are*. Retrieved May 10, 2019 from https://www.eea.europa.eu/about-us/who

Emas, R. (2015). *Brief for GSDR 2015*. Florida International University. Retrieved May 10, 2019 from https://sustainabledevelopment.un.org/content/documents/5839GSDR%202015_SD_concept_definiton_rev.pdf

EPA. (2015). *FY 2015 EPA Budget in Brief*. United States Environmental Protection Agency. Retrieved May 10, 2019 from https://www.epa.gov/sites/production/files/2014-03/documents/fy15_bib.pdf

European Commission. (2006). *Environment Fact Sheet: Energy For Sustainable Development*. Retrieved May 10, 2019 from http://ec.europa.eu/environment/archives/wssd/pdf/fs_energy.pdf

Hart, M. (1999). *Guide to sustainable community indicators*. North Andover, MA: Hart Environmental Data.

Kanianska, R. (2017). *Green Growth And Green Economy*. Matej Bel University Banská Bystrica Faculty Of Natural Science. Retrieved May 10, 2019 from http://enviroportal.sk/uploads/files/zelene_hospodarstvo/publikacie/2017SkriptaGreen-Growth-and-Green-Economy.pdf

Meadows, D. H., Meadows, D. L., Randers, J., & Behrens, W. W., III. (1972). *The limits to grow. A Report For The Club Of Rome's Project On The Predicament Of Mankind*. A Potomac Associates Book. Retrieved May 10, 2019 from http://www.donellameadows.org/wp-content/userfiles/Limits-to-Growth-digital-scan-version.pdf

Munasinghe, M. (2002). The Sustainomics Trans-disciplinary Meta-framework for making Development more Sustainable: Applications to energy issues. *International Journal of Sustainable Development*, *4*(2), 6–54.

Ocampo, J. A. (2012). The Transition to a Green Economy: Benefits, Challenges and Risks from a Sustainable Development Perspective Summary of Background Papers. *The Transition to a Green Economy: Benefits, Challenges and Risks from a Sustainable Development Perspective Report by a Panel of Experts, to Second Preparatory Committee Meeting for United Nations Conference on Sustainable Development*.

OECD. (2001). *The DAC Guidelines Strategies for Sustainable Development*. Retrieved May 10, 2019 from https://www.oecd.org/dac/environment-development/2669958.pdf

OECD. (2008). *2008 annual report on sustainable development work in the OECD*. Retrieved May 10, 2019 from https://www.oecd.org/greengrowth/42177377.pdf

Pearce, D. (1992). Green Economics. *Environmental Values*, *1*(1), 3–13. doi:10.3197/096327192776680179

Pearce, D., Markandya, A., & Barbier, E. B. (1989). *Blueprint for a Green Economy*. London: Earthscan.

Puppim de Olivera, J. A. (2012). *Introduction: Framing the debate on the green economy and governance from different angles. In Green Economy And Good Governance For Sustainable Development: Opportunities, Promises And Concerns*. United Nations:University Press.

Stone, S. (2010). *Ad Hoc Expert Meeting on The Green Economy: Trade and Sustainable Development Implications*. Chief of Economics and Trade Branch United Nations Environment Programme - UNEP. Retrieved May 10, 2019 from http://www.biotrade.org/MeetingsEvents/GreenEco/GER_Trade%20and%20Sustainability.pdf

Strowbridge, C. (2012). *Sustainable Development in Kenya: Keeping the Culture*. Retrieved May 10, 2019 from http://www.tacoma.uw.edu/sites/default/files/global/documents/travel/2012-kenya-strowbridge-paper.pdf

Sustainable Development Goals. (n.d.). *About the Sustainable Development Goals*. United Nations. Retrieved April 10, 2019 from https://www.un.org/sustainabledevelopment/sustainable-development-goals/

Sustainable Development Goals - Goal 1. (n.d.). *Goal 1: End poverty in all its forms everywhere*. Retrieved April 10, 2019 from https://www.un.org/sustainabledevelopment/poverty/

Sustainable Development Goals - Goal 10. (n.d.). *Goal 10: Reduce inequality within and among countries*. Retrieved April 10, 2019 from https://www.un.org/sustainabledevelopment/inequality/

Sustainable Development Goals - Goal 11. (n.d.). *Goal 11: Make cities inclusive, safe, resilient and sustainable*. Retrieved April 10, 2019 from https://www.un.org/sustainabledevelopment/cities/

Sustainable Development Goals - Goal 12. (n.d.). *Goal 12: Ensure sustainable consumption and production patterns*. Retrieved April 2019 from https://www.un.org/sustainabledevelopment/sustainable-consumption-production/

Sustainable Development Goals - Goal 13. (n.d.). *Goal 13: Take urgent action to combat climate change and its impacts*. Retrieved April 10, 2019 from https://www.un.org/sustainabledevelopment/climate-change-2/

Sustainable Development Goals - Goal 14. (n.d.). *Goal 14: Conserve and sustainably use the oceans, seas and marine resources*. Retrieved April 10, 2019 from https://www.un.org/sustainabledevelopment/oceans/

Sustainable Development Goals - Goal 15. (n.d.). *Sustainably manage forests, combat desertification, halt and reverse land degradation, halt biodiversity loss*. Retrieved April 10, 2019 from https://www.un.org/sustainabledevelopment/biodiversity/

Sustainable Development Goals - Goal 16. (n.d.). Goal 16: *Promote just, peaceful and inclusive societies*. Retrieved April 10, 2019 from https://www.un.org/sustainabledevelopment/peace-justice/

Sustainable Development Goals - Goal 17. (n.d.). *Goal 17: Revitalize the global partnership for sustainable development*. Retrieved April 10, 2019 from https://www.un.org/sustainabledevelopment/globalpartnerships/

Sustainable Development Goals - Goal 2. (n.d.). *Goal 2: Zero Hunger*. Retrieved April 10, 2019 from https://www.un.org/sustainabledevelopment/hunger/

Sustainable Development Goals - Goal 3. (n.d.). *Goal 3: Ensure healthy lives and promote well-being for all at all ages*. Retrieved April 10, 2019 from https://www.un.org/sustainabledevelopment/health/

Sustainable Development Goals - Goal 4. (n.d.). *4 Quality Education*. Retrieved April 10, 2019 from https://www.un.org/sustainabledevelopment/education/

Sustainable Development Goals - Goal 5. (n.d.). *Goal 5: Achieve gender equality and empower all women and girls*. Retrieved May 10, 2019 from https://www.un.org/sustainabledevelopment/gender-equality/

Sustainable Development Goals - Goal 6. (n.d.). *Goal 6: Ensure access to water and sanitation for all*. Retrieved April 10, 2019 from https://www.un.org/sustainabledevelopment/water-and-sanita

Sustainable Development Goals - Goal 7. (n.d.). *Ensure access to affordable, reliable, sustainable and modern energy*. Retrieved April 10, 2019 from https://www.un.org/sustainabledevelopment/energy/

Sustainable Development Goals - Goal 8. (n.d.). *Promote inclusive and sustainable economic growth, employment and decent work for all*. Retrieved April 10, 2019 from https://www.un.org/sustainabledevelopment/economic-growth/

Sustainable Development Goals - Goal 9. (n.d.). *Goal 9: Build resilient infrastructure, promote sustainable industrialization and foster innovation*. Retrieved April 10, 2019 from https://www.un.org/sustainabledevelopment/infrastructure-industrialization/

Sustainable Development Goals Knowledge Platform. (n.d.). *United Nations Conference on Sustainable Development, Rio+20*. Retrieved April 10, 2019 from https://sustainabledevelopment.un.org/rio20

UNCTAD. (2012). *UNCTAD Annual Report 2011*. Retrieved April 10, 2019 from https://unctad.org/en/PublicationsLibrary/_en.pdf

UNDESA. (2012). *A Guidebook to the Green Economy: Issue 2: exploring green economy principles*. Retrieved April 10, 2019 from https://sustainabledevelopment.un.org/content/documents/743GE%20Guidebook%202%20-%20Principles_final.pdf

UNEP. (1972). *Report of the United Nations Conference on the Human Environment*. Retrieved April 10, 2019 from http://www.un-documents.net/aconf48-14r1.pdf

UNEP. (2011). *Formative Evaluation of UNEP's Programme of Work 2010-2011*. Retrieved April 10, 2019 from http://wedocs.unep.org/bitstream/handle/20.500.11822/290/Formative_Evaluation_of_the_UNEP_Programme_of_Work_for_2010-2011.pdf?sequence=1

UNEP. (2013). *World Economic and Social Survey 2013, Sustainable Development Challenges*. United Nations. Retrieved April 10, 2019 from https://sustainabledevelopment.un.org/content/documents/2843WESS2013.pdf

UNEP. (2016). *UNEP Frontiers 2016 Report. Emerging Issues of Environmental Concern*. Retrieved April 10, 2019 from https://environmentlive.unep.org/media/docs/assessments/UNEP_Frontiers_2016_report_emerging_issues_of_environmental_concern.pdf

United Nations. (2011). *The Green Economy: Trade And Sustainable Development Implications*. United Nations Conference on Trade and Development. Retrieved April 10, 2019 from https://unctad.org/en/Docs/ditcted2011d5_en.pdf

United Nations Economic Commission for Africa. (2012). *A Green Economy in the Context of Sustainable Development and Poverty Eradication: What are the Implications for Africa?* Retrieved April 10, 2019 from http://www1.uneca.org/Portals/rio20/documents/cfssd7/1AfricaGE-BackgroundReportEN.pdf

WCED. (1987). *Our Common Future. World Commission on Environment and Development*. Oxford, UK: Oxford University Press.

WGEO. (2018). *2018 World Green Economy Report*. Retrieved April 10, 2019 from http://worldgreeneconomy.org/wp-content/uploads/2018/10/report.pdf

Yıldırım, S., Yıldırım, D. Ç., & Coltu, S. (2019). The Role of Education in Women's Career Life in Emerging Economies: A Case of Turkey. In E. T. Pereira & P. Paoloni (Eds.), *Handbook of Research on Women in Management and the Global Labor Market* (pp. 46–62). IGI Global. doi:10.4018/978-1-5225-9171-9.ch003

Yıldırım, S., Yıldırım, D. Ç., & Gedikli, A. (2016). Sustainable Consumption Trends in the World in the Context of Green Economy and Sustainability. In M. M. Erdoğdu, T. Arun, & I. H. Ahmad (Eds.), *Handbook of Research on Green Economic Development Initiatives and Strategies* (pp. 66–84). IGI Global. doi:10.4018/978-1-5225-0440-5.ch004

KEY TERMS AND DEFINITIONS

2030 Sustainable Development Goals (SDGs): Seventeen future goals for the world to reach sustainable development point by 2030.

AECEN (The Asian Environmental Compliance and Enforcement Network): An organization that including 13 Asian countries to guide and help them for having legal requirements for environmental sustainability in Asia.

EEA (European Environment Agency): Being one agency of European Union that works for providing reliable and independent information about environment.

EPA (United States Environmental Protection Agency): It is an organization for Americans that works to protect human health and natural environment.

Green Economy: An economic approach that working with sustainable development.

OECD (The Organisation for Economic Co-Operation and Development): It is an organization for member countries to have better economic and social policies for development.

Sustainability: A term that means an ability to be permanent.

Sustainable Development: A development type that meeting today's need with taking care of next generation's needs.

WGEO (World Green Economy Organization): It is an organization which is established based on Rio+20 UN Conference on sustainable Development in 2012 to support global actions through general sustainable development goals.

Chapter 2
Bio-Economy at the Crossroads of Sustainable Development

José G. Vargas-Hernández
University Center for Economic and Managerial Sciences, University of Guadalajara, Mexico

ABSTRACT

This study aims to review, analyze, and systematize the knowledge created on bio-economy to develop a conceptual and theoretical framework based on the transdisciplinary study of biology and socioeconomy to be used in further research. It begins from the questioning of the benefits that bio-economy has compared to the neoclassical economy. The methods employed are critical analytic, descriptive, deductive-inductive, and it suggests holistic and transdisciplinary approaches. As a result, the core of the study presents the principles under which this new scientific paradigm in sustainable development can continue creating more scientific knowledge to be used in the formulation and implementation of strategic choices for the bio-production, bio-distribution, and bio-consumption processes.

INTRODUCTION

Any nation of the World faces major environmental, economic and social challenges to be addressed to change for sustainable development and the better the way to live and work. Bio-economy is a 'greener' alternative that have impacts on natural and environmental resources, food, soil, land and livelihoods. Bio-economy has a relevant impact in important bio products such as textiles, cosmetics, bioenergy,

DOI: 10.4018/978-1-5225-9562-5.ch002

biofuels, building products, and other byproducts and bio power. Bio-economy serves a market of environmentally sustainable satisfactors, products and services and to keep in pace in the long term to become global, it requires more research and development. Bio-economy is globally influencing biotechnological research and development, business models and market structure.

Bio-economics is considered as a more advanced scientific development than economics because it relies on the evolutionary process of humanity and nature. The advance of economic science extends to consider biological evolution, biology and thermodynamics as important foundations of the economic process. The bio-economy connects and expands economics and biology to anchor in its empirical prediction to give it the power of regeneration and sustainability to the activities of the socioeconomic and biological systems.

This study analyzes the recent developments on bio-economy. It reviews the conceptualization of bio-economy, green economy and ecological economics to analyze the deficiencies of classic economy leading to present the bio-economics as the new epistemological paradigm inextricable linked to sustainable development. From this framework, there are derived at the core of the subject and object of study some principles offered as the basis for further research: Circular economy, sustainable development, holistic and transdisciplinary approaches, innovation culture and capacity creation, knowledge-based economy, global ethics, social capital and culture of peace.

Finally, the study considers the importance of formulation and implementation of the bio-economy as a strategy to enable and ensure results in terms of contributions for the sustainable development of renewable resources. Also some concluding remarks are offered.

CONCEPTUALIZATION OF BIO-ECONOMY

The concept of bio-economy is relatively new to name those economic activities derived from the biosciences advances and surge in the scientific knowledge in biotechnology, genetics, genomics, etc., to achieve practical applications from biological processes. The term *bio-economics* was coined by Georgescu-Roegen to explain the biological origin of the economic process and thus spotlight the problem of mankind's existence with a limited store of *accessible* resources, unevenly located and unequally appropriated (Georgescu-Roegen 1977: 361). Bio-economy is the sustainable production and conversion of biomass into a range of goods and services, among others food, health, fiber and industrial products and energy. The term 'bio-economic' is used to indicate both economic and biophysical components (Knowler 2002).

Bio-economy is a concept related to the economic activities derived from utilizing natural and biological resources or bioprocesses to produce bio products. Bio-economy is an aggregated set of economic operations and activities related with biological products to capture economic value, growth and welfare benefits for human development. The concept of a bio-economy refers to that economy where the basic components of materials, chemicals and energy come from renewable biological resources, such as plant and animal sources. This type of economy can meet many of the requirements for sustainability from environmental and social aspects as it is designed and implemented intelligently.

Returning to the definition of the concept of bio-economics, the OECD suggests that it can be understood as -the aggregate set of economic operations in a society that uses the latent value of biological products and processes to capture new benefits of growth and well-being for citizens and nations. This first definition, from the year 2006, essentially includes the same idea with regard to the means to achieve growth and prosperity, as is clear from the description of the OECD from 2009 (OECD 2009).

Turning to a European vision, the EC defines the bio-economy in its policy package as the production of renewable biological resources and the conversion of these resources and waste streams into value-added products such as food, feed, bio-based products and bioenergy (European Commission, 2015). The bio-economy encompasses agriculture, forestry, fisheries, food and biotechnology, as well as a wide range of industrial sectors, ranging from energy and chemical production to construction and transportation.

The concept of bio-economics has several meanings: It is the efficient management of human resources (Clark, 2010) and is considered as an analogy of biology to explain economic theory. The concept of bio-economics as the biological analysis of economic relations, which as dynamic systems can be effected, for example, through frames of reference, mental schemes and instruments of thought analysis.

The concept of bio-economy is under debate (Levidow, Birch, Papaioannou 2012). A bio-economy can be defined as an economy in which the basic building blocks for materials, chemicals and energy are derived from renewable biological resources (McCormick & Kautto, 2013). Bio-economy is defined as the global industrial transition of sustainably utilizing renewable aquatic and terrestrial biomass resources in energy, intermediate, and final products for economic, environmental, social, and national security benefits (USDA 2015). The bio-economy is defined as an economy based on the sustainable production and conversion of renewable biomass into a range of bio-based products, chemicals, and energy (de Besi and McCormick, 2017).

Awareness on the concept of the bio-economy as potential in biosciences and biotechnology.

While the concept of bio-economics began initially from the science of biotechnology, then it has expanded to incorporate other ideas. Biotechnology can be understood as the science of using living things to produce goods and services. Therefore, it involves manipulating and modifying organisms to create new and practical applications for primary production, health and industry.

Another meaning of the concept is the one that considers the bio-economy as the influence that has the satisfaction of the human needs like the biological conditions in the economic behavior.

Bio-Economy as Green Economy

Bio-economy also called green economy can be defined as one that has low carbon emissions, uses resources efficiently and is socially inclusive (PNUMA, 2016). The bio-economy sector is a warrantor for a green economy.

The 'bio-economy' agenda has developed the concept 'green economy' that emerged at the 2012 Rio+20 summit and is promoted by the United Nations Environment Programme to pursue natural renewable resources bioenergy and sustainable biological products (Socaciu, 2014). The agenda for bio-economy has been pushed by large corporations and developed states linked to green economy and the Knowledge-Based Bio-Economy (Hall, and Zacune, 2012). The Rio+20 agenda 'Towards a Green Economy' gave rise to the bio-economic strategy for sustainable development and economic growth (European Commission 2012). The European Union promotes among its Member States the commitment to the agenda of "Green economy", bioenergy (Paul, 2013) and agro fuels as an alternative to fossil fuels (Hall and Zacune 2012, OECD, 2009).

Bio-economics biologicalises the natural environment and the biological resources of business activities as intrinsic and inextricable elements of mutualistic coevolution. The bio-economy integrates the green economy that seeks to respond to the challenges of food security and clean bioenergy.

Bio-Economy as Ecological Economics

However, bio-economics is also called ecological economics. For some authors the bio-economy is the ecological economy that reconciles the economy and the ecology, that at the same time that looks for the economic efficiency, takes care of the natural resources that are essential for the humanity. The bio-economic approach calls for a change in values on the use of available resources and energy to be conserved for the use if future generations. The bio-economy is the basis of the business of ecological projects, agricultural, etc. Bio-economics studies the biological origin of economic process and the human activities associated with a limited stock of available and accessible resources that are unevenly located and unequally appropriated (Mayumi, 2001).

Ecological disasters in recent years as a result of the subordination of the laws of nature to the laws of the market economy and that has demonstrated the destructive capacity of the forces of nature, to the point that has created an awareness by the environmental care. Some analysts consider that the bio-economy approach is destructive and should be restructured from an agro ecological perspective.

THE DEFICIENCIES OF NEOCLASSICAL ECONOMICS

The economy as a science oriented by the competition has serious methodological deficiencies that the bio-economy tries to overcome through bio centric processes and of bio-economic balance centered in the cooperation for the sustainable development and the conservation of the nature and the environment in their interactions with the humanity. From a holistic perspective, the interactions between biological and socioeconomic systems result in the field of bio-economics. The interactions of the natural biological and economic processes that give rise to the bio-economy have an impact on the complex and uncertain phenomena of the biosphere.

The Physiocrats subordinated reproduction and economic transformation to nature, classical economics to capital, later to the goal of market equilibrium and the financial system with economic neoliberalism. The heterodox economy is more oriented to the human aspect with approaches such as humanist socialism that resists the clashes of the liberal economy and analyze the contradictions of economic liberalism with the argument that the labor force is not a commodity that separates from the human being.

The market economy reduces natural, social and moral values but cannot regulate the behavior of nature. The First Report of the Club of Rome (Club de Roma, 1972) which warns about the limits of economic growth and the Brundtland Report (Brundtland Gro Harlem, 1987) that reports threats to the mechanisms that regulate nature, emerges the issues for sustainable development to maintain the balance between the interdependence of the economy, nature and the biosphere.

BIO-ECONOMY: A NEW ECONOMIC EPISTEMOLOGY PARADIGM

Bio-economics as a discipline is a new paradigm in environmental economic development (Soedigdo et al. 2014). The emergence of Bio-economics as a different science to economics and biology represents a new paradigm in scientific disciplinary evolution for the study and analysis of the bio-economic causes of the environmental impacts of human actions (Mohammadian 2000). The interactions of biological and economic systems are integrated in the bio-economy from a new perspective that represents a paradigm shift. As an interdisciplinary science, bio-economics synthesizes sciences based on the empiricism of biology and the humanism of economics, resulting in a new, more holistic paradigm because it attempts to explain the interactivity of biological systems and nature with economics and the social.

Bio-economics represents a paradigmatic change in the evolution of disciplines whose main task is to investigate the problems that arise from the impact of human enterprise on the environment. These problems are not only due to purely biological causes, or to purely economic causes. Bio-economics has been the result and in turn is provoking paradigmatic change in the epistemology of research for the generation of innovative theoretical and empirical knowledge with applications that are highly significant for their contributions. The paradigm focused on bio-economic development is based on the holistic perspective that results from the interaction of biological, socioeconomic and environmental development to explain the coevolution of human development that guarantees the provision of resources for present and future generations.

The bio-economic development paradigm (Mohammadian, 2000) is an alternative to prevent the accelerated depletion of natural biological resources, mitigate environmental degradation, reduce economic inequality and social inequity. The community participation and paradigm has been changing with the bio-economy process (Henry and Roche 2013). Sustainability preserves the identity and integrity of bio-economic systems by enhancing self-sufficiency and equity and respect for biospheric equilibria as the criteria for regulation of trade and economic activity in opposition to the neoclassical economic paradigm endorsing global trade to stimulate economic growth.

The new paradigm complements the tangible and intangible resources, the objective with the subjective and the feelings with the facts with a sustainable and sustained growth orientation, with a material and economic operational benefit. The new paradigm of production and market, which has been call cognitive capitalism and bio-economics, in a word, bio-capitalism (Fumagalli 2007). Bio-economics makes aware of the interactions of biological and socio-economic systems, to reach a conciliation, to adopt a holistic research. The three disciplines of the economy-environment have offered a change of perspective, and a non-paradigm shift as bio-economics does.

PRINCIPLES OF BIO-ECONOMY

Circular Economy

Bio-economy links economic growth with environmental sustainability under the guiding principle of a circular economy. Bio based circular economy is bio-economy for a sustainable policy agenda which can solve the challenges of climate change, eco-technologies, agriculture and food security, blue growth, etc. For example, the wood-based bio-economy is a bio-based circular economy that originates from processing and recycling timber, pulpwood and other forests utilized for material and energy sources. Bio-economy innovation is shaping the new social economy combining elements of circular economy and social inclusion

Sustainable Development

Bio-economy is a transitional step towards sustainable development. Bio-economy promotes sustainable development by protecting biodiversity and reducing dependence on fossil natural resources. The White Paper the European bio-economy in 2030 sustains that bio-economy has to face challenges such as the sustainable management of natural resources, sustainable production, public health, mitigating climate change, integrating and balancing social developments and global sustainable development.

The neoclassical model of the economy supports neoliberal capitalism while the bio-economically centered sustainable development model encourages people to engage in cooperative socio-economic activities that benefit in the long run. The bio-economy reduces dependence on fossil natural resources, prevent biodiversity loss and creates economic growth and employment in line with the principles of sustainable development.

The bio-economy provides benefits for the increasing sustainable development by economic growth and outputs, replacing fossil fuels with renewable natural resources, biodiversity conservation, increase energy self-sufficiency. Some contributions of bio-economics to sustainable development are in global food security, renewable raw materials, mitigation of climate change, etc. The utilization of bio-economic resources to promote sustainable development of marine fisheries resources requires empirical research on fisheries biology and economics. Bio-economic analysis of fisheries is scarce despite that there are some reports on economics, biological and resource management (Habib, Ullah, and Ngoc Duy2014).

The bio-economic analysis is based on calculation of reference points (Thunberg, Helser, and Mayo, 1998). Mathematical bio-economics is used to study of the management of renewable resources, such as differential equations to model resource processes based on guiding principles to determine profits (Clark, 1990). One of this principles is the tragedy of the commons. Indicators for bio-economy sustainable development are required to be defined (Fritsche, Iriarte, 2014).

The bio-economy agenda has already presented several limitations in all principles of ensuring food security, harvest limited to the capacity of regeneration, use of biomass for the highest value and reducing, recycling and reusing waste. The European Union imports aromas expanding the use of bio-economy, despite that its policies are being questioned and criticized. A good example is agro fuels, which are not actually renewable resources and therefore, have failed to deliver the promises.

One of the main challenges of the bio-economy is to change the current production, distribution and consumption systems to those that are more environmentally friendly and provide sustainable development for the conservation of natural resources, while meeting human current needs.

Holistic Approach

According to Mohammadian (2005) bio-economics is a holistic interdisciplinary science, also called biological economics is a new epistemology for the investigation of the interrelationships between biological and socioeconomic systems beyond the different approaches of environmental economics, economics of natural resources and the ecological economy. Bio-economics aims to narrow biology as an empirical science and economics as a social science.

Bio-economics aims to achieve a harmony between the holistic balance of economic, social-human and natural and environmental conditions. Thus conceived, this bio-economic balance of holistic character gives rise to the happiness of a life balanced in all the orders. Achieving the balance between the price and the quantity of the economy that is short-term with the quality and the bio-economic value that is maintained in the long run is also to maintain a holistic perspective that balances selfishness and altruism.

Bio-economic education should focus on a holistic and transdisciplinary learning process that results from the scientific experimentation of new cognitive processes and synthesis of the interactions and interrelations of biological, economic, social and environmental processes. To achieve this new mentality, the educational process must undergo a scientific-academic revolution through the synthesis of theories of Biology, Economics and Cognition, to promote an integrated education in the form of a bio-economic educational process. Such an educational process is holistic and interdisciplinary, and helps to dismantle reductionist education to promote the synthesis culture in addition to facilitating the art of learning to learn.

Transdisciplinary Approach

Modern scientific research during the last centuries has suffered from the premises of simplicity, objectivity and positivism. In addition, its Cartesian reductionist methodology has divided biospheric and socioeconomic systems into separate compartments, to be investigated by various disciplines, forgetting the unity of human life with its biological basis. It is evaluating interactive problems with an outdated mindset, evolved for a world it has left behind decades ago. Bio-economics is born as a response to the incremental advances of the other economics-environment disciplines through which the pathologies of capitalism and its industrial system have been investigated individually and separately.

The analysis from the bio-economy is based on the transdisciplinary interrelations between the human, natural and economic areas (Nicolescu, 1996). In addition, the reflections of Georgescu-Roegen (GR) helped to establish links between different disciplines and to address the economic issue beyond money, managed to introduce the biophysical dimension, so that the currents of industrial ecology, agro ecology or urban ecology have in the proposals of GR a precedent (Carpintero 2006).

Bio-economy is a transdisciplinary approach that encompasses biology, economics, physics, genetics, forestry, marine sciences, etc. Bio-economics as a transdisciplinary science proposes the integration of biophysical subsystems of nature and environmental, biological, bio-spherical with economic, social and human subsystems with long-term orientation to ensure the happiness of future generations. Bio-economics is a transdisciplinary science that seeks to study and analyze biological and socioeconomic systems from a perspective of cooperation and solidarity for the conservation of physical, natural, biological and social capital. Bio-economics proposes among its transdisciplinary principles for the creation of bio-economic capital through biology and economics as the integrated solution to sustainable bio-economic development.

Heuristics is a method used by the bio-economy that is based on transdisciplinary and holism for the generation of knowledge through absence or reordering of existing information. The functional method in research starts from emerging properties in the interaction of problems such as climate change in biological and socioeconomic systems. The transdisciplinary of the principles of Bio-economics and the knowledge economy raises its character of postmodernity.

Sustainable bio-economy needs transdisciplinary capabilities and expertise. The bio-economy is not only a transdisciplinary branch, but also contributes to change the mentality of people, passing from a greedy, guided by the power that grants the money to a person who uses resources in a rational way, thinking about the future and the conservation of the planet.

Innovation Culture and Capacity Development

The bio-economic theory is based on the value of complex innovations based on an ethical - economic - humanist balance. Business culture to foster innovation is essential in bio-economy aligned with the needs of sustainable development and with the collaboration of all the stakeholders involved on strategic alliances or other forms of cooperation between different sectors are essential. Education, research and innovation skills are critical factor for development of bio-economy. However, the basis for the bio-economy comes from previous strategic agendas of the European Commission (EC), including the 1993 White Paper which highlighted the need for non-physical investments based on knowledge and the role of biotechnology in innovation and growth or the 2000 Lisbon Agenda by stimulating the knowledge-based economy to ensure competitiveness and economic growth.

It can be pointed out convincingly that discoveries, ideas and innovations play an important role in economic growth. Bio-economy is driven by material innovations. Bio-economy innovation emerges from research and bio-economy. The bio-economy web is created to integrate all the sectors involved in sustainable growth, including all bio products, food and nonfood and facing the challenges to become a major driver of innovation.

Small and medium-sized enterprises (SMEs) are drivers of innovation in bio-economy, thereby driving SMEs in bio-economy. SMEs and groundbreaking innovation emerges in the bio-economy. Not only large corporations, but also SMEs in all sectors are important for the development and implementation of bio-economy because they may be able to develop the capability to absorb the knowledge, produce in accordance and marketing innovations of the new bio products. Bio-economy offers opportunities to promote innovations, market access and ensure operations and functioning solutions.

A transition towards bio-economy requires the innovation and development in biotechnology. The transition towards a bio-economy founded on biomass has being designed by different strategies but on a common direction based on technological research and innovation on biotechnology de Besi and McCormick, 2017). Biotechnology R&D requires bio-economy innovation to attend an increasing market demanding sustainable products and services.

Bio-economy initiatives contribute to shape a sustainable economy away from fossil resource dependency, prompting governments and firms to develop strategies aimed to conduct research and innovation. Bio-economy makes possible de-carbonization which in turn supports innovations. Thus, biotechnology innovation drives bio-economy innovation and technology transfer from scientific institutions to industry through cooperation and networks with private firms, academic, social and governmental institutions.

Bio-economy obtains biological natural resources from agriculture, forestry, and fishery providing innovations that are vital for biotechnology growth. Sustainable bio-economy objectives are based on research and innovation into breeding, feeding, health and housing of livestock and fish. Some key influence factors identified for the wood-based bio-economy development are the biomass availability/forest structure, globalization and global economic development, energy and climate policies, supply and demand for wood, willingness to pay for bio-based products and innovations along the value chain of wood (De Besi and McCormick, 2015). Bio-economy innovation is driven by other influence factors such as the demand for biomass that may be reducing due to utilization of waste materials.

Urban green spaces are potentially development environments for sustainable bio-economy innovations in products and services that provide solutions in air quality, water, energy, health, waste management, etc. Interactions between urban green spaces and communities derive bio-economy benefits in areas such as renewable energies, food, health, etc. Bio-economy is already a major driver of rural and coastal development playing a key role in societal innovation.

Sustainable bio-economy activities of new business require investments in innovation and equity financing for growth of bio-economy services and products entering into global markets. Bio-economy growth business may be government funded, cooperation and public finance for research innovation and improve the bio-economy base products and services market position. An innovation system supported by institutional infrastructure and supportive mechanisms embedded within the waste-based bio-economy enable transition from traditional market to bio-economy-based market.

Sustainable bio-economy innovations require capabilities and competences development in research and expertise in product and services development. Development of bio-economy business expertise in some sectors still in their infancy is driven by the market attractiveness, risk investments for innovation and growth and target of demand. Further research on bio-economy innovation is needed. The circulate nature of bio-economy processes influence the economics of energy use and raw materials as it is required to build a capacity for future development based on research, innovation and market conditions.

Research, development and innovation on diverse sustainable technologies, facilities, processes and skilled workforce maximize environmental sustainable bio-economy. Innovations along the value chain to reduce costs are necessary. Institutional and technological innovations are essential for bio-economy product and process. A deficient innovation system may lead to weak innovative firms. Innovative innovation by the increase of bio-economy-based raw materials, and thus, increasing the diversification and variety supply for the bio-economy. The development of the bio-economy integrates alternative forms of agriculture and social innovation to achieve a more distributed bio-economy with relationships between firms and community's involvement.

Certain conclusions are drawn from the strategic analysis and recommendations for the future of bio-economy based on research, development and innovation. The bio-economy transition requires changes at the level of system involving social, political, government and industry actors in the strategy formulation and implementation on research and innovation, land use, biomass, social change and governance.

Bio-economy research and innovation strategy across the landscape resources meeting the scientific criteria is needed. Future opportunities of bio-economy applications for markets are the duties of research policies shaping the innovation and creativity as a framework conditions for the bio-economy locations.

Knowledge-Based Economy

To date, the progress of the bio-economy has been made possible by a recent search for knowledge and technical expertise to use biological processes for practical applications. The human enterprise based on the principles of bio-economics and novel ideas is really the knowledge economy. The dominant view of the bio economy considered as a hard science based on knowledge and technological innovation has a life sciences perspective that is based on the argument that global value chains increase the efficiency and productivity of natural agriculture bio products.

The bio-economy is based on the knowledge economy and green economy for an efficient management of renewable biological resources, the production of bio products, agro fuel agro-fuels. The new bio-economic sustainable growth theory is an alternative theory to neoclassical growth theory that emphasizes knowledge and ideas as the most relevant production factor.

The European Commission adopted the agenda 'Innovating for Sustainable Growth: A Bio-economy for Europe' in 2012 under the life sciences strategy to address environmental, biological and natural bio products and bioenergy. However, the life sciences approach to Knowledge-Based Bio-Economy (KBBE) dominates bio-economy research more than the agro ecology perspective. Life sciences is one of the dynamic sectors of bio-economy. The agro ecological perspective of the knowledge bio-economy stands as an alternative under the premise that organic farming with fewer levels of supply chains gives more value to producers (Levidow, Birch and Papaioannou 2012).

The OECD further states that the bio-economy involves three elements: the use of advanced knowledge of genes and cellular processes to design and develop new processes and products; the use of renewable biomass and efficient bioprocesses to stimulate sustainable production; and the integration of knowledge and applications of biotechnology in a range of sectors. According to the White

Paper, the implementation of bio-economy needs coherent an integrated policy for a sectorial and multidisciplinary investment on bio-economy research, knowledge development and innovation, entrepreneurship in bio-economy, and development of skilled workforce in bio-economy. However, it is highly debated and contested the top-down target-oriented approach to implement knowledge-based bio-economy as a programmatic framework.

The bio-economy pivots on the basis of the new knowledge economy with objectives of economic growth and competitiveness in close relation with the strategies of public policies that emerge from the neoliberal narrative. The bio-economy agenda is sustained by the Knowledge-Based Bio-Economy (KBBE) as an approach that emerged from the life-sciences research focusing on bio agriculture. The dominant version of bio-economics is the life sciences approach which commodifies both nature and knowledge reinforcing dysfunctional behaviors and patters instead to solve their causes.

Bio-economy is the knowledge-based bio production and use of renewable resources to make bio products, processes and services. The knowledge-based bio-economy develops biological processes technologically to provide a wide range of bio products from renewable raw materials. The knowledge-based bio-economy promotes strategic research and innovation to support the transition from an oil-based to a bio based economy that enables economic prosperity with ecological and social compatibility. Efficient and sustainable biological resources rests on bio-economy knowledge-based innovation aimed to business and large corporations to concentrate control over natural resources, production processes and distribution chains.

Knowledge-based bio-economy supports research and innovation for the transition from oil-based economy to bio based economy to foster ecological and social compatibility in a wide range of sectors. Bio-economy, bio-based economy, and knowledge-based-bio-economy (KBBE) are similar concepts used to describe the transition from a fossil fuel based economy towards an economy based on renewable biomass for bio products and bioenergy (Schmidt, Padel & Levidow *2012*, Birch and Tyfield (2012) and Staffas, Gustavsson & McCormick 2013).

Knowledge-based bio-economy is translating into economic growth by bio based research and innovation, accelerating bio based products and services, energy, health, food, IT sector, agriculture and manufacturing, and strengthening competitiveness. The bio-economy is expanding knowledge on biosciences and biotechnologies based on Nano molecular structures to genetic science. The knowledge-based bio-economy is scattered among the industrial sectors and nations. Knowledge-based research in the area of the bio-economy has been conducted and substantially covered in agriculture and food policy.

Bio-based innovations promoted by a knowledge-based research strategy is centered around competitive bio-economy sectors, such as sustainable agricultural production, the global food security, healthy and safe foods, the development of biomass-based energy carriers and the industrial application of renewable resources. Bio-economy involve the use of knowledge of genes and cell processes to develop new products and services.

Biotechnology benefits from bio-economy knowledge spillover contributing to a significant increase of economic growth. Bio-economics can maximize economic efficiency, social and human benefits from a sustainable use and maintenance of nature and environment through knowledge spillovers and commercial applications.

For the knowledge-based Bio-economy to create sustainable development is required to include sectoral components at all levels, that is at local, national, regional and global level. The economic, ecological, and social contributions of the bio-economy can be realized through knowledge of the biological processes and systems and their interactions with the ecosystem, as well as the associated bio technology and social implications. The knowledge-based bio-economy combine economic growth and prosperity with environmental sustainability and compatibility. The knowledge-based bio-economy contributes to global responsibility in the present, and to appropriate foresight for future generations.

Bio-economy knowledge can be taking for granting by emerging the information channels. The bio-economy transformation process driven by technological knowledge and supported by structures of innovation networks are taking commercial advantages in global markets. Integrated bio-economy combines entrepreneurship with corporate responsibility and identity with other stakeholders and firms sharing knowledge networks. Incorporation of renewable natural resources in bio-economy programs aimed for creation of business and new jobs requires the expertise of research multidisciplinary models to generate bio-economy knowledge in creating business.

Bio-economy knowledge can be transferred from research centers to different sectors, including to business in different organizational forms among which can be joint ventures for development and innovation. Innovative developments in bio-economy technologies and products are stimulated for investments on research and development and knowledge transfer and exchanges, combined with a created demand of bio products are important components of bio-economy policy (Grubler, Aguayo, Gallagher, Hekkert, Jiang, Mytelka, Neij, Nemet, Wilson, 2001; Borrás and Edquist, 2013; Foxon, Gross, Chase, Howes, Arnall, Anderson, 2005).

The knowledge-based bio-economy accommodates results between technology, the economy, and ecology. Knowledge-based bio-economy competencies expertise is developed by research infrastructure extended in bio-economy research centers, information and communication technologies such as the one supported by platform technologies and institutional funding.

The knowledge-based bio-economy requires the implementation of complex interrelationships of training and research agents committed to the creation of sustainable bio-based economy in accordance to demographic and socio-economic changes. Bio-economy requires well trained and educated talent with multidisciplinary and interdisciplinary qualifications.

Opportunities for a knowledge-based bio-economy, biomass-based raw materials and global food security are enormous in growing markets with the increasing demand of bio products and services. The Bio-economy is knowledge-based science requiring further collaborative intra and interdisciplinary research and development to increase the innovation capable to elicit and solve the global societal challenges.

Global Ethics

Bio-economics represents a fundamental change in ideology in everything that is related to socioeconomic, biological, and ethical activities. Business, industry and society can contribute to and benefit from bio-economics by considering the socio-economic and ethical implications. Homo bio-economicus is based on biological principles of conservation, recycling, regeneration and respect, as well as on the socioeconomic principles of equity, equality and under the ethical principle of exploiting natural and biological resources, but living off of its income management provided.

From a different perspective, bio-economics complements analyze of the neoclassical economics of socioeconomic, biological, and ethical activities. The principles of biological sustainability, environmental integrity, social equity, economic equality and global ethics sufficiency of the bio-economy that underpin socioeconomic activities.

The bio-economy supports economic activities based on the principle of an ethical practice to benefit all participants, thereby reducing transaction costs. The science of bio-economics is considered a postmodern science that considers the participation of all interest groups around the concepts of sustainability, quality, value, ethics, equality, social justice, fraternity and compassion. Ideas and knowledge as intangible resources of the bio-economy emanate from heuristics as a tool for sustainable economic growth that is based on biological, environmental, economic, social and ethical resources.

The implications of bio-economy for economy, society and ethics have to be addressed such as long-term health care, food, etc. The framework of bio-economy interdisciplinary research projects contributes to discussions on social, legal and ethical issues. Sustainable bio-economy global demand of bio products and bio services requires to be framed by ethical consumer behavior and legislation.

Social Capital and Culture of Peace

The business bio-economic activities have as components in bio-economic capital and social capital. Bio-economics is based on the cultural, non-economic and intangible dimensions of social capital such as trust, cooperation, solidarity, reciprocity, etc., values that validate the humanist and transformative vision of biology and socioeconomic activities of bio production with use value (Mohammadian, 2003). Social capital facilitates the relations of solidarity and compassionate cooperation that contribute to the formation of a more generous and altruistic society.

For organizations and companies with a bio-economic orientation, social capital, biological capital and financial and monetary capital have the same importance in their scale of values. In other words, a bio-economic enterprise attaches as much importance to social capital and biological capital as to money capital (Mohammadian, 2005). At the center of social capital is trust and cooperation, also the main ingredients of a culture of peace.

The bio-economy is based on solid principles of trust and cooperation, fraternity, justice and compassion to achieve the creation of bio-economic value and economic growth through the internalization of costs that produce the externality attached to the care of the biological foundation. The new institutional economy promotes the cultural principles on which the bio-economy is based, so that they coincide in the sustainable benefits obtained through just, cooperative, fraternal, reciprocal and trustworthy socio-economic transactions. For example, the non-economic components of bio-economic accounting enable the processes of transformation of economic activities with capitalist profit purposes to carry out more humanistic activities that harmonize the relations of cooperation and competition.

Bio-economy has an impact on the quality and level of employment and on building societal trust. The "Homo oeconomicus" is a being that seeks efficiency, focused on competition and is predatory, greedy and without any human feeling while "Homo bio-economicus" is a being that is sensitive to human needs and nature, centered on relations of cooperation and trust, in harmony with himself, with those around him and with nature and with a culture of sufficiency and conservation, with a sense of the values of solidarity and fraternity (Mohammadian, 2000, 2003) promoter of sustainability. Bio-economics is considered as a postmodern science in terms of the values of cooperation, trust and empathy on which it stands.

The institutionalization of bio-economics promotes the relationships of trust and cooperation between stakeholders and other groups of interest. To build consumer trust on bio products and bio-economy are required to implement high global standards of reliable quality, safety, efficiency, transparency and acceptability with the support from industry, society, policymakers, regulatory agencies.

The sustainable bio-economy encourages relationships of cooperation between different economic sectors and improves the well-being of society. Homo bio-economicus, unlike homo oeconomicus, is a being satisfied with the resources that he has access to and self-fulfillment in his life, sensitive to human needs and realities, in harmony and with an attitude of cooperation and care with environmental, economic, social and political situations. Bio-economy is sustained as the third path of economy because it is considered to be between the classical equilibrium economy and use value and the new global economy of complexity and exchange value, and therefore benefits both (Mohammadian, 2003) as models of competition and cooperation (Mohammadian, 2000).

Bio-economy organizations are using innovative business models based on relationships of cooperation to create new entrepreneurial structures to foster research and development and the applications. All type of organizations involved in bio-economy activities and practices have different entrepreneurship structures to accommodate the participation and cooperation of all the stakeholders to achieve the goals. Sustainable bio-economy services associated with industrial bio products contribute to develop efficient bio-economy value chains, create new bio-economy business and encourages relationships of cooperation and partnerships.

As such, development cooperation between business units, regions and nations demand sustainable bio-economy development activities in sustainable use and expertise of natural resources. Advancement requires active participation in relationships of international cooperation programs to strengthen support of bio-economy activities. A good example of sustainable bio-economy implementation is the cooperation with financial providers across sectoral boundaries. Bio-economy technologies, products and services can be standardized and certified to follow the rules of global markets by means of international cooperation and allocation. Technology transfer in bio-economy in science deliver economic and social benefits if scientific results are delivery through new forms of cooperation and strategic alliances between firms, science institutions, communities and government.

Although in fact, there is much to do and develop, the projects of bio-economy involve a more democratic attitude supportive of a culture of peace, such as the specific cases of free green spaces.

BIO-ECONOMY AS A STRATEGY

Bio-economy strategy aims on self-sufficiency in energy, raw materials and securing availability of biomass, low-carbon and resource-efficient society. A bio-economy strategy is aimed to identify energy, environment, water, food, health, social, etc., challenges and act upon the critical bio-economy research from using waste materials to gain market value and growth. A bio-economy strategy links bio-economy-based renewable resources with sustainability by ensuring sustainable production and use of biomass (Pfau, Hagens, Dankbaar, Smits 2014).

The knowledge-based bio-economy is a sustainable economic strategy for the creation of sustainable natural capital (Birch, Levidow, and Papaioannou, 2010) that is oriented towards the formulation of sustainability policies, in a way that attempts to link bio-economics projects with the knowledge-based economy and technological innovation for the design of public policies and institutional practices (Franco, Goldfarb, Fig, Levidow, and Oreszczyn, 2011).

Bio-economics is presented as a win-win strategy. Bio-economy has been identified as a strategy and defined as encompassing the production of renewable biological resources and the conversion of these resources and waste streams into value added products, such as food, feed, bio-based products and bioenergy. Its sectors and industries have strong innovation potential due to their use of science, enabling and industrial technologies, along with local and tacit knowledge (European Commission, 2012, p. 3). The European Union's strategy adopted in 2012 and announced as innovation in the service of sustainable growth: a bio-economy for Europe promotes sustainable production and consumption capabilities based on life sciences to address the challenges of the environment, the use of energy and food security.

The bio-economy as a greening strategy is advancing amid the debates on the so-called green economy proposed by the United Nations Environment Program (PNUMA) to promote bio production. Bio-economy as strategy has solutions to environmental concerns and sustainable economic growth moving forward to renewable biological resources in an increasing market share (European Bio-economy Panel and SCAR, 2014; European Commission, 2015). The European Union recommends the bio-economy to the Rio + 20 agenda 'Towards a green economy' as a strategy to promote the sustainable development of environmental and natural resources efficiently, thereby making economic growth compatible and the sustainable use of biological and environmental resources (European Commission, 2015).

To target specific markets, sustainable bio-economy must study and analyze the development and functioning of the environment, development of sectors, identify global trends and challenges, opportunities and changes in drivers of marketing of products and services, the specific needs to satisfy. The study of the bio-economy raises the need for a behavioral change of production systems called to play a strategic role in providing a response to a set of global challenges, uses the system approach to analyze related fields such as green economics and energy efficiency and productivity processes taking into account climate variations and increasing restrictions on the quality of biodiversity and natural resources such as air, water and soil. This analysis is necessary to formulate and implement a strategy and policy actions. Strategy formulation formulate priorities for future bio-economy development.

A favorable operating environment, strategic choices and policy actions are drivers for business bio-economy development, growth and achieving competitiveness in a setting to operate. Strategic choices and implemented sustainable bio-economy policy actions to produce efficient goods and services targeted to satisfy the needs of consumers in the marketplace and aimed to support the growth of bio-economy business. Strategy choices implementation and policy actions supported by agents in the bio-economy sector to set up a program aimed for resource efficiency and low-carbon society.

The bio-economy as part of a comprehensive global strategy including the renewable energies is able to solve the problems of sustainable development (Piotrowski, Carus, Essel, 2015). A sustainable bio-economy strategy is aimed to generate bio-economy business growth from added value bio-economy products and services while securing the nature´s ecosystems and providing sustainable global solutions for saving nature´s diversity, global warming, air pollution, consumption standards, etc. Sustainable bio-economy strategy aims to economic growth generation from high added value products and services in the competitive bio-economy business secured by natural ecosystems. Global bio-economy competitive strategy builds innovative firms supported by science and high technology research and structural conditions.

Productivity and performance of the bio-economy in sectors internationally competitive result in growing demand for innovative products, processes, and services.

Strategies for bio-economy development focus in priority areas related to research, development and innovation of new biotechnological and industrial bio products, relationships between firms, communities, research institutions and government to optimize the functioning of biomass use, funding the development of bio-based activities. Strategies on import of biomass as a raw material is required in some industries are related with the development certification process to ensure sustainability and not have negative economic, social and environmental impacts. Availability of biomass for the present and future of bio-economy is dependent on strategies on land use, agriculture, forest and the other natural and biological resources diversity. Also are important, technological development, economic and legal incentives (Welfe, Gilbert, Thornley, 2014).

Bio-economy strategies based on societal awareness and fostering research and innovation are aimed to the transition towards the development of a bio-based economy. To achieve a bio-economy transition, the development of some strategies and actions are required such as to invest in research and development, training human resources for innovative and completive skills and capabilities, to engage stakeholders in interactive processes of collaboration with bio-products to meet the market. A transition strategy towards a sustainable bio-economy has to face many factors with significant uncertainty, such as consumption patterns, climate change, sustainability risks, etc.

Some other important bio-economy strategies are designed more specifically to foster biotechnology, using biomass and waste residuals, promote collaboration relationships between different sectors and stakeholders, firms and research institutions, funding support, etc. A bio-economy research strategy should strengthen the interactions between the different stakeholders. Participation of stakeholders representing the bio-economy is vital to strategy formulation and implementation. The bio-economy research strategy is sustained by participation in research and development in collaborative projects between firms and science institutions aimed to achieve market leadership.

Research, development and innovation are the basis of the regional and industrial strategy for bio-economy development. Regional strategies for bio-economy development are different and contextualized in its own strengths, capacities and capabilities (Paterman, 2014). Deployment of bio-economics specialization strategies can foster regional economic development and support regional bio-economy clusters. Research on bio-economy strategies at regional level is very limited and provide little knowledge on the bio-economy development.

Regional strategies can improve coordination and communication between groups and industry´s platforms (BioPro Baden-Wuerttenberg, 2014), facilitates the role of local governments in supporting firms, research institutes to create bio-economy partnerships and developing standards for public procurement and labels for bio-based products, recognized by consumers (Carrez, 2014). Regional collaboration between the different actors in the different regions have strategies for bio-economy development sustained by biotechnology, health and life sciences. Regional bio-economy strategies are supported by the provision of funding and subsidies for research, development, innovation, communication, diffusion and commercialization of bio-based activities and bio-products.

The development of a network system to support bio-economy business is relevant for the strategy implementation to enter a new international market in such areas as food, health, energy, etc. The global strategy of the bio-economy as an agenda of multinational corporations that are linked to local governments is based on processes of innovation and the sustainable development of the agricultural sector and the highly questioned natural resources. The corporate-led bio-economy agenda is a global strategy linking public and private sectors based on innovation and sustainable development. Strategic alliances for collaboration between public and private sectors are critical instruments for information sharing, the research and expansion of bio-economics, and to encourage new programs of bio production.

A knowledge-based strategy intends to foster skills particularly for innovative start-ups and SMEs. Companies across bio-economy sector should encourage professional participation to gain experience in the field through different strategies and actions such as lifelong learning.

The benefits of bio-economy have to be communicated to consumers who may sift consumption away from fossil-based products and towards sustainable bio-products (FORMAS, 2012; TEM 2014). An external evaluation of the research bio-economy strategy assesses the positive effects and the impact on groundwork progress for the development of a knowledge-based competitive bio-economy activities. The bio-economic model is an integrated approach for evaluation of fishery management strategies (Anderson and Seijo 2010; Armstrong and Sumaila 2000; Clark,1995).

A strategic plan on bio-economy is required to map future potential and directions, matching economic and social needs and formulating policy agendas. The strategist of the bio-economy should be to gradually integrate small-scale ecological practices as an alternative to the expanding biomass production (ETC Group, 2015) with increasing independence of fossil fuels. However, some analysts consider that the bio-economy agenda has limitations and suggests that strategies should include more elements of agro ecology. The bio-economy strategy becomes essential to the concept of circular economy in such activities as separation of bio-waste collection and use, process of biodegradation, sustainable bio production, etc. This bio-economy strategy should be clear and transparent, engaging and involving all business, research and education institutions, community and social organizations and all levels of government institutions.

A sustainable bio-economic strategy requires an operating environment with access to sustainable biomass for the creation of new bio-economy business based on competence. Transition towards sustainable bio-economy needs strategies design and implementation for industrial biotechnological transformation from fossil fuels resources to biomass based production and the required consumer behavior changes (Birch, 2015).

These conditions can contribute to the creation of bio-economy business for sustainable development. Sustainable bio-economy development can be accelerated by systematic strategic choices and policy actions for achieving economic growth and well-being. Society structure must enable sustainable strategic choices and policy actions for bio-economy development targeted to offer alternative well-being services and products to consumer choices.

The bio-economy strategy should be more inclusive of ecological activities and techniques. The strategies of Bio-economy based on agro-industrial solutions needs to expand to include new forms of adding value and agricultural knowledge involving social and community innovation to biological resources (Birch and Tyfield, 2012; Schmidt *et al, 2012;* Levidow *et al. 2012).*

A research strategy should be based in a natural cycle of a bio based economy supported by a biological, ecology and technology systems in such a way that provide incentives to work and cooperate interdisciplinary. This strategy should develop the knowledge-based and innovation internationally competitive bio-economy.

Active dialogue, participation and relationships of cooperation among citizens, firms, new social movements and governments are required to support bio-economic initiatives embraced by public policies.

CONCLUDING REMARKS

The high dependence of today´s economic development supported on fossil-based resources increases environmental sustainability concerns of production systems and food security. This situation justifies the urgent need for a transition from neoclassical economy type of development based on fossil resources towards a more sustainable development supported by the bio-economy based on biological resources and bio biological products. Sustainable development based on bio-economy optimize the allocation of natural and biological renewable resources whilst increasing the environmental, food security, energy and health concerns.

The theoretical framework of bio-economics for sustainable development was created as an alternative to neoclassical economic development model. The economic development model based on neoclassical economics is being criticized for not addressing issues such as resource scarcity, environment, social institutions, social policy, social organization, entropy and bio-economics of economic activities.

The bio-economy sustainable development model focuses more on quality than on quantity as opposed to neoclassical economic development model. However, also the sustainable development model based on bio-economy is being under scrutiny. Some critical points addressed here regarding the sustainable development model are to consider natural resources as infinite goods which leads to an overexploitation, require massive inputs, and the production methods impact on agricultural land and the environment. This interpretation, which deals with similarities between economic and biological systems, has been harshly criticized. The explosive wave of bio-economics entails as policies the improvement in the quality of fuels and renewable energies, it is highly questioned and criticized for not delivering its promises.

This study has identified some principles of bio-economy which are critical issues affecting the prospects for the bio-economy based sustainable development. Therefore, the study concludes that bio-economy is at the crossroads of the sustainable development paradigm.

REFERENCES

Anderson, L. G., & Seijo, J. C. (2010). Bio-economics of Fisheries Management. John Wiley and Sons.

Armstrong, C. W., & Sumaila, U. R. (2000). Cannibalism and the optimal sharing of theNorth-EastAtlantic cod stock: A bio-economic model. *Journal of Bioeconomics*, *2*(2), 99–115. doi:10.1023/A:1011429907162

BioPro Baden-Wuerttenberg. (2014). *Bio-economy: Baden-Württemberg Path towards a Sustainable Future.* Available online: http://www.biopro.de/biopro/downloads/index.html?lang=en

Birch, K., Levidow, L., & Papaioannou, T. (2010). Sustainable Capital? The Neoliberalization of Nature and Knowledge in the European Knowledge-based Bio-economy. *Sustainability*, *2*(9), 2898–2918. doi:10.3390u2092898

Birch, K., & Tyfield, D. (2012). Theorizing the Bio-economy: Biovalue, Biocapital, Bio-economics or What? *Science, Technology & Human Values*, *38*, 299–327. doi:10.1177/0162243912442398

Borrás, S., & Edquist, C. (2013). The choice of innovation policy instruments. *Technological Forecasting and Social Change*, *80*(8), 1513–1522. doi:10.1016/j.techfore.2013.03.002

Brundtland Gro Harlem. (1987). *Our Common Future*. Oxford University Press.

Bundesministerium für Ernährung und Landwirtschaft (BMEL). (2016). *Nationale Politikstrategie Bioökonomie—Nachwachsende Ressourcen und Biotechnologische Verfahren als Basis für Ernährung, Industrie und Energie*. Available online: https://www.bmbf.de/files/BioOekonomiestrategie.pdf

Carpintero, Ó. (2006). *La bio-economía de Georgescu-Roegen*. Madrid: Montesinos.

Clark, C. W. (1985). Modelling and Fisheries Management. John Wiley and Sons.

Clark, C. W. (1990). *Mathematical Bio-economics: The Optimal Management of Renewable Resources*. John Wiley & Sons.

Clark, C. W. (2010). Mathematical Bio-economics: The Mathematics of Conservation (3rd ed.). Wiley.

Club de Rome (1972). *Halte à la croissance?* Traduction Française Fayard.

De Besi, M., & McCormick, K. (2015). Towards a bio-economy in Europe: National, regional and industrial strategies. *Sustainability*, *7*(8), 10461–10478. doi:10.3390u70810461

de Besi, M., & McCormick, K. (2017). *Towards a Bio-economy in Europe: National, Regional and Industrial Strategies International Institute for Industrial Environmental Economics (IIIEE)*. Lund University.

ETC Group. (2015). *The Bio-economy*. Retrieved from http://etcgroup.org/issues/bio-economy

European Bio-Economy Panel and SCAR. (2014). *What Next for the European Bio-economy?* Available from: http://ec.europa.eu/research/bio-economy/pdf/where-next-for-european-bio-economy-report-0809102014_en.pdf

European Commission. (2012a). *Innovation for Sustainable Growth: A Bio-economy for Europe*. Available from: http://ec.europa.eu/research/ bio-economy/index.cfm?pg=policy&lib=strategy

European Commission. (2012b). *Innovating for Sustainable Growth: A Bio-economy for Europe*. Luxembourg: Publication Office of the European Office.

European Commission. (2015). *Bio-economy Strategy*. Retrieved from http://ec.europa.eu/research/bio-economy/policy/strategy_en.htm

FORMAS. (2012). *Swedish Research and Innovation Strategy for a Bio-Based Economy*. Stockholm, Sweden: FORMAS.

Foxon, T. J., Gross, R., Chase, A., Howes, J., Arnall, A., & Anderson, D. (2005). UK innovation systems for new and renewable energy technologies: Drivers, barriers and systems failures. *Energy Policy*, *33*(16), 2123–2137. doi:10.1016/j.enpol.2004.04.011

Franco, J., Goldfarb, L., Fig, D., Levidow, L., & Oreszczyn, S. M. (2011). *Agricultural Innovation: Sustaining What Agriculture? For What European Bio-Economy? Project-wide final report*. CREPE.

Fritsche, U. R., & Iriarte, L. (2014). Sustainability criteria and indicators for the bio-based economy in Europe: State of discussion and way forward. *Energies*, *7*(11), 6825–6836. doi:10.3390/en7116825

Fumagalli, A. (2007). *Bioeconomia e capitalismo cognitivo: Verso un nuovo paradigma di accumulazione*. Roma: Carocci.

Georgescu-Roegen, N. (1977). Inequality, Limits and Growth from a Bio-economic Viewpoint. *Review of Social Economy, 35*(3), 361–375. doi:10.1080/00346767700000041

Grubler, A., Aguayo, F., Gallagher, K., Hekkert, M., Jiang, K., Mytelka, L., ... Wilson, C. (2001). Policies for the Energy Technology Innovation System (ETIS). In Global Energy Assessment—Toward a Sustainable Future. Cambridge University Press.

Habib, A., Ullah, H., & Ngoc Duy, N. (2014). *Bio-economics of Commercial Marine Fisheries of Bay of Bengal: Status and Direction*. Ahasan Thanasis Stengos.

Hall, R., & Zacune, J. (2012). *Bio-economies: The EU's real 'Green Economy' agenda?* World Development Movement and the Transnational Institute.

Henry, M., & Roche, M. (2013). Valuing lively materialities: Bio-economic assembling in the making of new meat futures. *New Zealand Geographer, 69*(3), 197–207. doi:10.1111/nzg.12021

Knowler, D. A. (2002). Review of selected bio-economic models with environmental influences in fisheries. *J Bioecon, 4*(2), 163–181. doi:10.1023/A:1021151809501

Levidow, L., Birch, K., & Papaioannou, T. (2012). EU agri-innovation policy: Two contending visions of the bio-economy'. *Critical Policy Studies, 6*(1), 40–65. doi: 10.1080/19460171.2012.659881

Mayumi, K. (2001). *The Origins of Ecological Economics.The bio-economics of Georgescu-Roegen Routledge Research in Environmental Economics*. London: Routledge.

McCormick, K., & Kautto, N. (2013). The Bio-economy in Europe: An Overview. *Sustainability, 5*(6), 2589–2608. doi:10.3390u5062589

Mohammadian, M. (2000). *Bio-economics: Biological Economics*. Madrid: Interdisciplinary Study of Biology, Economics and Education. Entrelíneas Editores.

Mohammadian, M. (2003). What is Bio-economics: Biological Economics. Journal of Interdisciplinary Economics, 14(4), 319-337.

Mohammadian, M. (2005). La bio-economía: un nuevo paradigma socioeconómico para el siglo XXI. Encuentros multidisciplinares, 7(19), 57-70.

Nicolescu, B. (1996). La Transdisciplinarité. Ed. Du Rocher.

OECD. (2009). *The Bio-economy to 2030: Designing a Policy Agenda*. Retrieved from http://www.oecd.org/futures/bio-economy/2030

Pfau, S., Hagens, J., Dankbaar, B., & Smits, A. (2014). Visions of Sustainability in Bio-economy Research. *Sustainability*, *6*(3), 1222–1249. doi:10.3390u6031222

Piotrowski, S., Carus, M., & Essel, R. (2015). Global bio-economy in the conflict between biomass supply and demand. *Nova Pap.*, *7*, 1–14.

PNUMA. (2016). *Programa de las Naciones Unidas para el Medio Ambiente*. Retrieved from http://www.pnuma.org/eficienciarecursos/economia.php

Schmidt, O., Padel, S., & Levidow, L. (2012). The bio-economy concept and knowledge base in a public goods and farmer perspective. *Bio-Based and Applied Economics*, *1*, 47–63.

Socaciu, C. (2014). Bio-economy and green economy: European strategies, action plans and impact on life quality. *Bulletin UASVM Food Science and Technology*, *71*(1).

Soedigdo, D., Harysakti, A., & Usop, T. B. (2014). The elements driving local wisdom on the architecture Nusantara. *J Perpect Archit*, *9*(1), 37–47.

Staffas, L., Gustavsson, M., & McCormick, K. (2013). Strategies and Policies for the Bio-economy and Bio-Based Economy: An Analysis of Official National Approaches. *Sustainability*, *5*(6), 2751–2769. doi:10.3390u5062751

Thunberg, E. M., Helser, T., & Mayo, R. (1998). Bio-economic analysis of alternative selection patterns in the United States Atlantic silver hake fishery. *Marine Resource Economics*, *13*(1), 51–74. doi:10.1086/mre.13.1.42629218

USDA. (2015). *An Economic Impact Analysis of the U.S. Biobased Products Industry - A Report to the Congress of the United States of America*. USDA.

Welfe, A., Gilbert, P., & Thornley, P. (2014). Increasing biomass resource availability through supply chain analysis. *Biomass and Bioenergy*, *70*, 249–266. doi:10.1016/j.biombioe.2014.08.001

Chapter 3
A Value for the Non-Valued:
Valuation of Ecosystem Resources

Kappina Kasturige Kamani Sylva
University of Peradeniya, Sri Lanka

ABSTRACT

The ecosystem has its intrinsic value while offering an extrinsic satisfaction to humans. Ecosystem resources are devalued in the economic valuing process when a monetary value is difficult in assigning to the 'non-use' effects of the separated functions of the ecosystem. There is a tendency to forego the value of the ecosystem, the bequest or existence values, although it offers some utility of satisfaction. This trade-off decision leads to detrimental effects on the survival of organisms. The chapter allows the decision-maker to identify the non-use ecosystem resources with an 'off-trade' value for the production process through Reflective Analysis, systems theory and feed-in indicators. The off-trade decision would enable the sustainability of organisms in the ecological system with their interwoven functions intact and not exposed to bargaining as separated parts. As a result, it would help the regeneration of the valued resources for economic valuing process.

INTRODUCTION

"Non-valued" are the ecosystem resources that are affected by the economic valuing process when economic value is difficult in assigning due to the "non-use" effect of these resources. Ecosystem resources generate services while offering some utility of satisfaction to individuals. A change agent would decide the value of the ecosystem resource: an individual, a firm, or a government and will depend on the technology in hand, the framework in operation including the social forces linked

DOI: 10.4018/978-1-5225-9562-5.ch003

with the utility of satisfaction (Sullivan & Arias, 1972). The decision, therefore, would permit the value to significantly vary on the above factors due to the connected subjectiveness. If ecosystem resources are inputs to the economic decision, as raw material, the limits of the methods and techniques associated with the extraction of those resources will decide its cost. If these resources provide only satisfaction, the value could be judged through an indirect assessment, using the alternative to the satisfaction of these resources. But, the difficulty in value judgment of bequest and existence values leads to a trade-off decision. This trade-off will support the sanction to proceed with no economic value added to these resources, leading to the extinction of non-use valued resources. They become the non-valued. Authors argue that the natural environment considered as a form of capital (Barbier & Markandya, 2013). However, one of the questions posed is, will the natural capital, once valued, be exposed to trading?

Another method is to assign preferences to natural capital (Loomis, 1996; Costanza, 2003, 2000). Without much scientific input, these preferences could result in the loss of the intrinsic value of the system (Zimmerman & Bradley 2019). Besides, manipulation of choices could happen (Costanza, 2003, 2000). But, if a value is not assigned, the resources are taken for granted as a continuous flow of nature. Nature has no capability in reproduction at the rate at which humans use and misuse them. This reduction of natural capital leads to environmental degradation unless an economic barrier is created to lessen the rate at which exploitation of natural resources is taking place. Sustainability of humans, in terms of both social and financial capital, and other organisms will depend on the sustainability of the ecosystem, the natural capital (Naeem et al., 2016; Lin, 2012; Morelli, 2011). As Lin (2012) points out, a wide range of ecosystem services are required to satisfy the demands of humans. These demands could vary from fertile soil for intensive agriculture, delivered by profoundly transformed ecosystems, to a steady supply of high-quality water, which depends on the maintenance of quasi-natural ecosystems. Evaluating trade-offs and valuing ecosystem resources are becoming concerns of the researches (Lin, 2012). As Naeem et al. (2016) point out, biodiversity is a foundation of ecosystem processes. For some people, it is like social cohesion, happiness and connections to nature, which is related to human well-being.

This chapter will enable economic decision-maker to identify the non-use resources in the ecosystem with economic value for the production process through Reflective Analysis. The valuing process would depend on contextual factors and professional judgment rather than a preference of a layman to ecological resources or manipulated choices for the satisfaction of a few elites. The valuing process for non-use resources will be supported and developed through systems theory and feed-in indicators. The introduction of an "off-trade" value assigned contextually would enable the sustainability of non-use valued resources with their interwoven functions. By reducing the usage to a rate at which nature could reproduce, it would be possible to secure the intrinsic value of the ecosystem. Introducing a regenerative price such as a feed-in tariff (Barbier & Markandya, 2013), will encourage the generation of organisms in the ecological system while development takes place. As a result, it would help the production of natural capital during the life-cycle of the regeneration process, supporting the economic needs of society. This cyclic process would support sustainability. Developing indicators for their trade-offs will allow the decision-maker to identify the non-use resources as another input to the production process. Strong policies would strengthen ecological sustainability while providing socially just and economically optimum solutions.

BACKGROUND

The history of valuation has had many attempts to establish a value for moral judgment, classically distinguishing between intrinsic and extrinsic benefits (Fanning, 2016). Fanning (2016) define the non-derivative value assigned to some characteristics such as life, pleasure, sentience or happiness as the intrinsic value. Extrinsic value is the derivative value that something has for the sake of some other, which is not essential for sustaining life (Fanning, 2016; Zimmerman & Bradley, 2019). Extrinsic value is termed as instrumental value and is created to make life easy such as transportation facilities, technological products. People were more concerned with the valuation of intrinsic goods that leads to the satisfaction of individuals. Furthermore, lately, it has been questioned whether the concept of "extrinsic value" is justifiable due to the dependency existing between intrinsic and extrinsic satisfaction related to the valuation of these resources (Zimmerman & Bradley, 2019). The value placed on neoclassical economic goals argues that the morally "right" action is the utility maximisation process that produces the most goods for the highest number of people (Costanza, 2000). The expectation was getting the ultimate satisfaction of intrinsic rights for human wellbeing or utility for social equity (Costanza, 2000).

However, with the society-level decisions to reach the goal for intrinsic satisfaction that compromises the sustainability of ecosystem services, justification of conventional economic models have been failing (Fanning, 2016). They are too simplistic in their approach and do not allow space for complex ecosystem goals. Neoclassical Homo economicus in the valuation of ecosystem services uses efficiency as the primary goal for services or individual preferences for the intrinsic value (Costanza, 2000). The only focus here is the willingness to pay (WTP) without much scientific input and a lesser level of discussion (ibid). After realising the value of ecosystem services to sustain life on earth, a border set of goals including ecological sustainability were given priority to in comparison to the traditional economic goal of efficiency

(Costanza, 2000). As stated by Costanza (2000, p. 4), "the evolution of the human economy has passed from an era in which human-made capital was the limiting factor in economic development to the current era in which remaining natural capital has become the limiting factor".

In the process of decision making for development, valuation of input resources was habitually made forgoing the ecosystem valuation. The "valuation" process had detrimental effects on the "non-valued" resources beyond borders in the trade-off decision with difficulty in the valuing process as either intrinsic or extrinsic goods. Constant devaluation led to threatening the survival of organisms, ultimately affecting the valued resources as well. The scarcity of resources and related consequences of ecosystem damages were an eye-opener for further studies in assessing the non-value in the decision-making process due to the interaction and trade-offs at the level of the decision. It was clear that the capital, land and labour and the indirectly connected resources such as different climates and soils, bodies of water, and living beings will determine the quality of life of organisms and their ultimate form of survival (Sullivan & Arias 1972).

In the process of economic decision-making, ecosystem resources were traded off as either inadequately valued raw material or ignorantly exhausted, non-valued, ecosystems. Land, including its ecosystem services, was considered as a primary factor of production and value was only based on the market value of the space provided and any resources that identify as inputs to a production system such as soil or minerals. Consumption related to individual utility, welfare, and investment to increase capital stocks were the considerations that were made related to land as a primary factor of production, ignoring intrinsic values associated to its ecosystem services (Costanza 2000). Valuation process consists of both intrinsic and extrinsic value judgment related to human wellbeing. But, the decision process did not consider "intrinsic value of the ecosystem" until the lost balance of the ecosystem was affecting human life on earth. Lately, to value ecosystem resources, many studies have been carried out on areas such as marine biodiversity (Beaumont et al., 2007) and rare and endangered species (Loomis &White, 1996). These Ecosystem Approaches initiated consideration of the direct and indirect benefits that the ecosystem could offer to its users, primarily focusing on people as the utility holders. There was an attempt to understand ecological services in terms of goods and services where a monetary value could be assigned to the environmental functions, translating the complex environment into a series of inputs, which could be readily understood by policymakers and laymen as the scientific nature of the ecological resources (Beaumont et al., 2007). The identification of ecosystem resources as a benefit for humans has its extrinsic value highlighted and not its intrinsic value as being present for the sustainability of the whole system.

The ecosystem approach, introduced during Earth Summit in Rio in 1992 uses integrated management of land, water, and living resources in an equitable way to promote both conservation and sustainable use simultaneously (Beaumont et al., 2007). As it assesses ecological processors in terms of goods and services for both direct and indirect benefits of ecosystems, this approach enables policymakers and nonscientists to readily understand the complex environmental system (Beaumont et al., 2007). But, the difficulties associated with the identification of "what is being gained and lost when exploitation and development take place" (Beaumont et al., 2007, p. 254), concerning the ecosystem resources, makes it difficult to be realistic and understand the usefulness of the approach.

Rare and endangered species have been measured using the Contingent Valuation Method (CVM) where an open market or a referendum is used to get the value people would pay to protect the species in a particular location (Loomis & White, 1996). Three elements identified are the description of the species, the habitat proposed for preservation, form, and frequency of payment and the amount one would be willing to pay (WTP) to protect the identified species. As Fanning (2016) presents, monetary valuations on both conceptual and methodological grounds are criticised by many. Some others point out that a non-trivial loss of information is associated with the process of reducing multifaceted ecosystem characteristics to a single, monetary metric. Separating the ecosystem services in financial valuation would not have a meaning. Summation of parts would not identify the intrinsic value of the ecosystem as a whole with its functions interwoven with each other (Zimmerman & Bradley, 2019). Individual preferences given either as deliberate or for separated parts will not preserve the purpose of the ecosystem as a whole. But, the conscious choice may have a vote on better models for sustainability and prevent corruption in the decision-making process.

ECONOMIC VALUATION OF THE NON-VALUED

In economic valuation, ecosystem values were based on its functions as a raw material provider, and lately, the preference given to indirect benefits for humans. The direct valuation of resources was simple and depended on the process associated with the extraction of resources for primary factors of production. In the indirect assessment of value, a relative change in inputs to the overall system was necessary. It was to be identified by the management subsystems and followed with action required for the whole system to achieve its objectives. Introducing a tax system as an indirect valuation may reduce the usage of non-renewable resources and will change the relative cost of output in a production process. But, "a change in the relative cost of 'green energy' will not, in itself, solve the problem" (Andrew & Kaidonis, 2011,

p. 2) related to the resource scarcity and associated ecosystem damages. What is needed is a behavioural change in engineering solutions with the sanction and backup of climate scientists (Andrew & Kaidonis, 2011). It would be difficult to achieve a behavioural change with a focus on end-of pipe-solutions of a system. Introduction of renewable resources with a "feed-in" solution rather than an end-of-pipe solution to avoid the mismanagement of the ecosystem related to its "intrinsic value" is necessary (Sylva, 2018).

"Feed-in" indicators will verify a process to identify any mismanagement of ecosystem resources by questioning any impacts to the ecosystem resources at the level of the input to a system (Sylva, 2018). A systems approach considers a contribution to the system and an output from the system. To accommodate the subsystem thinking necessary to fulfil the overall objective of reduction of resource scarcity and pollution, a linking of many subsets may be required (Churchman, 1968). The environmental indicators such as natural forest cover, air, water, and soil quality in an existing context are considered to be source controlling indicators which are from the Natural Capital (NC) rather than allowing the system to depend on end-of-pipe solutions such as percentage of waste to be recycled and water purification necessary after the process. Damage to any sources identified through these feed-in indicators will compel the decision-maker to investigate different alternatives in the decision-making process (Sylva, 2018). Since the "subset is an open one in the sense that inputs generate production of outputs for consumption" (Sullivan & Arias 1972, p. 609), the input to the subset of "world economy" will depend on its "total ecosystem including all people, capital, land, organizations, etc." (Sullivan & Arias 1972, p. 609). These inputs could be verified before any detrimental effects take place.

The three distinguished flows of information, energy, and material in the whole ecosystem, therefore, has to be linked with the subsystems through the entire system to provide the inputs to one subsystem to prevent a crisis related to the output of another subsystem or the whole system. The control of the whole system will then depend on the inputs to many subsystems, preventing any output that is harmful to the entire system. The circular economy with an aim for "zero waste" should be generated by the linking of these subsets (Korhonen et al., 2018; Kirchherr et al., 2017; Murray et al., 2017; Ghisellini et al., 2016;). The importance of the overall feed-in has to be determined by the feed-in indicators (Sylva, 2018) of the whole system and each subsystem as appropriate at different levels. These feed-in indicators have to decide the value for the non-valued as its intrinsic value of the entire ecosystem. Regeneration should be encouraged in decision making for the inherent value building of the ecosystem for the benefit of the whole system. The trade-off decision should be replaced with an "off-trade" choice where the non-valued resources are not bought or sold in the market. A valued scientific judgment should prevail in decision-making to prevent any damage at any cost where the extra cost associated with this decision would identify the non-valued cost of ecosystem resources related to the context which would become the "off-trade" value introduced in this chapter.

Sullivan and Arias (1972, p. 608) state that, "favourable movement of one indicator may be accompanied by an equal or larger unfavourable movement of another indicator caused by the complex and sometimes confusing interrelationships within an environmental system". The trade-off between agricultural food production with environmentally harmful pesticides and effects on wildlife and water quality could be considered for environmental, economic analysis in decision making. The detrimental pesticide usage will not be reduced or banned since it affects the quantity of production and consequently, the economy. A value for environmental resources is not counted in this process. Contrariwise, environmentally friendly pesticides could be developed for food production to protect the non-valued items that would be affected if the feed-in indicators depict the harm at entry-level to the system. Such identification would provide a feed-in solution for the process rather than depending on an end-of-pipe answer such as cleaning water sources with an additional energy requirement (Sylva, 2018). Although this is a decision to be made by policymakers and implemented by supplementary industries, it will not be encouraged as it is an additional burden to be initiated by the new industry or introduced by the existing industry replacing the existing processors. Besides, it would be a threat to the existing industries as well. But, for new industries that would find alternatives could be encouraged by feed-in tariff and enable the regenerative economies to stabilise (Boselli, 2016).

Considering all aspects of complex valuation, a better method to value the ecosystem resources forgone in the economic valuation process is crucial. The method should not further complicate the decision-making process and be a burden on the decision-maker as a layman to aspects related to ecosystem and its intrinsic value. The non-valued should be identified at an early stage by a method which enables reflection on human activities that had caused environmental misuse and degradation. The possibility of rebuilding ecosystem resources should be addressed concurrently with the protection of the resources in further developmental activities for human comfort and intrinsic satisfaction. Life not limited to humans should be the goal of securing ecosystem organisms for a cyclic process of human survival.

SOLUTIONS AND RECOMMENDATIONS

Any human problem should have a solution to the intrinsic satisfaction of humans while not damaging its intrinsic value of the ecosystem with its living organisms. A reflection of the economic production processors leading to essential satisfaction of humans while meeting the goals of sustainability has to be focused. Detrimental effects of the past decisions are soliciting for this equitable solution for both the living ecosystem and humans. Following sections of the chapter discusses how Reflective Analysis, systems theory, and feed-in indicators could reach an off-trade value for ecosystem resources to be intact with their intrinsic values and interwoven functions for the sustainability of organisms including human survival in the long-run.

Reflective Analysis as a Solution

Reflective Analysis is a method that enables an individual to reflect on the nature of the core structure of a problem and to judge the implied similarities on relatedness to the whole that this individual is living in (Boxer, 1979). One element of reflection is the notion of the problem being a puzzling, curious, or perplexing situation (Loughran, 2002). Reflective Analysis enables the user to explore their experience related to the nature of a problem context and connect that to the experience of other users to create relevant design criteria for different options commanding a consensus among all users (Boxer, 1979). It encourages examining one's practice through others' eyes (Loughran, 2002). Objectives of a Reflective Analysis are to be genuinely reflective, decisions to be evidence-based and coverage to be comprehensive for the evidence to be valid (Sharp & Sigurðsson, 2017). A genuine attempt to analyse experience avoiding groundless claims is encouraged to conclude from available, substantial evidence (ibid). Reflection requires contextual anchors for the learning process to be meaningful, and the relationship between time, experience, and expectations of learning through observation considered as an essential element (Loughran, 2002).

Reflective Analysis could be used in decision-making for intuitive, qualitative and judgmental aspects of projects and especially when there is something beyond rational, analytical and objective decision-making which is suited for practical purposes rather than academic theorisation (Boxer, 1979). In comparison to sound decision making, which is objective, judgmental decisions will depend on the experience of the decision-maker (ibid). Selecting well-experienced individuals to make decisions using reflective thinking would enable a quality decision. Reflective Analysis could become highly versatile in environmental economics since ecosystem related issues are complex and could relate to many phenomena. In the case of decision-making on any specific function of the ecosystem, the interwoven characteristics with many other services of the ecosystem considered. In Reflective Analysis, independent action of different professionals expected in analysing the problem at hand and then these independent decisions are taken as a whole to come up with the best strategy. "Reflection on experience enhances learning through experiences such that divergent rather than convergent learning outcomes are encouraged" (Loughran, 2002, p. 35).

The process of Reflective Analysis is in three steps: enabling the decision-maker to recognize his/her own subject-referenced knowledge related to the problem context, then generate consensus to provide a way for each decision-maker to explore their relatedness to other decision-makers' knowledge areas and finally, reaching the strategic decision sharing the knowledge and examining the trade-offs of different alternatives (Boxer, 1979). In using Reflective Analysis in the ecosystem valuation, diverse groups of specialists, economists, ecologists, and technical specialists may be able to reflect on the experience of a similar solution adopted. As Reflective Analysis insists on using a case study of good illustration (Sharp & Sigurðsson, 2017; Loughran, 2002) of a relatively recent problem as the contextual anchor for decision making, it would enable the decision-makers to reflect on such a challenge to modify any negative aspects related to the valuation of the present problem. This type of analysis would not depend on individual preferences where the preferences may deviate from the best solution, like in the case of elite manipulation of a situation through totalitarian Governments (Costanza, 2000).

Reflective Analysis would be versatile in complicated valuation in the case of social or cultural capital. A further complication could arise with natural capital where damage to the ecosystem could take place in a comparison process of proposed alternatives. Several factors affecting the ecosystem are considered concerning each option. The decision affecting one function of the ecosystem may have unseen and unidentified connections with many other services of the ecosystem. If a non-specialist to the knowledge on ecosystem functions does the comparison, identification of such diverse factors may be inadequate. For example, changes in the hydrological patterns with any proposed solution may affect wildlife habitats and biodiversity of the area. The input of well-experienced individuals may be necessary for reflecting the associated consequences in the selection of the alternative. Representation of professionals in all three pillars of sustainability: economy, society, and environment are essential in the decision-making process to balance the ecosystem resource usage, any effects on social and financial capital.

In Reflective Analysis, complex ecosystem goals could be well established in a Repertory Grid for analysis (Boxer, 1979). Then this matrix could be analysed by individuals who are professionally competent to give the best opinion on selected aspects. This process would be different from considering the ecosystem based on efficiency and WTP as in neoclassical economics (Costanza, 2000). The decision then would enable many options and alternatives to come up with the best solution to be fair by all parties, including the living ecosystem. The users of a Repertory Grid have to be cautious about the design and elicitation of grids since this requires skill and sensitivity (Easterby-Smith, 1980). To get useful results, the appropriateness of the model is essential since it can be a very delicate matter. A Repertory Grid contains three components: elements, construct and a linking mechanism ((ibid).

The grid will base on the elements selected, and the constructs will differentiate between elements for grouping. The linking mechanism allows each element assessed on each construct. Depending on the complexity of the problem the Repertory Grid could be used as full, partial or fixed grids (Edwards et al., 2009) A *full* Repertory Grid allows the individual to identify both the elements and constructs whereas a *partial* Repertory Grid will provide elements for an individual, but the constructs decided by personal experience. A *fixed* grid will give both elements and constructs for an individual to assess the problem.

Systems Theory and Conceptual Model

Reflective Analysis would enable the decision-makers to identify the whole system with its inputs and outputs of the selected alternative solutions for a problem. With these findings, a Conceptual Model could be developed to assess the best alternative incorporating systems theory to this solution. Both inputs and outputs identified under the three pillars of sustainability: economy, society, and environment. These may go as natural, human, manufactured and social capital (Costanza, 2000). Social capital could be linked to social aspects of sustainability, whereas manufactured capital would be directly related to the economic accumulation of wealth for sustainability. Human capital would be related to all three pillars of sustainability in terms of know-how providers of financial wealth production, environmental protection and in uplifting themselves for social sustainability. Manufactured capital would have both input and output items such as machinery and infrastructure (Costanza, 2000) depending on the problem addressed in the analysis. Natural capital would provide economic benefits while relating to environmental sustainability. According to Costanza (2000), the natural capital inputs to a system identified as the ecosystem services: mineral deposits and land, and other natural resources which also include existence and bequest values (Loomis & White, 1996). Land and mineral deposits contribute to economic goods and services that could be marketed and quantified in financial analysis. The ecosystem resources will be identified as services implicit or explicit and as functions affected in input and output in the process model. Social capital would enable the decision-maker to select the best options for sustainability by its institutional arrangements, rules, and norms (Costanza, 2000). A robust institutional agreement with its rules and standards in place would enable better decision-making for sustainability with the imposing of taxes to reduce any detrimental effects. Figure 1: Conceptual Model for the Introduction of an 'Off-Trade' value for Ecosystem Resources, will demonstrate the decision-making process to preserve ecosystem resources intact.

As demonstrated in the Conceptual Model (Figure 1), the results of the Reflective Analysis will allow identifying any disturbances to Ecosystem Resources, either as disturbance or separation. Without further complicating the issue at hand, the decision-maker then would divert the solution to the next possible alternative, either fully or partially, with higher financial capital investment. The cost difference associated with the following option could value the ecosystem resource that should be intact and preserved for the benefit of the whole system. This cost termed the "off-trade" value is not marketable in the value-adding process for development. Since the cost would depend on context-specific factors, if there are no disturbances to the ecosystem, the decision-making process could continue in a standard method of decision making for community development projects.

The Conceptual Model depicted in Figure 1 gives allowances for incorporating "feed-in" indicators for choosing the correct alternative. In the case where any indicator identified as detrimental in any project alternative, according to the policies established, the decision-maker could take a step forward to divert the decision to the next best alternative. For example, if the percentage of Toxic Waste (TW) or percentage of consumption of Natural Capital (NC) is too high leading to pollution and resource depletion respectively, the decision-maker could recommend the next possible alternative with lesser effects on the environment.

Application of the Conceptual Model

In an example, such as a problem related to building community connectivity for enhancement of living standards, there would be past experiences to reflect for the decision-maker to come up with the best alternative. The examples selected for discussion are common problems where the ecosystem will be damaged while the construction of roads, rails or similar means of connectivity. In identifying a solution to this nature of problems, one will not only depend on hard-headed analysis, but qualitative subject-referenced values will be involved to come up with the best alternative (Boxer, 1979). The connectivity decision could vary between many basic options such as roads, rails, or tunnels. The selection of the best primary alternative could support with Reflective Analysis as the first step. The decision whether to go for a road, rail or tunnel will depend on many fundamental factors such as cost, resettlement, and possible damage to the ecosystem. The pricing would need the hard-headed analysis, and it would be comparatively easy for the decision-maker to find the essential unit cost of the elements that have to support a road, rail, or tunnel. Reflective Analysis, up to some extent, is needed to find relative components and come out with a relatively reasonable direct cost associated with the selection. But, since the parts associated are explicit, it would not be identified as Reflective Analysis in the general terminology.

A project on community connectivity could have many alternative solutions such as roads, rails or tunnels as discussed previously, and this discussion leads

Figure 1. Conceptual model for the introduction of an 'off-trade' value for ecosystem resources

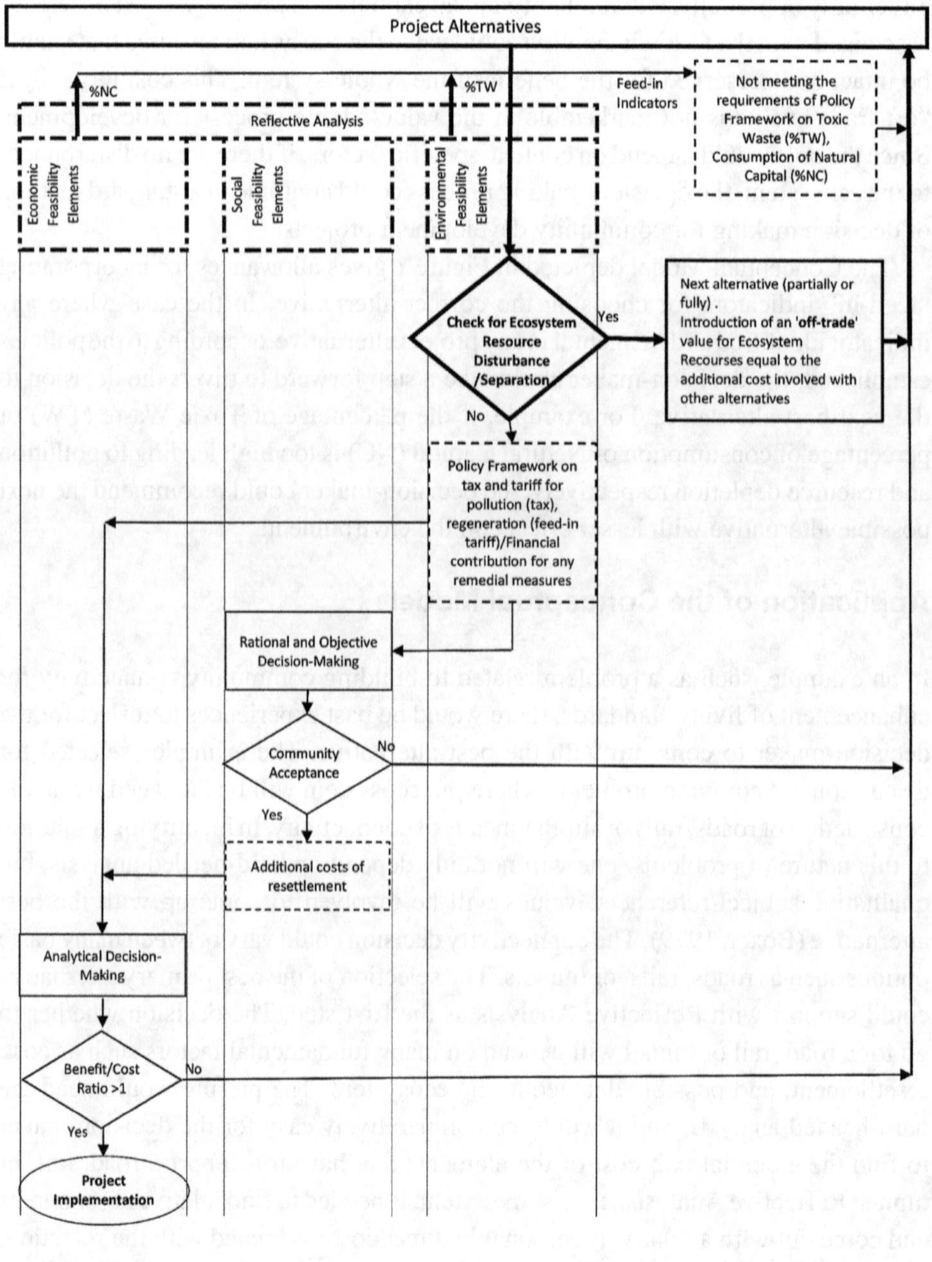

to the application of the proposed conceptual model in selecting the best option. Construction of a road, from within primary alternatives, is chosen to illustrate the model. Any alternative selected will have many inputs identified as financial, human resources, and other ecosystem services, including land to the system. The consequences or output of the project will have both positive and negative trends in the outcomes. These could be identified using Reflective Analysis by a group of professionals. Any factor that may be determined to be associated with indirect cost and quantified in monetary terms is taken for the comparison of alternatives in economic analysis. But, factors that are difficult to be quantified, such as social or cultural capital (Kay, 2006; Costanza, 2000) should be taken care of with public participation processors. Upon acceptance, additional costs associated incorporated in economic analysis. Resettlement is as an indirect cost and analysis related to explicit and implicated variables such as compensation and relocation of a part of the community or providing connectivity to their relatives will be decided after community participation processors. Many other social factors, such as social capital would be complicated, and it would be difficult to get a direct cost but dealt with community participation and acceptance as appropriate.

According to the proposed model, after selecting the primary alternative for a project on community connectivity, Reflective Analisis is used to verify relative damage that could occur to the ecosystem. Simultaneously social and economic factors gathered as information through a fixed, partial or fully designed Repertory Grid. Since the identification process of factors is highly context-specific and subjective, careful consideration given to selecting professionals in the decision-making process. The best type of road that may fulfil the requirement of connectivity while not damaging the ecosystem resources would be the goal of the decision-maker in this process. Following the example, the type of roads that are available for selection are "at grade controlled" or "uncontrolled" highways, or "above grade controlled-access" highways as preferred for further inspection (Samuel, 2006). The professionals are allowed to study a similar context, with different backgrounds are considered for comparing ecological sustainability, social fairness and economic efficiency (Costanza, 2000, p. 9) in the respective order of application. In addition to the fundamental costs associated with the unit cost and resettlement, many other factors are related to a road project. The selection criteria of the best alternative could go in-depth in identifying existing crossings, possibilities of new settlements in the vicinity of the road, the intersection of protected wetlands, pedestrians or wildlife in the region, etc. Each factor may have to be considered separately in the decision-making process.

A simple fixed Repertory Grid (Easterby-Smith, 1980; Boxer, 1979) with items identified by professionals through Reflective Analysis and systems theory as demonstrated in Figure 2 could be used to list the inputs and outputs/outcomes that would have a significant influence. Depending on the complexity of the project manual or automated processors could be selected for analysing alternative options

Figure 2. The inputs and outputs of the system of a project on community connectivity

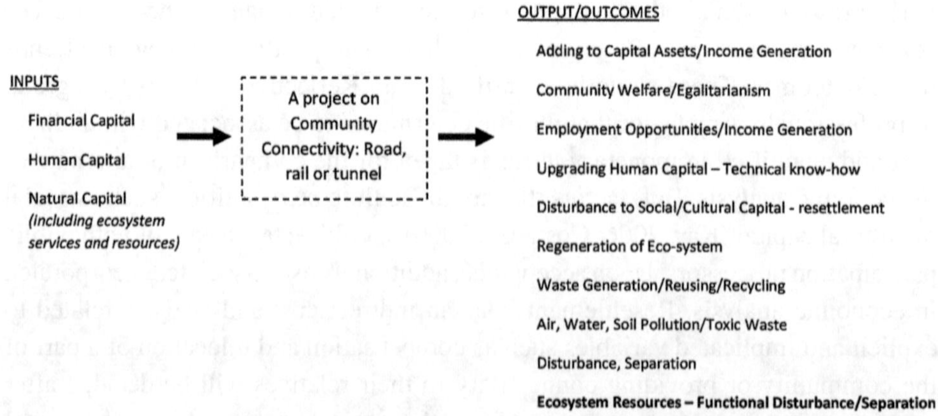

of a project once the Repertory Grid is in place. The elements selected with the Reflective Analysis and the constructs are appropriately adjusted, incorporating available policies as in standard processors of project analysis. As the most important phenomenon that is to highlight in this chapter is the encounter of non-valued ecosystem resources during a project, the general inputs and outputs identified are illustrated in Figure No. 3. The reader should notice that there could be many other consequences in a project of this nature, specifically contextual factors, and the selected aspects are only for the illustration of the model to value the non-valued ecosystem resources.

Direct contribution to economies such as infrastructure capital and the development of businesses is the identified positive economic outcomes of a road project. Employability and community connectivity can be positive social contributions of a road project, whereas resettlement could be a negative social outcome. Almost all economic and social consequences are explicit in a road project, although some ambiguous factors may remain in the relocation of communities related to social capital. They would lose their already established relationships with neighbours in the previous context. The identified social consequences would be the effects on the web of interpersonal connections and institutional arrangements that were maintaining relationships in the affected community (Kay, 2006). Generally, the issue of impact on social capital addressed by providing easy access to them to have the already established contacts or resettle them in the vicinity of the former neighbourhood. Although this nature of problems may have complex connections to many factors, they could be identified and solutions suggested through public participation and community meetings, possibly affecting societies due to the selected best alternative solution. Identifying the ecosystem functions, as inputs and output, becomes more complex and considering them in an economical decision relative to the previously discussed factors would be difficult. Other than the ecosystem service inputs such as land and raw material, which could be quantified and purchased in the market, many other functions are associated in this decision, which cannot be quantified or valued. For example, damage to an ecosystem in constructing an at grade road over a wetland will be detrimental and quantifying the damage will not be straightforward with its interwoven functions associated within the ecosystem. The loss will not be quantifiable with one feature such as flooding in the filling of wetlands since this function will intervene with many other functions in a complicated manner. Biodiversity and endangered spices would be affected in case of flooding. Many other ecosystem functions would be at a threat in separating the system with a barrier of road embankment. Quantification would be difficult in such a situation since a chain of other functions would be connected to one such identified service. Valuing and purchasing power becomes irrelevant in such cases, and the intact intrinsic value should dominate. Figure 3 depicts the application of the Conceptual Model for a Community Connectivity Project.

As discussed in the previous paragraph, some factors are unquantifiable in the effect that a selected alternative may have in disturbing the existing context. In this case, the only option is to avoid disturbing such factors as much as possible in the final decision since the valuation of such factors become complex. To prevent the damage of that particular unquantifiable factor, the decision-makers should be able to agree upon the best avoiding practice, deciding the next best alternative, to suit the whole scenario. For example, in the case of a road which is considered as a solution for social connectivity, if an at grade level road is selected, crossing a wetland would be a situation where quantification may be complicated in separated functions of the ecosystem. In this case, the decision-makers should be willing to come to a consensus to have a portion of the road changed in a manner to avoid damaging the wetland. Above grade controlled highway would be the best option for this part of the road as a better alternative to prevent the damage to the ecosystem. The most suitable choice may be an avoidance technique for the non-valued while meeting the demand for connectivity. But in the final decision, this solution may have a higher cost associated during the economic valuation process. The decision-makers should be able to justify the additional cost associated with the change of the portion of the road concerning the interwoven functions of the wetland that are unquantifiable in economic terms. The extra cost associated could be identified as the price paid for the "non-valued" of the precious resources that may have to be protected as existing or bequest valued resources (Loomis & White, 1996). These resources may have a different valuation in the process of assessment depending on the context and the alternative solutions selected by the decision-makers. But they would be protected for the sustainability of the system since the best solution would have minimal damage

Figure 3. Application of the conceptual model for a community connectivity project

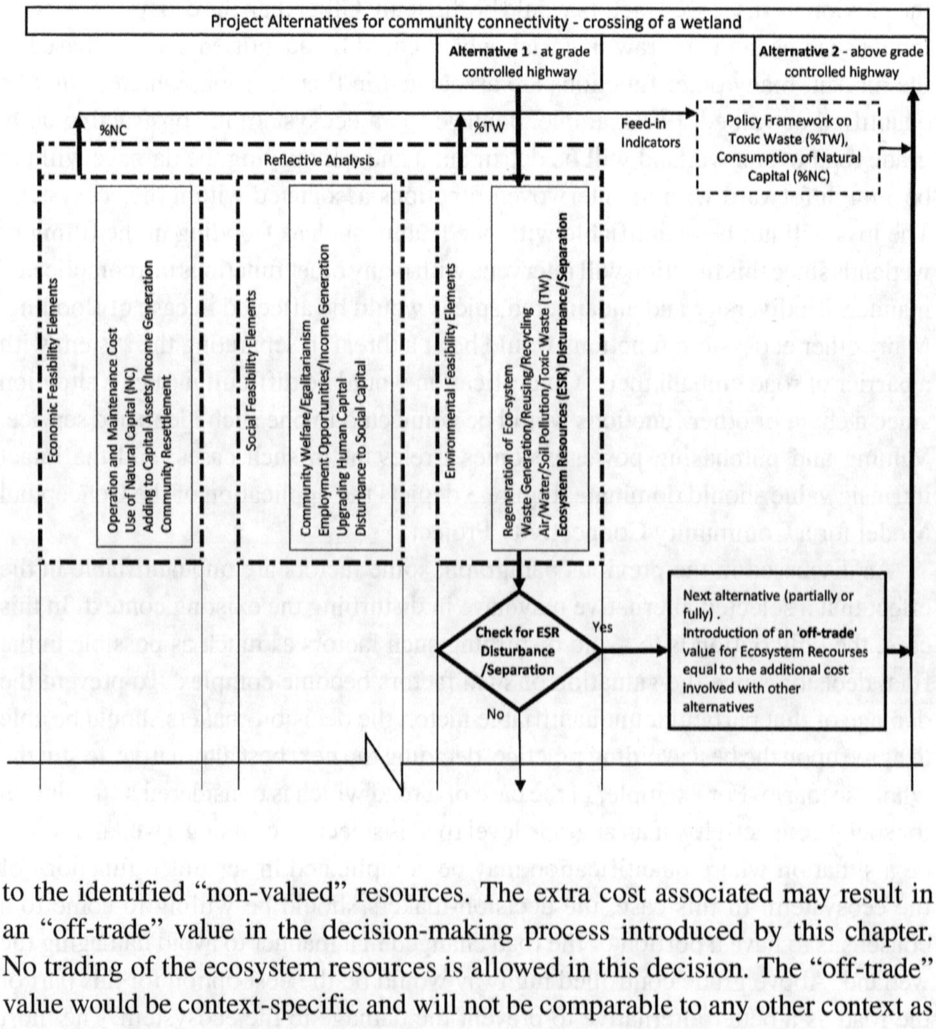

to the identified "non-valued" resources. The extra cost associated may result in an "off-trade" value in the decision-making process introduced by this chapter. No trading of the ecosystem resources is allowed in this decision. The "off-trade" value would be context-specific and will not be comparable to any other context as it would reflect the interwoven complexity and the best option selected.

Feed-In Indicators and Policy

The Conceptual Model with inputs and outputs could then be considered to identify the feed-in indicators of a particular problem. The reflection would enable the professional to recognise the value process related to not only economic factors, but also social and environmental factors. These factors, then, could be used to identify feed-in indicators that may be used to reduce any harmful effects to the environment or any other contribution to the society and economy. The developed feed-in indicators could then be used to construct policies related to similar problems. As stated by

Loomis (1996), "through various laws, society has declared that T&E species are not commodities to be bought and sold in markets", rather than creating a buy and sell market for ecosystem services or Threatened and Endangered (T&E) species, policies could be developed to secure the resources for fairness and sustainability of future generations. A hypothetical market (Loomis, 1996) will allow investors to buy any ecosystem product if they are WTP, whereas, a policy well established and implemented will not allow any ecosystem service to be unfairly bargained in the market or any other manipulation in economic terms. Even if a deliberate preference is identified in a WTP market, it does allow the market to bargain resources which should be protected for the benefit of the whole system. Developing indicators with Reflective Analysis would not involve any unprofessional preferences made by laymen considering separated functions of an ecosystem. The involved individuals will be professionals who would decide the value of any environmental service related to many other associated complex functions in the ecosystem as a whole. "Hypothetical market or a referendum which an individual user to reveal or state his or her WTP for protection of a specific species in a particular location" (Loomis, 1996, p. 198) will be based on individual preferences of laymen to other ecosystem functions and their complex interrelations. The intrinsic value of the whole ecosystem cannot be determined by adding the parts of the value of separated functions (Zimmerman & Bradley 2019). The individual preference of one species adding to a similar species and further summation will not give the whole value of the ecosystem. The intrinsic value rather than the extrinsic value of the ecological system as a whole should be taken into consideration rather than getting the summation of parts of an ecological system to get WTP preference value (Zimmerman & Bradley 2019).

Indirect compensation methods may be used in valuing the functions that are affected where direct valuation is not possible through the developed indicator systems. For example, application of feed-in tariff for renewable resources and a substantial tax for non-renewable alternatives may reduce the unsustainable usage patterns of non-renewable resources (Barbier & Markandya, 2013). The input indicator system for the process, feed-in indicators, should be able to judge the amount of resource usage or any possible adverse impacts (Sylva, 2018). Any product which comes out as the output of the process would have a price associated with this process of production and raw materials used. The waste of a procedure or any other adverse consequence to the ecosystem should, therefore, have a tax associated with it, if identified as outputs of the process. Process redesign is possible to reduce overall consequences. A set of robust policies should support the process for sustainable development. As presented by Costanza (2000, p.4), "the evolution of the human economy has passed from an era in which human-made capital was the limiting factor in economic development to the current era in which remaining natural capital has become the limiting factor". Therefore, in a process, reduction of the usage of natural capital or reduction of waste associated with a process should count high in the selection of alternatives. Appropriate feed-in indicators for the encouragement of either of these two goals: waste reduction and preserving natural capital is essential. The process extended to the regeneration of natural capital wherever possible in the decision-making process, too is vital.

The Realisation of Regenerative Economies

The answers to the present problems, addressed through regenerative economies would enable the growth of the natural capital. Any challenging process were a solution is expected for the demand, if redesigned to contribute to regenerate natural capital simultaneously, should be recognised and positively graded for sustainability. Regeneration seeks to mimic a circular metabolism found in nature in comparison to linear metabolism (Boselli, 2016). The circulation would encourage the use of waste as resources in a system of production, minimising raw resource usage. Whether the using waste in the same process or a different means of the solution demanded or energy production, it should count positively in the analysis of alternatives. A feed-in tariff associated with this process would encourage the investors to contribute to better options which are of higher cost.

Support of substantial policies could encourage large and small scale ecosystem regeneration in projects undertaken for any community needs. For example, while constructing a small housing unit, a Brownfield, could be regenerated to an ecosystem with a strategy on regeneration. A regulation of around 25 per cent of the land to be restored as ecosystem resources would encourage the reverse flow of the ecological habitat. Innovative project designs to preserve this land with the maximum utility to both humans, as well as ecosystem microorganisms, will satisfy the goals of sustainability in social as well as ecological aspects. Optimisation of the cost by the introduction of a feed-in tariff could lead to economic balance as well in the process. A large project such as a road project where a significant ecological imbalance may arise could have environmental context extended on either side of the road with adequate connectivity as over or underpasses. Organic agricultural projects and the elimination of the usage of toxic chemicals are examples of such development. Many such cases are available for the regeneration of ecological resources in the process of sustainable development.

Many methods are available in changing preferences over conventional economic solutions to realise and value the regenerative process of ecological resources. Influence of education, advertising, changing cultural assumptions can change preferences in reaching a sustainable outcome in the long run. Changing preferences with social dialogue and consensus would reach a higher long-term goal in ecological benefits than unconscious manipulation by dictatorial governments or by big businesses acting through advertising to come up with short-term solutions (Costanza, 2000). Preventing the manipulation of 'preferences to conform to the desires of a few sets of the elite rather than the society as a whole' (Costanza, 2000, p. 6) is one of the goals of the valuation techniques in addition to constructing of appropriate policies and regulations.

FUTURE RESEARCH DIRECTIONS

Case study research on applications of solutions to human problems such as a connectivity problem discussed in the chapter or any other issues such as human settlement or resettlement can be conducted to collect the data available on what nature of solutions are applied and how to avoid ecosystem damages through the application of Reflective Analysis. Possible cost differences could be obtained and verified for the "off-trade" value of the related ecosystem resources forgone in the economic valuation process. Furthermore, developing feed-in indicators to simple projects such as residential units or community buildings to be built in Greenfields in comparison to Brownfield development for expansion in utility could be verified as research studies. The construction of policies in regenerative ecosystems in Brownfield development too is essential. Feed-in tariff or a tax system to compensate for positive and negative contribution, respectively, for regenerative ecosystem resources could be developed through research studies to be adopted by the decision-makers.

CONCLUSION

The complex valuations involved with non-valued resources have become unavoidable in the economic decision-making process to keep the ecosystem intact and for its intrinsic values preserved. Different valuation techniques, in monitory value assignment, are implemented with their malfunctioning effects of either on the applicability or ignoring ecosystem resources. These methods involve preferences of a layman to ecosystem resources and have the possibility of misuse by the elite or manipulating according to political needs. An approach to value the non-valued resources with a practical and straightforward way, incorporating substantial professional, scientific judgment is crucial. This chapter provides a means to identify the value of non-use ecosystem resources with an "off-trade" value, which prevents the bargaining of these resources for intrinsic or extrinsic satisfaction of humans. The model suggests the use of Reflective Analysis to identify any damage ecosystem resources and direct the decision-maker to better alternatives with an additional cost in the investment, which is introduced as the "off-trade" value to assign a value to the non-valued. Feed-in indicators, policies through system analysis and incorporation of regenerative economic concepts further supports the valuation process. The expectation is to build a viable, fair solution for the protection of the intrinsic value of the ecosystem to benefit humans as well as all living beings in the whole ecosystem.

REFERENCES

Andrew, B., & Kaidonis, M. (2011). Policy instruments for reducing greenhouse gas emissions. In *The RMIT Accounting for Sustainability Conference* (pp. 1-12). Melbourne, Australia: RMIT.

Barbier, E. B., & Markandya, A. (2013). *A New Blueprint for a green economy*. New York: Routledge. doi:10.4324/9780203097298

Beaumont, N. J., Austen, M. C., Atkins, J. P., Burdon, D., Degraer, S., Dentinho, T. P., ... Zarzycki, T. (2007). Identification, definition, and quantification of goods and services provided by marine biodiversity: Implications for the ecosystem approach. *Marine Pollution Bulletin*, *54*(3), 253–265. doi:10.1016/j.marpolbul.2006.12.003 PMID:17266994

Boselli, F. (2016). *Cities must be Regenerative. But what kind of Regeneration are we actually talking about?* Retrieved from https://www.worldfuturecouncil.org/cities-must-regenerative-kind-regeneration-actually-talking/

Boxer, P. J. (1979). Reflective analysis. *International Journal of Man-Machine Studies*, *11*(5), 547–584. doi:10.1016/S0020-7373(79)80010-3

Churchman, C. W. (1968). The systems Approach. Dell Pub.Co., Inc.

Costanza, R. (2000). Social Goals and the Valuation of Ecosystem Services. *Ecosystems (New York, N.Y.)*, *3*(1), 4–10. doi:10.1007100210000002

Costanza, R. (2003). Social goals and the valuation of natural capital. *Environmental Monitoring and Assessment*, *86*(1/2), 19–28. doi:10.1023/A:1024045221992 PMID:12858996

Easterby-Smith, M. (1980). The design, analysis and interpretation of repertory grids. *International Journal of Man-Machine Studies*, *13*(1), 3–24. doi:10.1016/S0020-7373(80)80032-0

Edwards, H. M., McDonald, S., & Young, S. M. (2009). The repertory grid technique: Its place in empirical software engineering research. *Information and Software Technology*, *51*(4), 785–798. doi:10.1016/j.infsof.2008.08.008

Fanning, A. L. (2016). Contrasting values in the sustainability debate: Limitations of economic valuations and their role in decision-making. *International Journal of Sustainable Development*, *19*(2), 185–200. doi:10.1504/IJSD.2016.077205

Ghisellini, P., Cialani, C., & Ulgiati, S. (2016). A review on circular economy: The expected transition to a balanced interplay of environmental and economic systems. *Journal of Cleaner Production*, *114*, 11–32. doi:10.1016/j.jclepro.2015.09.007

Kay, A. (2006). Social capital, the social economy and community development. *Community Development Journal: An International Forum*, *41*(2), 160–173. doi:10.1093/cdj/bsi045

Kirchherr, J., Reike, D., & Hekkert, M. (2017). Conceptualizing the circular economy: An analysis of 114 definitions. *Resources, Conservation and Recycling*, *127*, 221–232. doi:10.1016/j.resconrec.2017.09.005

Korhonen, J., Nuur, C., Feldmann, A., & Birkie, S. E. (2018). Circular economy as an essentially contested concept. *Journal of Cleaner Production*, *175*, 544–552. doi:10.1016/j.jclepro.2017.12.111

Lin, Y. (2012). Sustainability of Ecosystem Services in a Changing World. *Journal of Ecosystem & Ecography*, *2*(2).

Loomis, J. B., & White, D. S. (1996). Economic benefits of rare and endangered species: Summary and meta-analysis. *Ecological Economics*, *183*(3), 197–206. doi:10.1016/0921-8009(96)00029-8

Loughran, J. J. (2002). Effective reflective practice: In search of meaning in learning about teaching (PDF). *Journal of Teacher Education*, *53*(1), 33–43. doi:10.1177/0022487102053001004

Morelli, J. (2011). Environmental Sustainability: A Definition for Environmental Professionals. *Journal of Environmental Sustainability*, *1*(1), 2. doi:10.14448/jes.01.0002

Murray, A., Skene, K., & Haynes, K. (2017). The circular economy: An interdisciplinary exploration of the concept and application in a global context. *Journal of Business Ethics*, *140*(3), 369–380. doi:10.100710551-015-2693-2

Naeem, S., Chazdon, R., Duffy, J. E., Prager, C., & Worm, B. (2016). Biodiversity and human well-being: An essential link for sustainable development. *Proceedings. Biological Sciences*, *283*(1844), 20162091. doi:10.1098/rspb.2016.2091 PMID:27928039

Samuel, P. (2006). *Innovative Roadway Design: Making highways more likeable*. Retrieved from http://americandreamcoalition-org.adcblog.org/highways/ps348.pdf

Sharp, N., & Sigurðsson, S. O. (Eds.). (2017). *Quality Board: Framework for Higher Education in Iceland* (2nd ed.). QEF. Retrieved from https://en.rannis.is/media/gaedarad/Final-for-publication-14-3-2017.pdf

Sullivan, J. J., & Arias, H. F. (1972). Concepts and Principles for Environmental Economics. *Environmental Affairs*, *2*(3), 597–613.

Sylva, K. K. K. (2018). A circular Economic Model for a Sustainable City in South Asia. In W. Leal Filho, J. Rogers, & U. Iyer-Raniga (Eds.), *Sustainable Development Research in the Asia-Pacific Region. World Sustainability Series* (pp. 345–359). Cham: Springer. doi:10.1007/978-3-319-73293-0_20

Zimmerman, M. J., & Bradley, B. (2019). Intrinsic vs. Extrinsic Value. *The Stanford Encyclopedia of Philosophy*. Retrieved from https://plato.stanford.edu/entries/value-intrinsic-extrinsic/#toc

Section 2

Integral Ecology, Climate Change, Waste, and Circular Tourism

Chapter 4
Integral Ecology and Educational Policies:
Axiological Convergences With SDG4

Giovanni Patriarca
Pontifical Athenaeum Regina Apostolorum, Italy

Diana M. Valentini
Marymount International, Italy

ABSTRACT

Education plays a major role in enabling us to become more active in the building of a better society, attacking the structural causes of inequality that creates an inhuman culture of waste and—from an ecological point of view—generates a unacceptable negligence with the care of our common home, causing environmental degradation and other disastrous consequences. This chapter explores integral ecology and education policies through axiological convergences with SDG4.

INTRODUCTION

"What kind of world do we want to leave to those who come after us, to children who are now growing up?" (Pope Francis, 2015, n.160). This is one of the most unequivocal questions raised by Pope Francis in his encyclical *Laudato Si'*. It is undoubtful that today, first and foremost, "we are faced with an educational challenge" (Pope Francis, 2015, n. 209). For these reasons, education achieves its purpose if it succeeds in forming people capable of walking together a path of honesty, mutual respect and esteemed acceptance.

DOI: 10.4018/978-1-5225-9562-5.ch004

In this way, it is possible to grow not only in humanity but also in intelligence and values, giving rise to new processes of social transformation. In light of the *United Nations 17 Sustainable Development Goals* all components of society are called to offer their specific contribution toward an integral development. Education plays a major role in the building of a better society by forming a holistic learner, while addressing the structural causes of inequality that creates an inhuman culture of waste and – from an ecological point of view – generates a unacceptable negligence with "the care of our common home", causing environmental degradation and other disastrous societal consequences.

The Second Vatican Council (1962-1965) had already brought new life to the Church's social teaching with a more pragmatic and ecumenical vision headed for the age. As it clearly states in the declaration *Gravissimum Educationis* (1965), an intensive educational effort is required to reach these goals. Education is not only a fundamental right of every human person, with a view to her or his own personal aim, but is also, and above all, the means by which everyone can contribute to building up the *common good* of our societies, thus promoting unity and peace on earth.

In an epoch of great technological change, there is the responsibility for the development of all peoples, says the encyclical *Populorum Progressio* (1967), in which Paul VI places a strong emphasis on the universal destination of resources and goods directed at individuals as a prerequisite for universal advancement: "[the] *development of the individual necessarily entails a joint effort for the development of the human race as a whole*" (Paul VI, 1967, n.43). More than fifty years later, this encyclical can be read as prescient in its ability to anticipate the relevant issues of poverty and wealth and of technological disruption and social development, all of which are earnestly discussed today.

INTEGRAL ECOLOGY AND EDUCATIONAL POLICIES

These aforementioned premises open the doors to an educational approach that has its roots in an integral vision of the person. In this way, the *educating community* does not fall into the trap of exclusivity but overcomes obstacles and goes beyond the walls of the class and integrates itself into society. A partial education – purely based only on technocratic skills – would be the cause of further fragmentation and confusion since it would educate one aspect of the person, sacrificing a more holistic development of the students. On the contrary, an all-encompassing pedagogy is based on *life skills education* that is – simultaneously – "personal, social, interpersonal, cognitive, affective, universal" (World Health Organization, 1999, p. 3).

An *integral education* cultivates curiosity and imagination as well as resilience and self-regulation and develops "a person's full potential, preparing him or her both for the world of thought and for that of work" (N. Capelle, 2015, p.5). In this way, pupils and students do not ignore their cultural background and spiritual quests. Fostering dialogue and encounter, they are able "to respect and appreciate the ideas, perspectives and values of others; and [...] to cope with failure and rejection, and to move forward in the face of adversity. Their motivation will be more than getting a good job and a high income; they will also need to care about the well-being of their friends and families, their communities and the planet" (Schleicher, 2018, p. 2).

The urgent call for the protection of the environment is a priority not only in the political agenda but also in educational policies. Even though it can be declined in different ways, the *integral ecology* testifies a fundamental interconnectedness because "the human environment and the natural environment deteriorate together; we cannot adequately combat environmental degradation unless we attend to causes related to human and social degradation" (Pope Francis, 2015, n.48)

Such an interrelated commitment highlights a global responsibility for a common sustainable future. To reach this goal and its transformative potential a *synergy between science, policy and religion* can be a step forward toward a "fundamental reorientation in our behavior and attitude" that generate positive externalities (Sanchez Sorondo-Ramanathan, 2016, p. 747). This integrated approach expands freedom, engagement and respect because "education also makes people healthier, and gives them more control over their lives. And it generates trust, boosts social capital, and creates institutions that promote inclusion and shared prosperity" (World Bank, 2018, p. 38).

A FAITH-BASED GLOBAL NETWORK

Faith-based education has always played a major role in providing education worldwide. Throughout the centuries, the fruitful encounter between cultures and religions has permitted an increase in the exchange of views and experiences. As recognized by the United Nations, *Faith-Based Organizations* (FBO) are "key and important players in eradicating poverty, improving people's health, protecting the environment and thus achieving sustainable development. Citizens see in such organizations as being trusthworthy and highly networked with dynamism that enables them to operate and achieve on the ground results where and when needed" (UN Environment, 2018, p. 2).

Catholic education is present in all continents and – albeit respectful of the national legal systems as well as the particular worldvisions of the pupils and their parents – the *core curriculum* is enriched by a series of teachings taken from sapiential tradition and the classical heritage. Through formal and informal education, it reaches all the continents and even those places in which institutional learning is less active for political and social reasons such as areas of conflicts and refugee camps. According to some data, over 60 million children are actually enrolled in Catholic schools and not less than 6 million in Catholic tertiary education worldwide.

Catholic education – as expressed in many documents throughout the history – is "an organic, critical, and value-oriented communication of culture" (Congregation for Catholic Education, 1982, n. 29).Through its schools, vocational centers and universities, it tends to form an integral human person which – though the synthesis of faith, culture and life – overcomes "[her/his] individualism and discover[s] [her/his] specific vocation to live responsibly in a community with others" (CEC, 1977, n. 45).

It is within this background that the guidelines "Educating to fraternal humanism. Building a "civilization of love" 50 years after *Populorum Progressio*" – published by the *Congregation for Catholic Education* in 2017 – should be read. The guidelines serve as an operative tool for understanding contemporary social issues and giving a practical response to them, inspired by a faith-based model of communion and identity.

A COMMON ACTION

The current geopolitical scenario is constantly in flux. The recent financial crises have triggered post-globalized economic processes with a revival of identity and protectionist sentiments in nations. The phenomenon and scale of migration and internal displacements, moreover, have affected and disrupted the old ways of social and educational cooperation.

In this framework, Pope Francis's Magisterium is undoubtedly inspired by Paul VI, easily recognizable in terms of *welcoming, protecting, promoting and integrating* (Pope Francis, 2017b). Through this *golden formula* the international community is called to share a common action for the human family. It is – as Benedict XVI affirmed – an anthropological emergency, which involves an educational component that can no longer be deferred. For this reason, it is necessary to build "a new trajectory of thinking in order to arrive at a better understanding of the implications of our being one family; interaction among the peoples of the world calls us to embark upon this new trajectory, in order that integration can signify solidarity rather than marginalization" (Benedict XVI, 2009, n. 75).

The hope in mind "is a full-bodied humanism" which bridges distances and creates opportunities. It is a globalization of hope based on a *culture of encounter* instead of a clash of civilizations. This step can be realized only through education, which – as the United Nations in the *Framework for Action for the Implementation*

Table 1. Trends in the number of students enrolled in k12 Catholic schools (thousands)

	1975	1980	1985	1990	1995	2000	2005	2010	2016
	Nurseries and Preschools								
Africa	-	162.4	312.5	484.6	646.2	1,147.9	1,149.4	1,277.5	2,194.9
Americas	-	514.0	800.6	968.7	1,042.1	1,331.1	1,541.7	1,409.6	1,379.1
Asia	-	607.0	840.0	1,058.6	1,327.0	1,369.8	1,651.4	1,761.1	1,841.3
Europe	-	1,634.4	1,796.5	1,845.1	1,901.3	1,681.0	1,714.5	1,923.4	1,835.1
Oceania	-	7.6	37.0	33.5	33.9	37.1	109.7	107.0	63.0
World	-	2,925.4	3,786.7	4,390.5	4,950.5	5,566.8	6,166.7	6,478.6	7,313.4
	Primary Schools								
Africa	4,221.0	5,610.7	7,052.5	8,393.8	9,356.4	10,158.4	12,435.8	15,821.3	19,174.4
Americas	7,101.5	6,838.6	7,118.2	7,380.6	7,198.3	7,554.7	7,045.0	6,766.0	6,285.6
Asia	3,215.1	3,752.6	3,929.0	4,289.9	4,539.6	4,668.9	4,907.5	5,023.8	5,967.6
Europe	4,552.5	3,979.0	3,810.3	3,569.2	3,607.6	3,099.4	3,003.7	2,846.0	2,948.5
Oceania	493.6	480.3	480.2	510.9	544.1	615.7	692.1	694.0	749.1
World	19,583.7	20,661.2	22,390.3	24,144.5	25,245.9	26,097.1	28,084.1	31,151.2	35,125.1
	Secondary Schools								
Africa	599.0	806.5	1,032.4	1,275.2	1,701.7	2,267.1	3,438.1	4,540.9	5,911.7
Americas	2,930.2	3,364.0	3,521.2	3,506.0	3,603.7	3,797.6	3,696.6	3,868.1	3,979.4
Asia	2,607.8	3,150.9	3,720.9	3,982.1	4,134.5	4,017.4	4,985.1	5,292.0	6,105.2
Europe	3,149.2	3,436.0	3,485.0	3,358.3	3,459.2	3,593.8	3,721.2	3,666.4	3,590.5
Oceania	236.0	257.6	306.8	319.3	333.3	350.8	391.1	426.1	459.6
World	9,522.3	11,015.0	12,066.3	12,440.9	13,232.4	14,026.7	16,232.1	17,793.6	20,046.3
	Total								
Africa	4,820.0	6,579.6	8,397.4	10,153.6	11,704.3	13,573.4	17,023.4	21,639.8	27,281.0
Americas	10,031.7	10,716.6	11,440.1	11,855.3	11,844.1	12,683.3	12,283.2	12,043.7	11,644.2
Asia	5,822.9	7,510.5	8,489.9	9,330.6	10,001.1	10,056.1	11,544.0	12,076.9	13,914.0
Europe	7,701.7	9,049.3	9,091.8	8,772.6	8,968.1	8,374.3	8,439.4	8,435.8	8,374.1
Oceania	729.7	745.5	824.0	863.7	911.3	1,003.6	1,192.9	1,227.1	1,271.6
World	29,106.0	34,601.5	38,243.3	40,975.9	43,428.9	45,690.6	50,482.8	55,423.4	62,484.8

Source: Q. Wodon, "Enrollment in K12 Catholic Schools: Global and Regional Trends", *Educatio Catholica*, IV, 3/2018, p. 193.

Note: Compiled from the annual statistical yearbooks of the Church.

Totals for 1975 are not comparable to subsequent years due to lack of data for nurseries and preschools.

of SDG 4 stated – must be "holistic, ambitious and aspirational, leaving no one behind" (UNESCO, 2017, p. 7).

An integral education starts, in the first place, with a personal and social transformation, which functions as the basis for an inclusive process that broadens

Figure 1.
Source: Q. Wodon, "Enrollment in K12 Catholic Schools: Global and Regional Trends", Educatio Catholica, IV, 3/2018, p. 195.

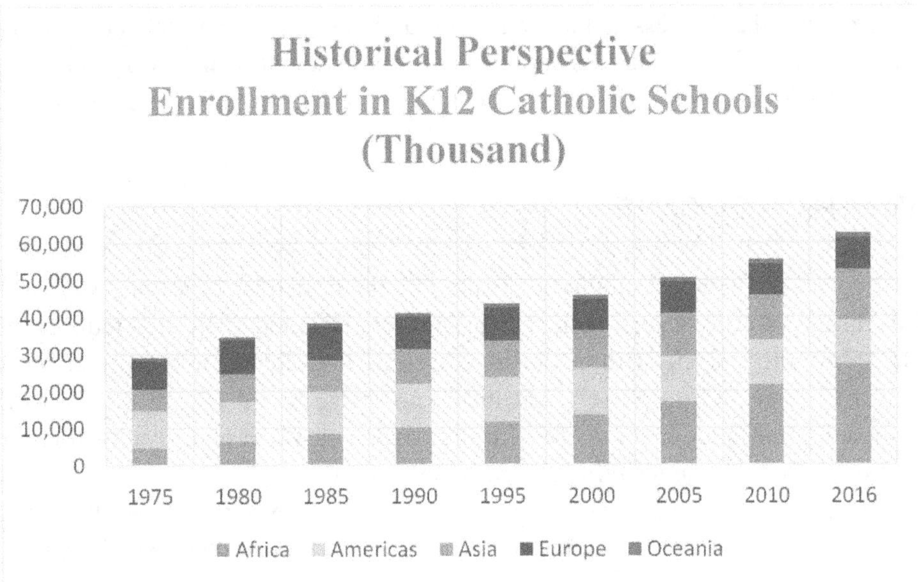

to influence lifestyles, as well as economic and environmental paradigms. It is a *humanizing education,* where the person is at the center but deeply connected to a planetary community, bound to a shared destiny. It is a discovery and a participation of a *fraternal humanism* based on mutual trust and reciprocity of duties.

In a similar effort, the *Incheon Declaration* affirms: "education is a public good, a fundamental human right and a basis for guaranteeing the realization of the other rights. It is essential for peace, tolerance, human fulfilment and sustainable development". To achieve all these results, it is required to focus all the efforts "on access, equity and inclusion, quality and learning outcomes, within a lifelong learning approach" (UNESCO, *idem*).

A *humanizing education*, therefore, deals with all the components of the personal, moral, aesthetic and social abilities of the human individual. It is the re-composition of an *educational alliance* with the family, the territory, the schools, and the entire society in all its expressions. This effort will rebuild the broken bonds with people with cultural and religious differences, with those in economic difficulty, and with institutions because "*a large proportion of the world's out-of-school population lives in conflict-affected areas*" where "*crises, violence and attacks on education institutions, natural disasters and pandemics continue to disrupt education and development globally*" (UNESCO, 2017, p. 9).

To respond to this situation, the entire human family needs an education – and at the same time – it must be sound and open, supportive and inclusive, responsive and resilient. Such an educational philosophy pulls down the walls of exclusivity and promotes the richness and diversity of individual talents. Formal and informal education extend from the classroom to outside of it, embracing every corner of social experience, with which it can generate solidarity, sharing, and communion.

AN ETHICS OF CARE

The educational policies should be inspired by the principles of an *ethics of care*. This means radically reversing the prevailing technical model, one that reduces the educational process only to the acquisition of skills, both conceptual and procedural, as if it were enough to possess scientific knowledge to act correctly. A holistic formation implies an openness to ethical horizons in which one matures through the assumption of responsibility and personal commitment.

The new generations, therefore, must "acquire the knowledge and skills needed to promote sustainable development," including "[a] sustainable lifestyle, human rights, promotion of a culture of peace and no violence, global citizenship and appreciation of cultural diversity" (*Sustainable Development Goal* 4, Target 4.7).

There is an urgent quest of a common language based on a "grammar of dialogue" and being able "to find answers to the challenges of our time" (Pope Francis, 2017c). Such a narrative can take place only within an ethical framework of requirements and attitudes, as well as common goals. In a *true dialogue* everyone must "be free from their contingent interests and must be prepared to recognize the dignity of all parties" (CEC, 2017, n.12). As a paradigmatic consequence, actions will match with words, linking the proclaimed ethical principles with active and pragmatic choices.

Such a dynamic responsibility for educational concern is "at the heart of the 2030 Agenda for Sustainable Development and essential for the success of al SDGs" (UNESCO, 2017, p. 24). Education for democratic citizenship, therefore, expresses itself through a constant reflection of the sense of co-participation both locally and globally. It "includes encouraging the responsible use of freedom to face issues with good sense and intelligence" so that people are able to understand "that their own lives, and the life of the community, are in their hands, and that freedom is itself a great gift" (Pope Francis, 2016, n. 262). But freedom must be cultivated through "ideas, incentives, practical applications, stimuli, rewards, examples, models, symbols, reflections, encouragement, dialogue and a constant rethinking of our way of doing things" in a process that is as demanding as it is virtuous (Pope Francis, 2016, n. 267).

According to these statements, the principles of peace and *common good* must beneficially and decisively become part of educational *curricula*. A unity of values will be the common ground where the "dialogical citizens" live, think and act. This approach is not lured into the *technocratic paradigm,* which "has, in some cases, downplayed historical, intellectual and humanistic knowledge," but it is based on the concept of the *human being* – with his or her psychological, cultural and spiritual inheritance (CEC, 2017, n. 23).

The United Nations agree on this peculiar point when they affirm that a true education is "embedded in its holistic and humanistic vision, which contributes to a new model of development. That vision goes beyond a utilitarian approach to education and integrates the multiple dimensions of human existence" (UNESCO, 2015, P. 10). This is the common root of a *fraternal humanism* that – declining any form of egocentrism and ethnocentrism – is called to build a "civilization of love" (CEC, 2017, n. 29).

A STRATEGIC APPROACH

To leave no one behind means, first and foremost, to expand this fundamental human right, ensuring "universal equal access to inclusive and equitable quality education and learning" (UNESCO, 2017, p. 28). It means to reach the children trapped in new forms of slavery and providing education for all, especially for girls and unaccompanied minors whose number is considerably growing. Aiming at the full development of a future citizen, an "educational alliance" – formed by parents, civil society, teachers, educators, the private sector, entrepreneurs, local communities and youth people – has an important role in "realizing the right to quality education" (UNESCO, *idem*)

According to articles 2 and 5 of the *Convention against Discrimination in Education* (1960) such a fundamental right cannot avoid "the wishes of the pupil's parents or legal guardians" to receive "the religious and moral education of the children" (Art. 2). To the family must be given and protected the essential liberty to choose a form of education in conformity with its own convictions.

This prior right is based on the Article 26 of the *Universal Declaration of Human Right* (1948). In the following article of the same document it is stated that "everyone has the right freely to participate in the cultural life of the community, to enjoy the arts and to share in scientific advancement and its benefits" (Art. 27). This demonstrates that there is a positive convergence of "hands, heart and mind." Such an interdependence is didactically fruitful and open the doors of informal educational activities through their pursuit of *fair play* and the "pedagogy of harmony" (Pope Francis, 2015b).

Therefore, education must integrate and harmonize "intellect, affections and hands, that is to say, head, heart and action. This will offer students a growth that is harmonious not only at the personal level, but also at the level of society. We urgently need to create spaces where fragmentation is not the guiding principle, even for thinking. To do this, it is necessary to teach how to reflect on what we are feeling and doing; to feel what we are thinking and doing; to do what we are thinking and feeling: an interplay of capacities at the service of the person and society" (Pope Francis, 2018).

Through *experiencing*, *conceptualizing, analyzing* and *applying,* the students invent alternative paths, use their creativity, solve problems and find integrated solutions. It does not deal with a merely *mechanic cycle* because experiencing is also *feeling*, conceptualizing is also *imagining*, actively analyzing means also practically *doing* and applying is *sharing* interventions and results. In this way, the cognitive and affective domains as well as the intellectual and social realms are not at all separated. In the learning process, feelings and knowledge, intellectual discovery and emotions, organization and compromise are on the same level in a strict relationship to an ethical standpoint.

Such an education will prepare the pupils and the students "to face the challenges of the near future. The *divorce* of fields of learning from languages, and illiteracy with regard to integrating the distinct dimensions of life, bring only fragmentation and social breakdown" (Pope Francis 2018). A mastery of technical skills – like complex problem solving, the perfect use of deductive and inductive logic or analytic reasoning – without any kind of empathy or the ability to work collaboratively would be cause of frustration and failure not only from a social but also personal perspective.

An up-to-date education increasingly requires an interconnection between *curriculum* and reality, inclusion and sympathetic responsiveness, learning and service, gift and communion, concepts and praxis, critical analysis and strategies for a fundamental change. It is a praxeological approach that investigates the real nature of social problems. It is an authentic lifelong partnership with all the components of society focused on "learning outcomes of children, youth and adults" to obtain good results "at every age and stage, such as school readiness for pre-school children, academic competencies of children in primary and secondary education, functional literacy and numeracy skills among young and adults, and skills for work" (UNESCO Institute for Statistics, 2018, p. 20). The sharing of responsibilities and tasks – based on realistic and interdisciplinary methods – fortify the social bonds, develop a sense of principled leadership, and gain individual maturity.

It is a *deeper and empathic learning* that lead students to understand the spectrum of diverse situations through not only team-working, imagination and inventiveness but also an *emotional literacy.* It is in this sphere where the "criteria of judgment, determining values, points of interest, lines of thought, sources of inspiration and models of life" are formed (Paul VI, 1975, n. 18). Focusing on equitable education and learning opportunities for all, these personal and societal efforts allow all forms of discrimination, exclusion and marginalization as well as of disparity, vulnerability and inequality to be addressed, especially when it occurs against children, youth and adults with disabilities.

It is an educational investment that involves "the provision of multiple and flexible learning pathways, and entry points and re-entry points at all ages and all educational levels, strengthened links between formal and non-formal structures, and recognition, validation and accreditation of the knowledge, skills and competences acquired through non-formal and informal education" (UNESCO, 2017, p. 33).

An integral education is capable of preparing autonomous subjects that respect the dignity of others, who are ready to dedicate themselves to "the global task of promoting and protecting all human rights and fundamental freedoms so as to secure full and universal enjoyment of these rights" (UN Vienna Declaration and Programme of Action, 1993, Preamble). To achieve these goals and put in action the necessary strategies, it is fundamental to have the contribution of teachers and educators, who "are open to change, and keen to learn and develop throughout their careers. At the same time they need to take more initiative to work with colleagues and school leaders and to take advantage of opportunities for professional development" (UNESCO, 2017, p. 54).

The integral formation for teacher and staff is a primary responsibility of a *leadership*, which is shaped by values and intimately connects the intellectual, professional, moral and spiritual dimensions. Its effectiveness is linked to the aptitude to understand the human condition of uncertainty and fragility. Such an *active leadership* generates organizational and multidimensional quality, forming "wise men in search of a new humanism, one which will enable our contemporaries to enjoy the higher values of love and friendship, [...] and thus find themselves" (Paul VI, 1967, n. 20). This approach, at the same time humble and complex, will benefit also all the pupils and students who – through tutoring, mentoring, coaching and other person-centered supports – will feel accompanied on their educational journey and not left behind.

A PLANETARY INTERDEPENDENCE

Hence, learning is a commitment towards self-improvement and common good. It is "an engagement with self and the others," in which *governance* is a means to "develop the value and attributes of trust, compassion, a sense of giving, empathy, wisdom and insight" (Bezzina, 2018, pp. 55/67). This outlook allows to "mobilize resources for adequate financing for education, ensure monitoring, follow-up and review all targets" as well as to "achieve effective and inclusive partnerships" (Bezzina, idem). This responds to the urgent need for "networking" in order to "improve educational policies and the way they work together" (UNESCO, 2017, p. 31). Such indispensable educational cooperation is a sign of the planetary interdependence and "obliges us to think of one world with a common plan" (Pope Francis, 2015, n. 164).

In order for all these efforts not to be lost, a positive atmosphere is needed that allows for authentic interaction and the creation of meaningful relationships. The centrality of the relational dimension is not only a psychological aspect, but it also deeply marks the structure of institutions and the success of the whole educational process, especially in a context of extreme digitalization. Through the interaction between individuals, the *contents' dimension* and the *school's organization* are based a set of strategic approaches "that enable all individuals to gain access to, participate in, learn through and complete a quality education, with a special focus on those who are the hardest to reach in all contexts" (UNESCO, 2017, p. 31).

Such an intergenerational dynamism is *per se* transformative and the backbone of an international civil society. This is a natural barrier to any form of egoism, arrogance and self-centered policy, as well as a mortal attack to the pervasive and perverse tentacles of corruption that "does not let civilization grow" (Pope Francis, 2017d). Our common civilization is – in fact – at risk and all "our efforts at education will be inadequate and ineffectual unless we strive to promote a new way of thinking about human beings, life, society and our relationship with nature" (Pope Francis, 2015, n. 215). There are alternative responses to the "culture of the waste." The ecological citizenship leads us to reduce excessive consumption, reuse materials and redesign all the economic chain through transparency, integrity, accountability and a responsible governance.

The development of new convictions, attitudes, and forms of life would enable a great cultural, spiritual and environmental challenge to occur. It is a long path of renewal in the wake of prudence, sobriety, temperance and soberness. A fraternal economy is primarily about the destiny of women and men in the real world and, from a moral point of view, it does not ignore the *time to come*. Therefore, all of humanity is called "to adopt *a circular model* of production capable of preserving resources for present and future generations, while limiting as much as possible the use of non-renewable resources, moderating their consumption, maximizing their efficient use, reusing and recycling them" (Pope Francis, 2015, n. 22).

Our common duty is to start "economic initiatives that witness [...] reciprocal fraternal relationships and gratuitous action" (Short, 2018). In this fertile intersection, a circular economic model emerges "as a beacon for moving away from a take-make-dispose culture and society. It also presents the opportunity to fundamentally address how we create value in our economies and minimize the liabilities that they create, hallmarks of a green and inclusive economy" (Stone, 2018).

This mission can be fulfilled through establishing transnational alliances "that create groups based on solidarity, in which the *common good* is connected virtuously to the good of each of their components, transforming the contents of knowledge in line with the full realization of the person and his or her belonging to humanity" (CEC, 2017, n. 18).

CONCLUSION

Theologically reflecting on globalization, Benedict XVI states in the encyclical *Caritas in Veritate* that "the risk for our time is that the de facto interdependence of people and nations is not matched by ethical interaction of consciences and minds that would give rise to truly human development" (Benedict XVI, 2009, n. 9). Beyond the logics of superficial consumerism with its inhuman culture of waste, an *integral education* sustains and supports a philosophically grounded ethical perspective in favor of the common good.

Inspired by the *Agenda 2030 five "P" principles* of *People, Planet, Prosperity, Peace and Partnership*, such an integrated approach can "facilitate the integration of religious, spiritual and cultural values to ensure inclusive green and transformative development through adopting value-faith-based lifestyles and behaviors to achieve sustainable consumption and production. Reaching to local, poorest and marginalized communities can significantly contribute to ending extreme poverty" and to promoting "innovative nature-based solutions, respect for traditional knowledge and cultural diversity, exercise environmental stewardship and duty of care" (UN Environment, 2018, p. 5).

In sum, it is evident that Catholic education does not only dispense "technical skills" but, by its very nature, lays the foundations for a new humanism, that – "sharing a "mystique" of living together, of mingling and encounter, of embracing and supporting one another" – becomes "a genuine experience of fraternity" (Pope Francis, 2013, n. 87). Catholic vocational centers, schools and universities are essential places of dialogue and mutual growth, within a process of *education for life*. By proposing the *centrality of human person,* Catholic education prevails over the unquestioned purely materialistic paradigms, while also proposing higher values for a truly *integral development.*

REFERENCES

Benedict, X. V. I. (2009). *Encyclical Caritas in veritate*. Vatican City: Vatican Library.

Bezzina, C. (2018). Teacher's Formation. Towards a Professional, Collaborative and Sustainable Development. In New Educational Horizons. Leadership in Catholic Schools and Universities. Vatican City: LEV.

Capelle, N. (2005). Integral Education. *MEL Bulletin, 19*.

Congregation for Catholic Education. (1977). *The Catholic School*. Vatican City: CCE.

Congregation for Catholic Education. (1982). *Lay Catholics in Schools: Witnesses to Faith*. Vatican City: CCE.

Congregation for Catholic Education. (1988). *The Religious Dimension of Education in a Catholic School: Guidelines for Reflection and Renewal*. Vatican City: CEE.

Congregation for Catholic Education. (1997). *The Catholic School on the Threshold of the Third Millennium*. Vatican City: CEE.

Congregation for Catholic Education. (2007). *Educating Together in Catholic Schools: A Shared Mission between Consecrated Persons and the Lay Faithful*. Vatican City: CCE.

Congregation for Catholic Education. (2014). *Educating Today and Tomorrow: A Renewing Passion*. Vatican City: CCE.

Congregation for Catholic Education. (2017). *Educating to fraternal humanism Building a "civilization of love" 50 years after Populorum Progressio*. Vatican City: CCE.

European Union. (2011). *Action Plan on Unaccompanied Minors (2010-2014)*. Retrieved from https://ec.europa.eu/anti-trafficking/sites/antitrafficking/files/action_plan_on_unacompanied_minors_en_1.pdf

Fiorin, I., Paletta, A., Bezzina, C., De Groof, J., & Zani, A.V. (Eds.). (2018). New Educational Horizons. Leadership in Catholic Schools and Universities. Vatican City: LEV.

OECD. (2018). *Education at Glance 2018*. Paris: OECD Publishing.

Office International de l'Enseignement catholique. (2018). *I Can. Children and Young People meet the Challenges of Laudato Si'*. Teacher's Guide. Rome: OIEC.

Paul, V. I. (1967). *Encyclical Populorum Progressio*. Vatican City: Vatican Library.

Paul, V. I. (1975). *Apostolic Exhortation Evangelii nuntiandi*. Vatican City: Vatican Library.

Pope Francis. (2013). *Apostolic Exhortation Evangelii Gaudium.* Vatican City: Vatican Library.

Pope Francis. (2015a). *Encyclical Laudato Si' on the care of our Common Home.* Vatican City: Vatican Library.

Pope Francis. (2015b). *Address for the Closing of the Fourth World Congress sponsored by Scholas Occurrentes.* Vatican City: AAS.

Pope Francis. (2016). *Apostolic Exhortation Amoris lætitia.* Vatican City: Vatican Library.

Pope Francis. (2017a). *Apostolic Constitution Veritatis gaudium.* Vatican City: Vatican Library.

Pope Francis. (2017b). *Address to Participants in the International Forum on "Migration and Peace".* Vatican City: AAS.

Pope Francis. (2017c). *Address to the Plenary Session of the Congregation for Catholic Education.* Vatican City: AAS.

Pope Francis. (2017d). *Address in Cesena (Italy).* Vatican City: AAS.

Pope Francis. (2018). *Address to the Pontifical University of Chile.* Vatican City: AAS.

Sanchez Sorondo, M., & Ramamanathan, M. (2016). Pursuit of Integral Ecology. *Science, 352*(6287).

Save the Children. (2018). *The Many Faces of Exclusion. End of Childhood Report 2018.* Fairfield: Save the Children.

Schleicher, A. (2018). Foreword. In *The Future of Education and Skills. Education 2030.* Paris: OECD.

Second Vatican Council. (1965, October 23). Declaration on Christian Education. *Gravissimum educationis.*

Short, W. (2018). *Reflections on the Present Economic Crisis from a Franciscan Perspective.* Retrieved November, 19, 2018 from http://www.franciscansforjustice.org/wp-content/uploads/2011/05/Franciscan-Economic-Perspectiveedited.pdf

Stone, S. (2018). *Closing the loop: how a circular economy helps us #BeatPollution.* Retrieved November 19, 2018 from https://www.unenvironment.org/news-and-stories/story/closing-loop-how-circular-economy-helps-us-beatpollution.html

The United Nations. (1948). *Universal Declaration of Human Right.* Author.

The United Nations. (1951). *Convention relating the Status of Refugee*. Author.

The United Nations. (1960). *Convention against Discrimination in Education*. Author.

The United Nations. (1979). *Convention on the Elimination of All Forms of Discrimination against Women*. Author.

The United Nations. (1989). *Convention on the Rights of the Child*. Author.

The United Nations. (1993). *Vienna Declaration and Programme of Action*. Author.

The United Nations. (n.d.). *Sustainable Development Goals*. Author.

Transparency International. (2013). *Global Corruption Report on Education*. New York: Routledge.

UN Environment, . (2018). *Engaging with Faith-Based Organizations*. Geneva: United Nations.

UNESCO. (2015). *Rethinking Education: Towards a global common good?* Paris: UNESCO.

UNESCO. (2017). *Education 2030. Incheon Declaration and Framework for Action for the Implementation of SDG 4*. Paris: UNESCO.

Unesco Institute for Statistics. (2018). *Quick Guide to Education Indicators for SDG4*. Montreal: UIS.

UNICEF. (2017). *State of the World's Chilfren 2017*. New York: UNICEF.

Wodon, Q. (2018). Enrollment in K12 Catholic Schools: Global and Regional Trends. *Educatio Catholica, 4(3)*, 189–210.

World Bank. (2018). *World Development Report 2018: Learning to Realize Education's Promise*. Washington, DC: World Bank.

World Health Organization. (n.d.a). *Partners in Life Skills Education*. Geneva: Department of Mental Health-WHO.

World Health Organization. (n.d.b). *World Report on Disability*. Geneva: WHO.

Chapter 5
Public Risk Perception Towards Power Generation by Municipal Waste Incineration:
Word-Frequency-Based Decision Making

Rui Zhao
Southwest Jiaotong University, China

Yuxin Huang
Southwest Jiaotong University, China

Yuyu Zhou
Southwest Jiaotong University, China

Meng Yang
Southwest Jiaotong University, China

Xinyue Liu
Sichuan Environment and Engineering Appraisal Center, China

ABSTRACT

Power generation by municipal waste incineration provides a template not only for waste reduction but also for energy recovery. However, incineration plants face considerably strong protests from local communities. In such context, this study investigates the public's risk perception towards an operating incineration plant by using a word-frequency-based decision making approach to provide insight into risk mitigation while enhancing public acceptance. An operating municipal waste plant located at Chengdu, Sichuan Province was used as a case study to examine the risk perception posed by the host communities. Face-to-face interviews through a structured questionnaire were applied to data collection. A word frequency analysis was used to identify the key factors that influence public's risk perception and construct a multi-attributive decision matrix for the risk assessment. Entropy-based fuzzy decision making was implemented to discriminate the risk semi-quantitatively. To alleviate possible conflicts, policy implications were given.

DOI: 10.4018/978-1-5225-9562-5.ch005

INTRODUCTION

China, because of its large population and rapid urbanization, is expected to achieve an 8% annual growth rate of municipal waste in 2020, with over 300 waste incineration plants coming into use (Lu, Zhang, Hai, & Lei, 2017; Makarichi, Jutidamrongphan, & Techato, 2018). Despite the rapid development of power generation by waste incineration, due to the potential environmental impacts in the course of operation, such as dioxin and odor, the public shows different degrees of risk perception (Lin et al., 2018; Qi et al., 2017).

Risk perception is the evaluation by the public towards any target objects, including the public's demand for risk information and corresponding emergency behaviors, thus determining the public's reactions to existing and unknown risks (Pennings & Smidts, 2000; 2003). Zegans (2008) clarified that the public might have different choices in terms of various risk perceptions. As far as waste incineration is concerned, individuals may have different subjective judgements resulting in different levels of acceptance that even transform into a Not-In-My-Back-Yard (NIMBY) notion (Omanga, Ulmer, Berhane, & Gatari, 2014).

A number of empirical studies have identified influencing factors of public risk perception on construction projects, which are classified into external and internal factors. Regarding external factors, the public concerns may come from the potential harm caused by changes in the ambient environment to their own health, such as noise pollution, air pollution, water pollution, etc. (Ren, Che, Yang, & Tao, 2016; Yu, Huang, Qin, & Chen, 2018). Omanga et al. (2014) found that air pollution and water pollution were the main concerns of the public through investigations of residents in the vicinity of the industrial zone in Kenya. A similar conclusion was reached in the study by Ma, Gong, Fang, Liu, and Liu (2018), which focused on the public's acceptance of the Para Xylene (PX) project and showed that air and water pollution were the main concerns for the public's opposition to the project construction. Rajgor (2011) found that the potential impact of noise from wind power projects might lead to residents' resistance. Paiva, Cardoso, and Zannin (2019) pointed out that the public's perception to traffic noise was significantly positively correlated with noise exposure. Further, prior studies have found that governmental credibility and media disclosure are external factors that influence public risk perception (Liu, Sun, Xia, Cui, & Coffey, 2018). By taking Hong Kong's nuclear power construction as a case, Mah, Hills, and Tao (2014) confirmed that information transparency was a prerequisite for risk communication between the government, operators, and the public. Liu, Lyu, Pan, and Wang (2017) and Wang, Wang, Lin, and Li (2019), respectively, took a coal-fired power plant in Hunan, China, and a nuclear power plant in Jiangmen as case examples, and found that the major reason for local residents' resistance to such plants was information asymmetry especially lack of risk communications. Study also indicated that the distance of residence affected the public's risk perception (Harclerode, Lal, Vedwan, Wolde, & Miller, 2016). When a project started construction, publics were more likely to experience strong psychological changes related to their living environments, thus aggravating their risk perceptions (Lima, 2004).

Internal factors are reflected by the fact that people in different genders, ages, educations, incomes, etc., may have various risk perceptions (Jenkins-Smith, Silva, Nowlin, & DeLozier, 2011). Huang et al. (2013) studied the chemical industrial projects of three representative cities in China and identified that the risk perception of people over 50 years old was relatively low, similar to that of less-educated people and retirees. Stoutenborough and Vedlitz (2016) further pointed out that there was a significant correlation between education and risk perception: the higher the public education level was, the lower was the expression of risk perception. Similarly, Hussey and Arku (2019) pointed out that risk perception varied greatly because of the different levels of public education. Additionally, both Lo (2014) and Geng, Liu, Zhou, and Yang (2018) took nuclear power projects as an example and found that residents' income levels were negatively correlated to their risk perceptions. In particular, the bottom class showed low support for such projects.

The above studies are largely based on the projects' verification period, and there is little concern about the public's risk perception towards the projects during their operations. Moreover, the existing methods applied to surveying risk perceptions are mainly based upon the Likert scale. But they are limited in that respondents may only pick the deterministic option, while the changes between the given options cannot be measured (Brouwer, Dekker, Rolfe, & Windle, 2010). It is thus difficult to fully reflect the behavioral motives related to risk perception (Hodge & Gillespie, 2003). This study takes an operating incineration plant in a mega city as a case area, to conduct in-depth interviews with its neighboring residents, and identify key semantic information involved in the interviews. On this basis, a statistical analysis of key words frequency is conducted to establish an evaluation system coupled entropy with fuzzy decision-making to discriminate public risk perception. It is expected the study to provide insight into reduction of public risk perception, mitigation of risk consequences, and assist policy making on implementation of governance projects by taking public appeals into account, thus promote sustainable development.

METHOD AND DATA

Design of In-Depth Interviews

This study selects residents living around an operating incineration plant in Chengdu, Sichuan Province, as interviewees. The plant was completed in 2011 and has been in operation for 7 years. An open questionnaire was used to conduct face-to-face interviews with the residents within a radius of 3 km around the plant. Questionnaires are a method of designing a series of questions to quickly understand respondents' opinions, which are characterized by low cost, wide coverages (Williams, 2003). However, they do not accurately reflect the feelings of respondents (Khushaba et al., 2013). In-depth interviews involve face-to-face contact between researchers and respondents by conducting a purposeful dialogue based on a certain topic (Bolderston, 2012). Its advantage is that only a small sample size is required to obtain in-depth information feedback (Qu & Dumay, 2011). The combination of the two methods may facilitate effective understanding of the true feelings of respondents on the operation of the incineration plant while covering sufficient information.

Given that public risk perception is mainly due to the direct and potential threats that incineration plants pose to the public, including perceived losses and benefits, the authors designed a number of open-ended questions to assist in interviews, including respondents' feelings about benefiting from power generation by waste incineration (Q1); respondents' understanding of power generation by waste incineration (Q2); respondents' feelings of environmental changes (Q3); respondents' feelings about the operation of the incineration power plant (Q4); respondents' feelings of changes in the infrastructures of the incineration power plant (Q5); respondents' feelings about information on waste incineration, including the extent of access to information, publicity, etc. (Q6); respondents' feelings about the communication between operators and the public (Q7); respondents' feelings about media reports on the incineration power plant (Q8); and respondents' feelings about government propaganda and communication with the government (Q9), as shown in Table 1.

Construction of an Indicator System

In this study, interview contents were first transcribed into text and entered into a document, and they were then coded according to grounded theory by using the QSR NVivo8 software. The specific operation steps are given as follows: ① open coding to extract possible categories that affect public risk perception from the original interview sentences; ② axial coding to compare and classify all categories again before extraction of main categories; ③ selective coding to dig out the core categories that govern all the main categories. By coding first-hand interview data

Table 1. Questionnaire design for public risk perception

Item	Subject Design	Variable
Interview	Respondents' understanding of power generation by waste incineration	Q1
	Respondents' understanding of power generation by waste incineration	Q2
	Respondents' feelings of environmental changes	Q3
	Respondents' feelings about the operation of the incineration power plant	Q4
	Respondents' feelings of changes in the infrastructures of the incineration power plant	Q5
	Respondents' feelings about information on waste incineration	Q6
	Respondents' feelings about the communication between operators and the public	Q7
	Respondents' feelings about media reports on the incineration power plant	Q8
	Respondents' feelings about government propaganda and communication with the government	Q9

word by word, the significant contents were extracted, summarized, and merged to achieve categorization. Eventually, 101 initial free nodes and 22 categories were obtained, as shown in Table 2.

Axial coding links the various categories obtained in the open coding step using conditions such as phenomenon, causality, and intermediary. This paper summarized the six main categories that affect public risk perception through the interrelationships and logical sequences between different categories, as shown in Table 3.

Selective coding was intended to select the core categories to be associated with the main categories to establish a conceptual model with logical relationships, as shown in Table 4.

All the above categories were constituted into an indicator system for evaluation of public risk perception, including three decision-making hierarchies, as shown in Table 5.

Fuzzy Decision-Making

This study assesses public risk perception through a fuzzy decision-making, which ranks objectives in terms of maximum membership degree (Zhao, Liu, Liu, Zhang, & Li, 2018). Specific steps are given as follows:

First, the set of evaluation factors was determined:

Table 2. Excerpt of open coding for public risk perception

Excerpt of Interview Data	Phenomenal Summary	Categories
I have lived here for more than ten years, and there is definitely an impact living next to the incineration plant. The garbage is stinky, especially in the summer.	Stinky garbage	Air pollution
Sometimes there will be stinky ditches beside the incineration plant, especially in summer.	Stinky ditches	Water pollution
Look at those vegetables; many are about to get withered and yellow, and they will soon die.	Reduced crop production	Influence on crops
I used to go into the streets, but now I don't like to go. My head keeps spinning, and it must be related to the incineration plant.	Physical discomfort	Physical and mental health
I am worried about my own child, because the air is not good . . .	Psychological stress	Physical and mental health
The houses around are not selling well. I thought that the price would go up. Now the incineration plant has come, and the housing prices have taken a hard fall.	Property depreciation	Income
I don't understand the emissions information published on the screen of the incineration plant.	Incomprehension of emissions information;	Operation information
I don't want it here any longer, and I am talking to other people about this.	Expectation of relocation;	Relocation appeal

$$U = \{u_1, u_2, \ldots, u_n\},$$

where $u_i\,(i = 1,2,\ldots,n)$ is the evaluation factor, and n is the number of individual factors at the same hierarchy. Then, the set of evaluation ranks was determined:

$$V = \{v_1, v_2, \ldots, v_n\},$$

where $V_j\,(j = 1,2,\ldots,n)$ is the standard of evaluation rank, and n is the number of levels. The evaluation ranges from extremely high to high, medium, low, and ultimately to extremely low.

The membership matrix R was constructed as follows:

$$R=\begin{pmatrix} r_{11} & \cdots & r_{1m} \\ \vdots & \ddots & \vdots \\ r_{n1} & \cdots & r_{nm} \end{pmatrix}, 0<<r_{ij}<<1 \tag{1}$$

Table 3. Axial coding for public risk perception

Main Categories	Categories	Connotation of the Relationship
Changes in the natural environment	Air pollution	Public perception of environmental change
	Water pollution	
	Noise	
	Influence on crops	
Influence on physical and mental health	Residential distance	Public perception of the influence on physical and mental health
	Physical health	
	Psychological stress	
Influence on income	Permanent assets	Public perception of the influence on their own income
	Wage earnings	
	Subsidies	
	Job opportunities	
Government behavior	Administrative penalties	Public perception of government behavior
	Force of supervision	
	Propaganda and report	
	Infrastructure improvement	
Individual behavior	Protest against operation	Public perception of individual behavior
	Relocation appeal	
	Complaint and advice	
Behavior of the incineration plant	Operation information	Public perception of the behavior of the incineration plant
	Emergency plan and disposal	
	Green space construction	
	Upgrade of pollution control technology	

Table 4. Selective coding for public risk perception

Core Categories	Main Categories
Perception of risk source	Changes in the natural environment
	Influence on physical and mental health
	Influence on income
Perception of risk communication	Government behavior
	Individual behavior
	Behavior of the incineration plant

Table 5. Indicator system for evaluation of public risk perception

Indicator System			
Public risk perception during the operation of the incineration plant (A_1)	Perception of risk source (B_{1-1})	Environmental changes (C_{1-1})	Air pollution (D_{1-1})
			Water pollution (D_{1-2})
			Noise (D_{1-3})
			Influence on crops (D_{1-4})
		Influence on physical and mental health (C_{1-2})	Residential distance (D_{1-5})
			Physical health (D_{1-6})
			Psychological stress (D_{1-7})
		Influence on income (C_{1-3})	Permanent assets (D_{1-8})
			Wage earnings (D_{1-9})
			Subsidies (D_{1-10})
			Job opportunities (D_{1-11})
	Perception of risk communication (B_{1-2})	Government behavior (C_{1-4})	Administrative penalties(D_{1-12})
			Force of supervision (D_{1-13})
			Propaganda and report (D_{1-14})
			Infrastructure improvement (D_{1-15})
		Individual behavior (C_{1-5})	Protest against operation (D_{1-16})
			Relocation appeal (D_{1-17})
			Complaint and advice (D_{1-18})
		Behavior of the incineration plant (C_{1-6})	Operation information (D_{1-19})
			Emergency plan and disposal (D_{1-20})
			Green space construction (D_{1-21})
			Upgrade of pollution control technology (D_{1-22})

where $r_{ij} = \sum_{k=1}^{H} u_{ij}^{k} / H$, and u^k is evaluation result of the ith object by the kth decision maker; H is the number of decision makers; m is the number of evaluation objects; and n is the number of evaluation levels.

Based on the different weights of each indicator, the result of fuzzy evaluation was obtained: $C = W \cdot R$.

$$C = W \cdot R = \lambda_{D1}, \lambda_{D2}, \ldots, \lambda_{Dn} \begin{pmatrix} r_{11} & \cdots & r_{1n} \\ \vdots & \ddots & \vdots \\ r_{m1} & \cdots & r_{nm} \end{pmatrix}$$

$$= \left(R_{C1}, R_{C2}, \ldots R_{Cn}\right) \tag{2}$$

where W refers to the set of weights.

Word frequency analysis was employed to calculate the frequency of each indicator mentioned in the interview and convert it into entropy. This might overcome the uncertainty of subjective judgment and achieve objective weighting of indicators (Zhao, Min, Geng & He, 2017). The entropy weight represented the extent to which each indicator affected public risk perception. If the number of evaluation indicators is n, and the frequency of each indicator is $f_i\left(i = 1, 2, 3, \ldots, n\right)$, the detailed transformation is given as follows (Wu et al, 2017):

1. 1. Normalization of the value of f_i:

$$fi^{'} = fi \,/\, \sum_{\mathrm{i}=1}^{n} fi \tag{3}$$

2. 2. The entropy of each indicator:

$$f_i^h = -\left(In\left(n\right)\right)^{-1} \sum_{i=1}^{n} fi'\, In\left(fi'\right) \tag{4}$$

3. 3. Degree of divergence of intrinsic information:

$$f_i^{div} = 1 - f_i^h \tag{5}$$

4. 4. The entropy weight of each indicator:

$$f_i^e = f_i^{div} \,/\, \sum_{i=1}^{n} f_i^{div} \tag{6}$$

Figure 1 (a) shows the frequency of indicators at different levels in the interview process. The frequency of each indicator is substituted in equations (3) to (6), and the weights of the indicators are shown in Figure 1(b).

RESULTS AND DISCUSSION

Results

Figure 2 shows the evaluation results of indicators at the first hierarchy. More than 30% of the respondents showed a strong risk perception to "environmental change," "health impact," "government action," and "individual behavior." In particular, 74.8% of the respondents showed an extremely high-risk perception of health impact, indicating that the public had the most concerns about its own physical and mental health. This was also a key indicator to determine whether the public would accept the incineration power generation project or not. This finding is similar to what Geelen, Souren, Jans, and Ragas (2013) have found, i.e., public concerns about projects regarding pollution control are mainly related to health hazards due to environmental changes.

Figure 3 shows the evaluation results of indicators at the second hierarchy. In particular, 61.6% of the respondents showed an extremely high perception to the risk source, suggesting that the perception of the damage to individual interest was caused by the risk source, whilst 33.5% of the respondents showed an extremely high perception of risk communication. A possible reason is information asymmetry, which may give rise to public distrust thus enhance their risk perception.

Figure 4 shows the evaluation results at the third hierarchy, which are the final evaluation results of the respondent's risk perception towards the power generation by incineration plant. A total of 43.1% of the respondents showed an extremely high risk perception, 19.3% showed a high risk perception, 16.0% showed a medium risk perception, 10.9% showed a low risk perception, and only 10.0% showed a very low risk perception. The results also indicate that effective measures are needed to mitigate possible risk consequences.

DISCUSSION

The above results indicated that most of the respondents had a strong risk perception towards the incineration plant. Particularly, the respondents showed strong concerns about the impact on their own physical and mental health, and the environmental quality. This is similar to the empirical findings of prior studies, i.e. the health and

Figure 1. (a) The frequency of indicators at different levels; (b). Weight distribution of indicators at different levels

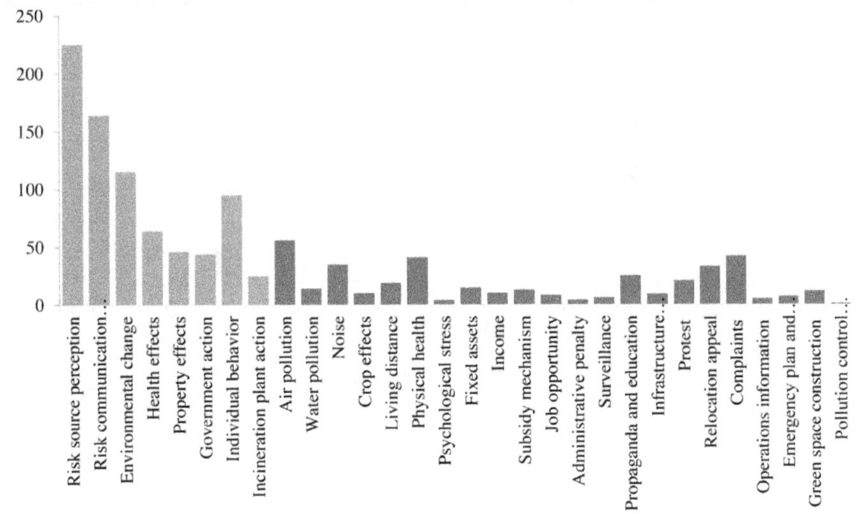

(a)

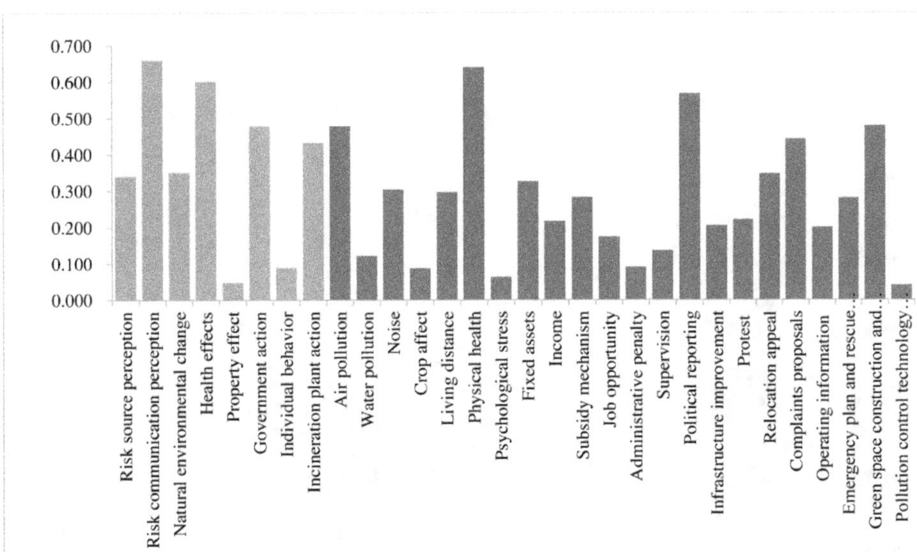

(b)

environmental impacts of construction projects are the main hazards perceived by publics (Shekdar, 2009; Kothari, Tyagi, & Pathak, 2010).

The results also reflected public confusions on the incineration plant operation, for which the respondents showed a high level of risk perception towards the indicators

Figure 2. Public risk perception evaluation results at the first hierarchy

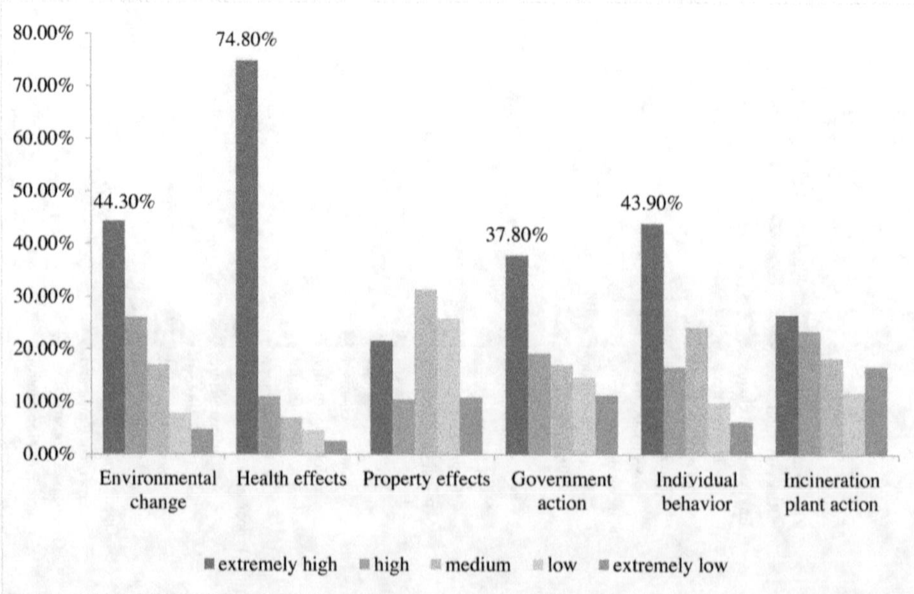

Figure 3. Public risk perception evaluation results at the second hierarchy

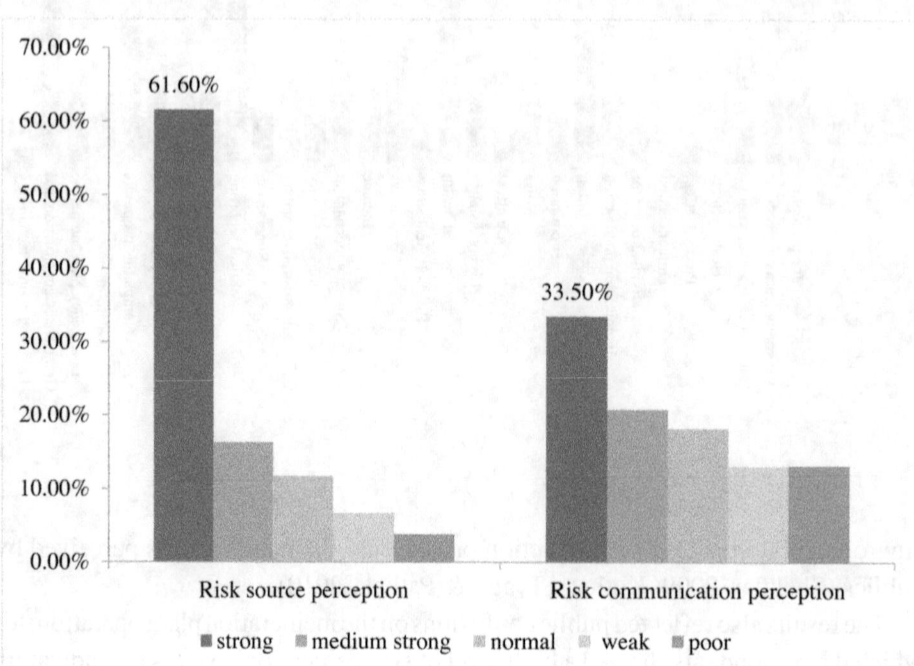

Figure 4. Public risk perception evaluation results at the third hierarchy

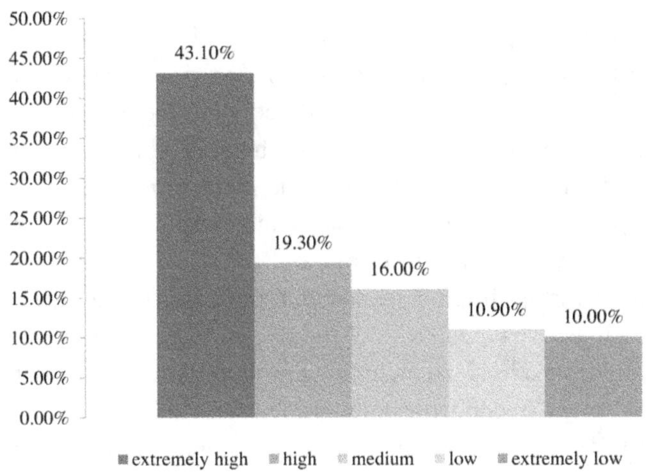

of both "government behavior" and "incineration plant behavior". On the one hand, publicity and education play an important role; the public is susceptible to lack of available accesses to incineration information thus exude negative feelings (Zhang et al., 2012; Che et al., 2013). In a case study of the Pingjiang Modern Coal-fired Power Plant in Hunan Province, China, and the Jiangmen Nuclear Power Plant Project, because of inadequate project-related publicity, the publics had no channels to express their concerns and opinions, resulting in widespread resistance (Liu et al., 2017; Wang et al., 2019). The public risk perception towards "administrative penalties" and "force of supervision" was also strong, which indirectly reflected the publics' expectations on local government to adopt effective surveillances on the incineration plant. Further, the risk perception towards the indicator of "green space construction" was strong. This indicated the publics' psychological appeal for environmental recovery. Prior studies have identified that increase of green space can effectively alleviate the individuals' stress (Thompson et al., 2011; Ohly et al., 2016).

The results provide insightful guidance for reduction of public risk perception and resolution of potential conflicts. From the perspective of local government, it is suggested that the authorities strive to achieve information transparency, listen carefully to public appeals, and lead well policy design for ecological compensation (Lockwood, 2010). For the incineration plant, the operator is recommended to improve its environmental management system, reinforce self-regulation, and communicate with publics in a timely manner (Nie, 2008). With regard to the publics, they are encouraged to be rational involved in project surveillance, to better understand its advantages and challenges.

CONCLUSION

This study conducted in-depth interviews of residents living around an operating incineration plant to establish an indicator system for risk perception evaluation. Based on a word frequency analysis, this study coupled the entropy method with fuzzy decision-making to rank the importance of the indicators. The results showed that the respondents' risk perception towards the incineration plant was at a high level, and the impacts on individual physical and mental health as well as the environmental quality were the key risk sources.

There is room for further improvement. First, the constructed indicator system was based on the subjective perceptions of the respondents. It did not consider the interactions with other stakeholders, including the operators of the incineration plant and the local government. Second, the demographics, including age, education, and income were not taken into the sampling of respondents, which might influence the evaluation results. Future study will consider applying game theory to analyze potential conflicts and interactions of different stakeholders, and improve the indicator system by introducing more scenarios that reflect the individual characteristics.

ACKNOWLEDGMENT

This study is sponsored by National Natural Science Foundation of China (No.41571520), Sichuan Young Talent Scientific Funding (No. 2019JDJQ0020), Sichuan Environment & Engineering Appraisal Center Fund (No. 2018H0729), Sichuan Province Circular Economy Research Center Fund (No. XHJJ-1802), the Fundamental Research Funds for the Central Universities (No. 2682014RC04).

REFERENCES

Bolderston, A. (2012). Conducting a research interview. *Journal of Medical Imaging and Radiation Sciences*, *43*(1), 66–76. doi:10.1016/j.jmir.2011.12.002 PMID:31052024

Brouwer, R., Dekker, T., Rolfe, J., & Windle, J. (2010). Choice certainty and consistency in repeated choice experiments. *Environmental and Resource Economics*, *46*(1), 93–109. doi:10.100710640-009-9337-x

Che, Y., Yang, K., Jin, Y., Zhang, W., Shang, Z., & Tai, J. (2013). Residents' concerns and attitudes toward a municipal solid waste landfill: Integrating a questionnaire survey and GIS techniques. *Environmental Monitoring and Assessment*, *185*(12), 10001–10013. doi:10.100710661-013-3308-y PMID:23793647

Geelen, L. M., Souren, A. F., Jans, H. W., & Ragas, A. M. (2013). Air pollution from industry and traffic: Perceived risk and affect in the Moerdijk region, The Netherlands. *Human and Ecological Risk Assessment*, *19*(6), 1644–1663. doi:10.1080/10807039.2012.749068

Geng, L., Liu, T., Zhou, K., & Yang, G. (2018). Can power affect environmental risk attitude toward nuclear energy? *Energy Policy*, *113*, 87–93. doi:10.1016/j.enpol.2017.10.051

Harclerode, M. A., Lal, P., Vedwan, N., Wolde, B., & Miller, M. E. (2016). Evaluation of the role of risk perception in stakeholder engagement to prevent lead exposure in an urban setting. *Journal of Environmental Management*, *184*, 132–142. doi:10.1016/j.jenvman.2016.07.045 PMID:27477350

Hodge, D. R., & Gillespie, D. (2003). Phrase completions: An alternative to Likert scales (Note on Research Methodology). *Social Work Research*, *27*(1), 45–56. doi:10.1093wr/27.1.45

Huang, L., Ban, J., Sun, K., Han, Y., Yuan, Z., & Bi, J. (2013). The influence of public perception on risk acceptance of the chemical industry and the assistance for risk communication. *Safety Science*, *51*(1), 232–240. doi:10.1016/j.ssci.2012.05.018

Hussey, L. K., & Arku, G. (2019). Conceptualizations of climate-related health risks among health experts and the public in Ghana. *Social Science & Medicine*, *223*, 40–50. doi:10.1016/j.socscimed.2019.01.026 PMID:30708170

Jenkins-Smith, H. C., Silva, C. L., Nowlin, M. C., & DeLozier, G. (2011). Reversing nuclear opposition: Evolving public acceptance of a permanent nuclear waste disposal facility. *Risk Analysis: An International Journal*, *31*(4), 629–644. doi:10.1111/j.1539-6924.2010.01543.x PMID:21175714

Khushaba, R. N., Wise, C., Kodagoda, S., Louviere, J., Kahn, B. E., & Townsend, C. (2013). Consumer neuroscience: Assessing the brain response to marketing stimuli using electroencephalogram (EEG) and eye tracking. *Expert Systems with Applications*, *40*(9), 3803–3812. doi:10.1016/j.eswa.2012.12.095

Kothari, R., Tyagi, V. V., & Pathak, A. (2010). Waste-to-energy: A way from renewable energy sources to sustainable development. *Renewable & Sustainable Energy Reviews*, *14*(9), 3164–3170. doi:10.1016/j.rser.2010.05.005

Lima, M. L. (2004). On the influence of risk perception on mental health: Living near an incinerator. *Journal of Environmental Psychology*, *24*(1), 71–84. doi:10.1016/S0272-4944(03)00026-4

Lin, P. Y., Lai, S. P., Wang, M. C., Liang, J. J., Chiang, C. F., & Kuo, H. W. (2018). Environmental health risks perception, attitude, and avoidance behaviour toward municipal solid waste incinerator. *International Journal of Environmental Health Research*, *28*(2), 159–166. doi:10.1080/09603123.2018.1453052 PMID:29564918

Liu, F., Lyu, T., Pan, L., & Wang, F. (2017). Influencing factors of public support for modern coal-fired power plant projects: An empirical study from China. *Energy Policy*, *105*, 398–406. doi:10.1016/j.enpol.2017.03.017

Liu, Y., Sun, C., Xia, B., Cui, C., & Coffey, V. (2018). Impact of community engagement on public acceptance towards waste-to-energy incineration projects: Empirical evidence from China. *Waste Management (New York, N.Y.)*, *76*, 431–442. doi:10.1016/j.wasman.2018.02.028 PMID:29475616

Lo, A. Y. (2014). Negative income effect on perception of long-term environmental risk. *Ecological Economics*, *107*, 51–58. doi:10.1016/j.ecolecon.2014.08.009

Lockwood, M. (2010). Good governance for terrestrial protected areas: A framework, principles and performance outcomes. *Journal of Environmental Management*, *91*(3), 754–766. doi:10.1016/j.jenvman.2009.10.005 PMID:19896262

Lu, J. W., Zhang, S., Hai, J., & Lei, M. (2017). Status and perspectives of municipal solid waste incineration in China: A comparison with developed regions. *Waste Management (New York, N.Y.)*, *69*, 170–186. doi:10.1016/j.wasman.2017.04.014 PMID:28408280

Ma, D., Gong, W., Fang, Q., Liu, D., & Liu, Y. (2018). Divergence between general public's risk perception and environmental risk assessment: A case study of p-xylene projects in China. *Human and Ecological Risk Assessment*, *24*(4), 859–869. doi:10.1080/10807039.2016.1239180

Mah, D. N. Y., Hills, P., & Tao, J. (2014). Risk perception, trust and public engagement in nuclear decision-making in Hong Kong. *Energy Policy*, *73*, 368–390. doi:10.1016/j.enpol.2014.05.019

Makarichi, L., Jutidamrongphan, W., & Techato, K. A. (2018). The evolution of waste-to-energy incineration: A review. *Renewable & Sustainable Energy Reviews*, *91*, 812–821. doi:10.1016/j.rser.2018.04.088

Nie, Y. (2008). Development and prospects of municipal solid waste (MSW) incineration in China. *Frontiers of Environmental Science & Engineering in China*, *2*(1), 1–7. doi:10.100711783-008-0028-6

Ohly, H., White, M. P., Wheeler, B. W., Bethel, A., Ukoumunne, O. C., Nikolaou, V., & Garside, R. (2016). Attention restoration theory: A systematic review of the attention restoration potential of exposure to natural environments. *Journal of Toxicology and Environmental Health. Part B*, *19*(7), 305–343. PMID:27668460

Omanga, E., Ulmer, L., Berhane, Z., & Gatari, M. (2014). Industrial air pollution in rural Kenya: Community awareness, risk perception and associations between risk variables. *BMC Public Health*, *14*(1), 377. doi:10.1186/1471-2458-14-377 PMID:24742166

Paiva, K. M., Cardoso, M. R. A., & Zannin, P. H. T. (2019). Exposure to road traffic noise: Annoyance, perception and associated factors among Brazil's adult population. *The Science of the Total Environment*, *650*, 978–986. doi:10.1016/j.scitotenv.2018.09.041 PMID:30308872

Pennings, J. M., & Smidts, A. (2000). Assessing the construct validity of risk attitude. *Management Science*, *46*(10), 1337–1348. doi:10.1287/mnsc.46.10.1337.12275

Pennings, J. M., & Smidts, A. (2003). The shape of utility functions and organizational behavior. *Management Science*, *49*(9), 1251–1263. doi:10.1287/mnsc.49.9.1251.16566

Qi, L., Ren, Y., Liu, A. M., Huang, Y. R., Zhao, Z., Wang, J., & Li, H. (2017). Pollution characteristics of PCDD/Fs in ambient air and exposure risk assessment around a municipal solid waste incinerator in Beijing. *Environmental Sciences (Ruse)*, *38*(4), 1317–1326. PMID:29965132

Qu, S. Q., & Dumay, J. (2011). The qualitative research interview. *Qualitative Research in Accounting & Management*, *8*(3), 238–264. doi:10.1108/11766091111162070

Rajgor, G. (2011). Fighting the NIMBY war with a gamble. *Renewable Energy Focus*, *12*(3), 28–30. doi:10.1016/S1755-0084(11)70059-X

Ren, X., Che, Y., Yang, K., & Tao, Y. (2016). Risk perception and public acceptance toward a highly protested Waste-to-Energy facility. *Waste Management (New York, N.Y.)*, *48*, 528–539. doi:10.1016/j.wasman.2015.10.036 PMID:26577458

Shekdar, A. V. (2009). Sustainable solid waste management: An integrated approach for Asian countries. *Waste Management (New York, N.Y.)*, *29*(4), 1438–1448. doi:10.1016/j.wasman.2008.08.025 PMID:19081236

Stoutenborough, J. W., & Vedlitz, A. (2016). The role of scientific knowledge in the public's perceptions of energy technology risks. *Energy Policy*, *96*, 206–216. doi:10.1016/j.enpol.2016.05.031

Thompson Coon, J., Boddy, K., Stein, K., Whear, R., Barton, J., & Depledge, M. H. (2011). Does participating in physical activity in outdoor natural environments have a greater effect on physical and mental wellbeing than physical activity indoors? A systematic review. *Environmental Science & Technology*, *45*(5), 1761–1772. doi:10.1021/es102947t PMID:21291246

Wang, S., Wang, J., Lin, S., & Li, J. (2019). Public perceptions and acceptance of nuclear energy in China: The role of public knowledge, perceived benefit, perceived risk and public engagement. *Energy Policy*, *126*, 352–360. doi:10.1016/j.enpol.2018.11.040

Williams, A. (2003). How to … Write and analyse a questionnaire. *Journal of Orthodontics*, *30*(3), 245–252. doi:10.1093/ortho/30.3.245 PMID:14530423

Wu, K. J., Liao, C. J., Tseng, M. L., Lim, M. K., Hu, J., & Tan, K. (2017). Toward sustainability: Using big data to explore the decisive attributes of supply chain risks and uncertainties. *Journal of Cleaner Production*, *142*, 663–676. doi:10.1016/j.jclepro.2016.04.040

Yu, C. H., Huang, S. K., Qin, P., & Chen, X. (2018). Local residents' risk perceptions in response to shale gas exploitation: Evidence from China. *Energy Policy*, *113*, 123–134. doi:10.1016/j.enpol.2017.10.004

Zegans, L. S. (2008). The psychology of risks. *Journal of Environmental Psychology*, *29*(4), 531–532.

Zhang, W., Che, Y., Yang, K., Ren, X., & Tai, J. (2012). Public opinion about the source separation of municipal solid waste in Shanghai, China. *Waste Management & Research*, *30*(12), 1261–1271. doi:10.1177/0734242X12462277 PMID:23045226

Zhao, R., Liu, S., Liu, Y., Zhang, L., & Li, Y. (2018). A safety vulnerability assessment for chemical enterprises: A hybrid of a data envelopment analysis and fuzzy decision-making. *Journal of Loss Prevention in the Process Industries*, *56*, 95–103. doi:10.1016/j.jlp.2018.08.018

Zhao, R., Min, N., Geng, Y., & He, Y. (2017). Allocation of carbon emissions among industries/sectors: An emissions intensity reduction constrained approach. *Journal of Cleaner Production*, *142*, 3083–3094. doi:10.1016/j.jclepro.2016.10.159

Chapter 6
Climate Change and Profit Loss:
A Case History of Salinity Intrusion in Rice Production

Huynh Viet Khai
https://orcid.org/0000-0001-8969-5387
Can Tho University, Vietnam

ABSTRACT

The chapter aims to evaluate the profit loss of rice farmers due to salinity intrusion by collecting the information of rice production in three regions with the same natural environment conditions, social characteristics (e.g., the same social and farming culture, ethnicity, type of soil), and only differed with respect to the level of salinity in Soc Trang province, one of the most salinity-affected areas in the Vietnamese Mekong Delta. The study estimated the profit loss in rice production due to saltwater intrusion by the difference in rice profit between the non-salinity and salinity regions and showed this loss was about VND 9.3-15.1 million per ha-1 a year.

INTRODUCTION

Salinity intrusion is a natural phenomenon occurring in the land, estuaries and groundwater adjacent to the sea. Salinity intrusion occurs when there is a difference in the flow of energy as well as specific weight between fresh and salt water. Salinity intrusion is caused by many factors such as river flow levels, topography,

DOI: 10.4018/978-1-5225-9562-5.ch006

geomorphology, the slope of river flow, the intensity of the sea tide, the wind speed and direction, water temperature and so on.

Salinity lands in the Vietnamese Mekong Delta are relatively large compared to the whole country due to the crisscrossing systems of river and canals resulting in saltwater easily penetrating further inland. Salinity intrusion lasts longer than normal and penetrates inland about 50 km if the raining season comes late, and $1\%_0$ salinity covers almost all the coastal estuaries. Most likely in the peak month, salinity could reach $1.0\text{-}1.5\%_0$ (DWRM, 2016a; 2016b). This problem greatly affects agricultural production, especially rice crop in winter-spring season. In the time of water shortages in the dry season and at the end of the rainy season, farmers use brackish water to irrigate their rice fields, especially in the rice flowering stage, which leads to loss their rice yield and profit.

Scientific evidence shows that the rice losses of salinity intrusion is not so small in terms of reducing the productivity and profit. Although there are many studies on analyzing the effects of salinity intrusion in rice production, very few studies have evaluated specific statistics about the decline of rice profit caused by salinity. In this study, we analyze the effect of salinity intrusion to rice production and identify how rice farmers deal with and adapt the problems of salinity. The effects of salinity intrusion to rice farmers are defined as the total economic losses of rice production in terms of reduced quantity, reduced quality and an increase in input costs, which are estimated by comparing the profits between selected areas (a salinity and non-salinity area). The differences in profits between these areas are considered reflecting the economic damage, caused by salinity, to rice production. The results of study could provide useful information to local authorities, for example the department of Natural Resources and Environment, to issue appropriate policies to help or support farmers who are affected by salinity. The results of the study are also necessary data used as the value of benefit transferring into other similar future projects in Vietnam.

This chapter is constructed as follows. The next section describes the concept to estimate economic loss caused by salinity intrusion and data collection. The results and some discussion related to the effect of salinity intrusion to rice farmers and their adaptation of salinity problems are reported in the focus of the chapter. The final section presents some main conclusions and policy implication.

EVALUATION CONCEPT AND EMPIRICAL MODEL

The total economic loss of rice production includes three factors. First, a reduction in crop quantity assumes that salinity decreases rice yield. Second, a reduction in rice quality, which is measured as price, assumes that the lower price of rice in a particular region could reflect reduced rice quality due to salinity. Third, an increase in input costs assumes that farms may attempt to compensate for the possible productivity losses by implementing activities that are capable of offsetting this possible loss but are costlier to implement. The expectation of the profit loss is summarized by the following formula:

$$\begin{aligned}
\pi_{salinity} &= \left(\bar{P} - \Delta P\right)\left(\bar{Q} - \Delta Q\right) - \left(\bar{C} + \Delta C\right) \\
&= \bar{P}\bar{Q} - \bar{P} \times \Delta Q - \Delta P \times \bar{Q} + \Delta P \times \Delta Q - \bar{C} - \Delta C \\
&= \left(\bar{P}\bar{Q} - \bar{C}\right) - \left(\bar{P} \times \Delta Q + \Delta P \times \bar{Q} + \Delta \bar{C}\right) + \Delta P \times \Delta Q \\
&= \pi_{non-salinity} - Profit\, loss \\
&=> Profit\, loss = \bar{P} \times \Delta Q + \Delta P \times \bar{Q} + \Delta \bar{C} \\
&= Quantity\, loss + Quality\, loss + Cost\, increase
\end{aligned}$$

where $\pi_{\text{non-salinity}}$ and π_{salinity} are the rice profits in the non-salinity and salinity areas. Because $\Delta P \times \Delta Q$ is small compared with the other parts of the equation, it can be ignored and assumed to be 0.

The profit loss is estimated by the following basic profit function:

$$\pi^* = \pi\left(W^*, C, Z, E, D_1, D_2\right) \tag{3}$$

where π^* is normalized profit defined as gross revenue minus variable cost divided by farm-specific output price, W^* is a vector of variable input prices divided by output price, C is a vector of fixed factors of the farm, Z is a vector of social-economic characteristics of farmers, E is a vector of farming conditions, and D_1, D_2 are the relative location of farms (D_1=1 if the farmers in Lieu Tu which is considered as the area little affected by salinity, D_2= 1 if the farmers in Lich Hoi Thuong which is considered as the area heavily affected by salinity; $D_1 = 0$ and $D_2 = 0$ if the farmers in Dai Tam which is considered as the area unaffected by salinity) .

The profit loss due to saltwater intrusion is defined by the difference in profit between the salinity and non-salinity areas. It is estimated by the equation:

$$\Delta\pi_1^* = \pi\left(\bar{W}^*, \bar{C}, \bar{Z}, \bar{E}, D_1 = 0, D_2 = 0\right) - \pi\left(\bar{W}^*, \bar{C}, \bar{Z}, \bar{E}, D_1 = 1, D_2 = 0\right)$$

$$\Delta\pi_2^* = \pi\left(\bar{W}^*, \bar{C}, \bar{Z}, \bar{E}, D_1 = 0, D_2 = 0\right) - \pi\left(\bar{W}^*, \bar{C}, \bar{Z}, \bar{E}, D_1 = 0, D_2 = 1\right) \tag{4}$$

where $\Delta\pi_1^*$ and $\Delta\pi_2^*$ is Profit loss in two salinity areas respectively; $\bar{W}^*, \bar{C}, \bar{Z}, \bar{E}$ are the average prices of inputs, the average of the fixed factors, the social-economic characteristics of farmers, the farming conditions, respectively.

We use the translog profit functional form. The formula is given as (Rahman 2002; Surjit and Carlos 1981):

$$\pi^* = \alpha_0 + \sum_{j=1}^{4} \alpha_j \ln W_j^* + \frac{1}{2}\sum_{j=1}^{4}\sum_{k=1}^{4} \tau_{jk} \ln W_j^* \ln W_k^* + \sum_{j=1}^{4}\sum_{l=1}^{2} \phi_{jl} \ln W_j^* \ln C_l + \\ + \sum_{l=1}^{2} \beta_l \ln C_l + \frac{1}{2}\sum_{l=1}^{2}\sum_{t=1}^{2} \varphi_{lt} \ln C_l \ln C_t + \sum_{m=1}^{3} \varpi_m Z_m + \sum_{n=1}^{3} \eta_n E_n + \gamma_1 D_1 + \gamma_2 D_2 + \varepsilon \quad (5)$$

where π^* is the restricted profit (total revenue minus total cost of variable inputs) normalized by price of output (P); W_j^* is the price of the jth input (W_j) normalized by the output price (P); j is the price of seed (1), the price of herbicide (2), the price of fertilizer (3), the price of pesticide (4); C_l is the quantity of fixed input, where l is the area of rice land (1), capital (2); Z_1, Z_2, Z_3, are the age (years), studying high school or above (1 = Yes, 0 = otherwise), and attending trainings (1 = Yes, 0 = No), and E_1, E_2, E_3, are the variables of Disease (1 = serious diseases happening during the year, 0 = otherwise), soil quality (1 = Vey no-fertile, 2 = No-fertile, 3 = Medium, 4 = Fertile, and 5 = Very fertile), and Irrigation (1 = located in the irrigation region, 0 = Otherwise), respectively.

Then, the following restriction is applied to test the existence of the Cobb-Douglass function (Khai and Yabe, 2013):

$$\tau_{jk} = \phi_{jl} = \varphi_{lt} = 0 \quad (6)$$

DATA COLLECTION

The study region covers the areas Soc Trang province, one of the most salinity-affected provinces in the Vietnamese Mekong Delta at the end of 2015. Farmers were randomly selected for interviews from three areas (Dai Tam, Lieu Tu and Lich Hoi Thuong district) with similar social and natural conditions (e.g., fertile soils, weather). The selection of the salinity and non-salinity area are based on the recommendation or suggestion of local authorities and farmers. The villages in Lieu Tu and Lich Hoi Thuong had problems with heavily saltwater intrusion at the period from the end of 2015 to the beginning of 2016, the most heavily salinity-affected time in the

Vietnamese Mekong Delta, while the villages in Dai Tam represent the non-salinity area (see Figure 1). In total, 214 rice farmers, consisting of 72 farmers in Lieu Tu and 72 farmers in Lich Hoi Thuong that were heavily affected by salinity and 70 farmers in Dai Tam near Lieu Tu and Lich Hoi Thuong regions, but not affected by salinity. The survey was conducted during the time from March and April 2016. Data was collected on household level information related to production costs and income as well as the social and economic characteristics of the farmers, and their perceived damages and losses due to salinity.

Table 1 shows the salinity level of the study areas during the period of saline intrusion in the Mekong Delta in 2015-2016. The regions of Lieu Tu and Lich Hoi Thuong are rather high salinity, up to 2.8%$_0$, while a level of salt water intrusion in Dai Tam is approximately from 0.0 to 0.3% $_0$, which the experts assessed almost not affected by saltwater intrusion. Moreover, to check the validity of the study area, we also asked farmers in these areas if their land is affected by salinity. Most farmers in Dai Tam answered that salinity have no impacts on their land, while a majority of farmers in Lien Tu and Lich Hoi Thuong confirmed their land had a problem with

Figure 1. Map showing study site

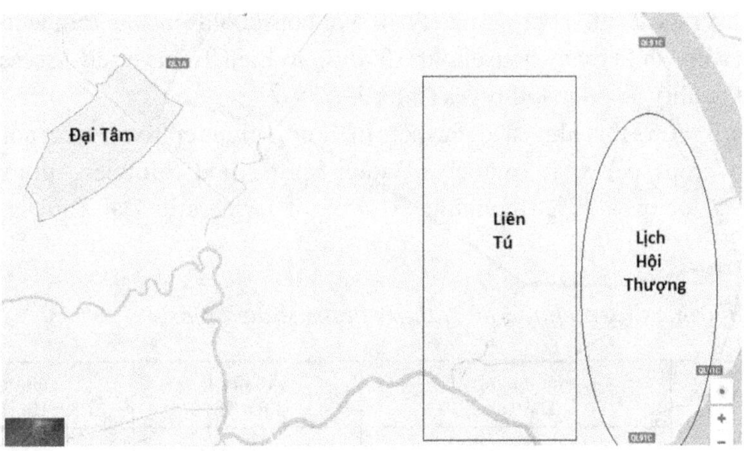

Table 1. The situation of salinity in the study areas in 2015-2016

	Unit	Non-Salinity (Dai Tam)	Salinity 1 (Lieu Tu)	Salinity 2 (Lich Hoi Thuong)
Period of salinity	month	December 12, 2015 – February 2, 2016		
Average level of salinity	%$_0$	0.0 – 0.3	0.8-2.8	1.7-2.8

Source: Department of Agriculture and Rural Development in My Xuyen and Tran De, 2016

salinity (See Table 2). This reveals the selected areas are suitable for the study on the economic loss of rice production due to salinity.

MAIN FOCUS OF THE CHAPTER

Socioeconomic Status, Cultivation, and Salinity Adaptation of Rice Farmers

Table 3 shows the overview of characteristics of rice farmers in the survey areas. The results of t-test show that almost all social-economic characteristics and farming conditions of rice farmers are not so different among the groups of the farmers in the study areas, showing selected study sites have the same social, natural condition. The interviewed households have the average age of about 47 years old and 27 years in rice farming. A household with averagely 4.5 members in selected regions produces rice of 2.12 ha on average. A half of rice farmers said that they have attended training provided by local authorities.

Soil quality is assessed by farmers through a questionnaire with 5-level scale from very infertile to very fertile. The results are shown in Figure 2. The results show that over half of farmers in three areas said their land quality to be fertile soil with the average level. Approximately 40% of households in Dai Tam who said soil quality fertile while many households (37.5%) in Lien Tu have self-assessments of their soil quality as poor soil types (infertile).

Figure 3 shows that almost all farmers in three regions cultivate rice monoculture with two crops per year (namely, Winter-Spring and Summer-Autumn crop), accounting for over 90% (including 91.43% of farmers in Dai Tam, 95.89% of

Table 2. Farmers' perception on salinity in the study areas

	Non-Salinity (Dai Tam)		Salinity 1 (Lieu Tu)		Salinity 2 (Lich Hoi Thuong)	
	Number	Percent (%)	Number	Percent (%)	Number	Percent (%)
Rice production is not affected by salinity	69	98.57	2	2.78	3	4.17
Rice production is affected by salinity	1	1.43	70	97.22	69	95.83
Total	70	100	72	100	72	100

Source: Own estimates; data appendix available from authors.

Table 3. Social and economic characteristics of rice farmers

Items	Unit	Non-Salinity (1)	Salinity 1 (2)	Salinity 2 (3)	Difference (1 vs. 2)	Difference (1 vs. 3)	Whole Area
Family members	Persons	4.37	4.37	4.84	0.00	0.43	4.60
Owner's age	Years	49.6	46.05	46.5	3.55	3.1	47.37
Agriculture labor	Persons	1.72	1.73	1.70	0.02	0.01	1.79
Rice area	Ha	2.47	2.09	1.78	0.38	0.69	2.12
Crop number	crop/ year	2	2	2	-	-	2
Owner's experience	Year	28.35	27.42	26.34	0.93	2.01	27.16
Education	Year	10.00	8.09	7.36	3.78***	2.64 ***	8.47
Training	-	0.64	0.46	0.42	0.18**	0.23***	0.050

Note: *** and ** represent statistical significance level at 1% and 5%

farmers in Lieu Tu and nearly 99% of households applied monoculture) while only 3.3% of farmers rotate rice with other crops or vegetables and apply intercropping model. The main reasons for most farmers applying rice monoculture are that this model is a traditional production one and most farmers have been producing for a long time and have extensive experiences on rice monoculture, so they are afraid to change other cultivation models.

Figure 2. The perception of farmers on the quality of their land
Source: Own estimates; data appendix available from authors.

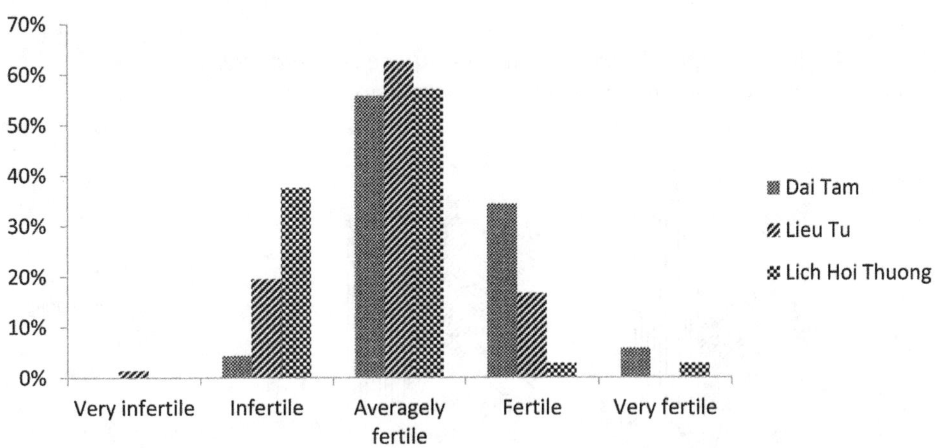

Figure 3. The cropping system of rice production in the study areas
Source: Own estimates; data appendix available from authors.

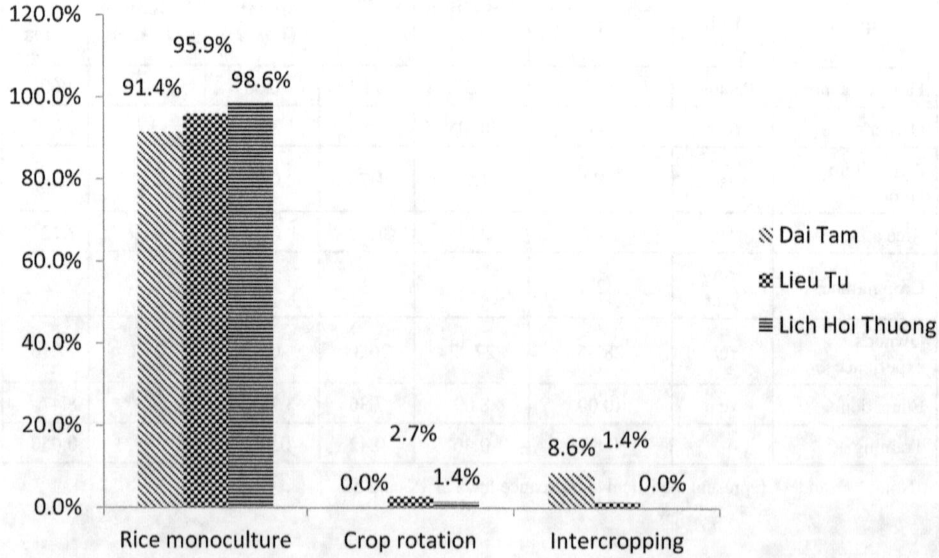

Figure 4 performs that the situation of serious diseases occurring in the rice field during the study period. Farmers were interviewed if any serious diseases occur for their rice cultivation during the survey period. The results show that over 40 percent of rice land occurred some serious diseases, of which, rice blast and red stripe disease is considered to be one of the main causes on rice damage during the study period.

Farmers in the two salinity areas (Lieu Tu and Lich Hoi Thuong) were also interviewed to assess their ability to adapt to the problems of saltwater intrusion. They were asked if they accepted to pay more for any technical improvements to

Figure 4. The situation of serious diseases during the study period
Source: Own estimates; data appendix available from authors.

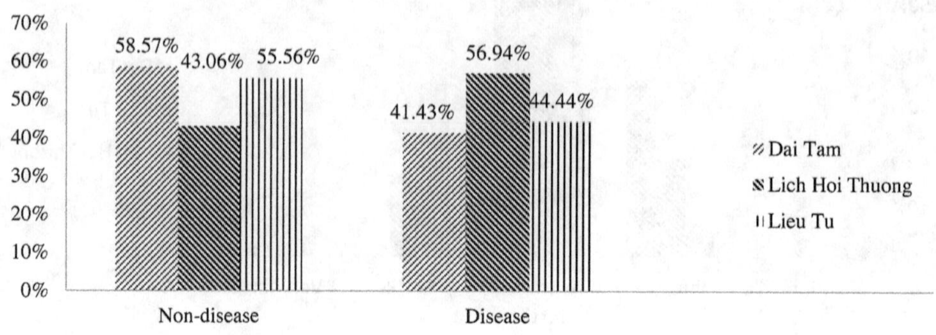

reduce losses in rice production due to salinity. The results of their answer with the 5 levels from completely disagree to completely agree are shown in Figure 5. A majority of farmers in the salinity regions accepted to pay more to reduce the damages caused by salinity intrusion. Up to 30 farmers (about 41.67%) in Lieu Tu and 40 farmers (about 55%) in Lich Hoi Thuong agreed to pay some extra costs that could partly mitigate or prevent the losses in rice production due to salinity. This reveals that farmers in the salinity areas are aware of the negative impact of salinization on rice productivity and profitability.

Rice farmers apply different measures to deal with saltwater intrusion depend on the social and natural characteristics of salinity areas. Based on the results of focus group discussion, some proposed adaptation measures listed in the questionnaire, including an increase in an amount of fertilizers, planting salt-tolerant varieties, application of new technologies, increasing an investment in irrigation infrastructure, dredging channels and weeding, and doing nothings are presented in Table 4.

The results show that the measure of dredging channels and weeding is mostly applied by farmers to reduce the damage caused by salinization, accounting for 68.06% and 61.11%, respectively, while about 47.22% farmers in Lieu Tu and 38.89% farmers in Lich Hoi Thuong are ready to improve irrigation infrastructure to mitigate the losses in rice production due to salinity. The interesting results show that very few farmers selected the measure of planting salt-tolerant varieties to mitigate the damage caused by salinity, but majority of farmers do nothings to deal with saltwater intrusion. Especially, farmers in Lich Hoi Thuong (accounting for 37.50%) have no preparations to deal with salinity because they said that saltwater

Figure 5. Farmers' willingness to pay more to reduce the losses in rice production due to salinity

Source: Own estimates; data appendix available from authors.

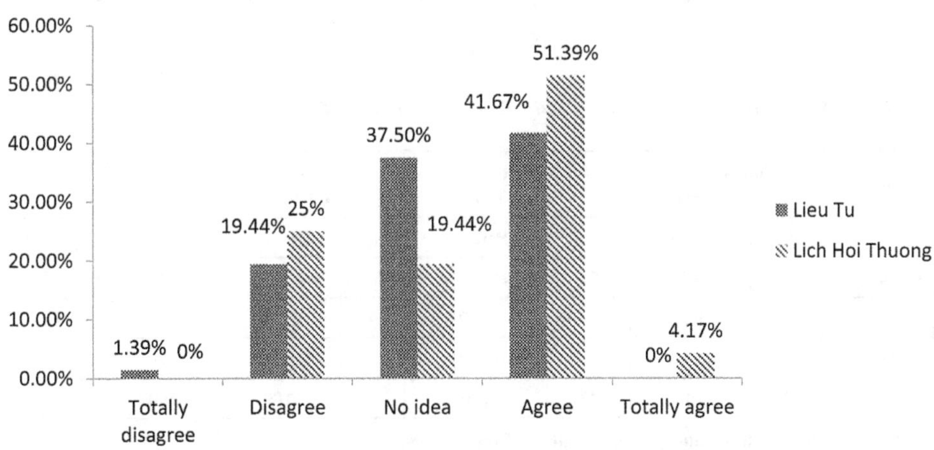

Table 4. The adaptive strategies of rice farmers in the salinity areas

Adaptation Measures	Salinity 1 (Lieu Tu)		Salinity 2 (Lich Hoi Thuong)	
	Number	Percent (%)	Number	Percent (%)
Increasing fertilizers	27	37,50	24	33,33
Dredging channels and weeding	49	68,06	44	61,11
Applying new technologies	6	8,33	3	4,17
Increasing an investment in irrigation infrastructure	34	47,22	28	38,89
Diversification of crops	27	37,50	16	22,22
Planting salt-tolerant varieties	2	2,78	5	6,94
Doing nothings	12	16,67	27	37,50
Other measures	5	6,94	5	6,94

Source: Own estimates; data appendix available from authors.

intrusion occurred very suddenly in 2015-2016, and they had no time to prepare or mitigate this problem.

Table 5 presents the main rice varieties are used by farmers in the study areas. Over half of farmers (62.9%) applied the variety of OM4900 (44.29% for Dai Tam, 44.6% for Lich Hoi Thuong and 86.11% for Lieu Tu), while only 26.8% farmers planted the variety of RVT. A majority of farmers preferred to grow OM4900 because this variety has good resistance to yellow dwarf disease, and especially alkaline resistance and salt-tolerance. The total cost of rice production showed in Table 6 included land preparation cost (machinery cost, labor hired cost), the cost of seeding (seed cost, labor hired cost), the cost of weeding (herbicide, labor hired cost), fertilizer cost (the cost of fertilizers, labor hired cost), pesticide cost (pesticide, labor hired cost), irrigation cost (machinery cost, labor hired cost) and harvesting

Table 5. Rice varieties used by farmers in the study areas

Rice Varieties	Non-Salinity (Dai Tam)		Salinity 1 (Lieu Tu)		Salinity 2 (Lich Hoi Thuong)		Whole	
	No.	Percent	No.	Percent	No.	Percent	No.	Percent
OM4900	31	44.29	62	86.11	64	88.89	157	62.9
RTV	20	28.57	7	9.72	4	5.56	67	26.8
Others	19	27.14	3	4.17	4	5.56	26	10.4
Total	**70**	**100**	**72**	**100**	**72**	**100**	**250**	**100**

Source: Own estimates; data appendix available from authors.

cost (machinery cost, labor hired cost). In the study area, almost all farmers have no processing cost because they sell fresh rice at their field.

Table 6 shows there are some differences in cost between the three regions, the cost of rice production in Lieu Tu is the highest, followed by the cost of rice production in Dai Tam and finally in Lich Hoi Thuong. The results of t-test also show there are differences in the total cost of rice production between non-salinity and two salinity areas at a statistically significant level of 1%. Harvest cost is contributed the most in the difference of the total cost. The cost of harvesting in Dai Tam (Non-salinity) is approximately VND 5.9 million and VND 4.9 million for Lich Hoi Thuong (Salinity 2) which makes the difference up to VND 1.035 million in harvest cost between two regions.

IMPACT OF SALINITY ON THE PROFIT OF RICE PRODUCTION

The translog profit function form of (5) is applied to identify profit reduction in rice production caused by salinity. Lagrange Multiplier (LM) test is also used to check the present of Heteroscedasticity in the profit function[1]. The result shows the existence of Heteroscedasticity in the data at the significant level of 5 percent, the OLS regression with robust standard error is estimated to solve the problem of Heteroscedasticity. Table 7 shows the OLS regression of rice profit function with robust standard error. The full model is statistically significant at the 1% level.

Table 6. The cost of rice production per hectare a year

Items	Non-Salinity (Dai Tam)		Salinity 1 (Lieu Tu)		Salinity 2 (Lich Hoi Thuong)		Difference (1 vs. 2)	Difference (1 vs. 3)
	In VND	%	In VND	%	In VND	%		
Land preparation	3,298.21	8.94	3,726.80	9.93	3,977.43	11.35	-428.54*	-697.22
Seeding	5,626.38	15.25	5,515.83	14.69	5,519.37	15.76	110.55	107.02
Weeding	909.14	2.46	827.10	2.20	764.28	2.18	82.05	144.87
Fertilizer	13,853.10	37.56	13,765.07	36.66	12,882.91	36.78	88.01	970.16
Pesticide	5,045.95	13.68	5,623.84	14.98	4,745.81	13.55	-577.9	300.14
Irrigation	2,272.66	6.16	2,381.89	6.34	2,294.50	6.55	-109.22*	-21.84*
Harvest	5,881.23	15.94	5,707.10	15.20	4,845.97	13.83	174.13*	1,035.25*
Total	**36,886.64**	**100**	**37,547.60**	**100**	**35,030.27**	**100**	**-660.94*** **	**1,856.37*** **

Notes: ***, **, * indicate statistical significance at the 0.01, 0.05 and 0.1 level respectively

Source: Own estimates; data appendix available from authors.

The estimated R-square revealed that 63% of the variation in the rice profit can be explained by the model.

Next, the null hypothesis of the Cobb-Douglass functional form is tested. The restricted function is estimated assuming the null hypothesis that the joint parameters in the equation (6) are 0. The computed F statistic of 1.66 is more than the critical $F(21,178)$ value of 1.62 at the 5 percent level). The null hypothesis is therefore rejected, which supports the use of the translog functional form in this study. The estimation of profit function also shows the absence of multicollinearity (the correlations of independent variables less than 70 percent) (Khai and Yabe, 2012).

The coefficient of *Salinity 1* and *Salinity 2* variables representing the effects of salinity are negative and significant ($P < 0.01$), which confirms that saline intrusion reduces the profit of rice cultivation. The reduction in rice profit can be calculated using the coefficients presented in Table 7. The estimated profit is approximately VND 15 million for rice cultivation in the area of *Salinity 1*, VND 9.1 million in the *Salinity 2* and VND 24.2 million for that in the area of non-salinity after the influences of other factors are eliminated. The loss of rice profit due to salinity can be estimated by subtracting the rice profit in the salinity region by the rice profit in the non-salinity region (equation 12). Using this approach, the loss of profit is calculated to be approximately VND 9.3 million per hectare in the *Salinity 1* (Luu Tu) and VND 15. 1 million per hectare in the *Salinity 2* (Lich Hoi Thuong).

CONCLUSION AND RECOMMENDATIONS

This study surveyed rice farmers in three areas with the same natural environment conditions and social characteristics, and only differed with respect to salinity. The rice profit loss caused by salinity was estimated by the difference in rice profit between the three areas. The results showed that the profit loss was about VND 9.3 - 15.1 million tons per hectare. Although official warnings of expected salinity and drought problems during the Dong Xuan season generally reach farmers early, these warnings did not translate into adjusted agricultural production on a large scale. High salinity during the late stage of rice growth (around maturity) was also a major problem during the 2015-2016 salinity crisis. Early cut-off dates for harvesting rice could help farmers avoid stretching the crop into periods of high salinity by late March and April. Suitable short-duration varieties for the adjusted growth window thus need to be identified and promoted. Additional investments should be made to further improve those varieties, and to improve late-stage salinity tolerance. This study only estimated the quantity reduction of rice production due to salinity.

The current salinity crisis has shown that a regional water management approach is crucial for minimizing damage to rice production. This includes better coordination

Table 7. The OLS regression of rice profit function

Variables	Symbol	Coef.	Robust St.Er.
ln(*Normalized price of seed*)	$Ln(W_1)$	68,217.87**	28,551.13
ln(*Normalized price of herbicide*)	$Ln(W_2)$	-39,744.84	34,211.88
ln(*Normalized price of fertilizer*)	$Ln(W_3)$	19,736.82	70,307.97
ln(*Normalized price of pesticide*)	$Ln(W_4)$	15,099.96	22,984.59
ln(*Land*)	$Ln(C_1)$	-2,039.17	19,169.39
ln(*Capital*)	$Ln(C_2)$	-62,253.83	173,696.30
½ ln(*Normalized price of seed*)^2	$\frac{1}{2}\ln(W_1)^2$	-821.21	703.56
½ ln(*Normalized price of herbicide*)^2	$\frac{1}{2}\ln(W_2)^2$	831.67	1,105.15
½ ln(*Normalized price of fertilizer*)^2	$\frac{1}{2}\ln(W_3)^2$	1,555.25	3,187.92
½ ln(*Normalized price of pesticide*)^2	$\frac{1}{2}\ln(W_4)^2$	-1,286.77*	715.75
½ ln(*Land*)^2	$\frac{1}{2}\ln(C_1)^2$	-565.05	412.96
½ ln(*Capital*)^2	$\frac{1}{2}\ln(C_2)^2$	8,868.86	17,943.29
ln(*Normalized price of seed*)× ln(*Normalized price of herbicide*)	$\ln(W_1)\times \ln(W_2)$	-201.95	780.47
ln(*Normalized price of seed*)× ln(*Normalized price of fertilizer*)	$\ln(W_1)\times \ln(W_3)$	-1,957.66	2,029.58
ln(*Normalized price of seed*)× ln(*Normalized price of pesticide*)	$\ln(W_1)\times \ln(W_4)$	166.82	869.13
ln(*Normalized price of seed*)× ln(*Land*)	$\ln(W_1)\times \ln(C_1)$	-506.24	624.79
ln(*Normalized price of seed*)× ln(*Capital*)	$\ln(W_1)\times \ln(C_2)$	-6,939.79**	2,857.41
ln(*Normalized price of herbicide*)× ln(*Normalized price of fertilizer*)	$\ln(W_2)\times \ln(W_3)$	-165.43	1,841.31
ln(*Normalized price of herbicide*)× ln(*Normalized price of pesticide*)	$\ln(W_2)\times \ln(W_4)$	-1,084.84*	646.76
ln(*Normalized price of herbicide*)× ln(*Land*)	$\ln(W_2)\times \ln(C_1)$	121.89	578.73
ln(*Normalized price of herbicide*)× ln(*Capital*)	$\ln(W_2)\times \ln(C_2)$	4,358.80	3,512.34
ln(*Normalized price of fertilizer*)× ln(*Normalized price of pesticide*)	$\ln(W_3)\times \ln(W_4)$	3,868.66**	1,569.46
ln(*Normalized price of fertilizer*)× ln(*Land*)	$\ln(W_3)\times \ln(C_1)$	69.38	1,226.36
ln(*Normalized price of fertilizer*)× ln(*Capital*)	$\ln(W_3)\times \ln(C_2)$	-2,012.26	7,001.07
ln(*Normalized price of pesticide*)× ln(*Land*)	$\ln(W_4)\times \ln(C_1)$	-652.51*	370.10

continued on following page

Table 7. Continued

Variables	Symbol	Coef.	Robust St.Er.
ln(*Normalized price of pesticide*)× ln(*Capital*)	ln(W_4)× ln(C_2)	-2,646.62	2,458.01
ln(*Land*)× ln(*Capital*)	ln(C_1)× ln(C_2)	410.67	1,999.21
Age	Z_1	9.53	15.94
Highschool	Z_2	-140.29	543.48
Training	Z_3	492.17	378.75
Disease	E_1	-523.28	394.14
Soil quality	E_2	943.02***	306.84
Irrigation	E_3	905.78**	445.12
Salinity 1	D1	-2,010.43***	486.93
Salinity 2	D2	-3,287.04***	606.61
Constant		191,484.50	852,974.40
R-square		0.63	
Included observation		214	

Notes: ***, **, * indicate statistical significance at the 0.01, 0.05 and 0.1 level respectively
Source: Own estimates; data appendix available from authors.

and communication of measures across different provinces of the Vietnamese Mekong Delta, as well as strengthening cooperation with other riparian states of the Mekong River. In the long term, all popular varieties planted in the Vietnamese Mekong Delta should carry multiple tolerances to abiotic stresses (i.e. salinity, drought and heat stress) and fit for the new cropping system. A forward-looking breeding program should be designed for the development of new 'designer' varieties that fit the new cropping systems and carry the package of traits required for climate resilience, such as combining tolerance to current and foreseen abiotic stresses like salinity, drought and heat stress. These recommendations are also considered in the new rice master plan recently approved by the MARD (Ministry of Agriculture and Rural Development) Minister as part of Prime Minister's decision (Decision No. 899/QD-TTg dated 10 June 2013) to restructure Vietnam's agricultural sector.

ACKNOWLEDGMENT

This study is funded in part by the Southeast Asian Regional Center for Graduate Study and Research in Agriculture (SEARCA) and the Can Tho University Improvement Project VN14-P6, supported by a Japanese ODA loan. Our warmest thanks go to the staff and students in the department of Environmental and Resource Economics, College of Economics, Can Tho University for assisting in data collection.

REFERENCES

DWRM. (2016a). *Summary of water sources, drought and salinity intrusion updated on 15 April 2016. Department of Water Resources Management.* Ministry of Agriculture and Rural Development.

DWRM. (2016b). *Salinity intrusion in the Mekong River Delta (2015-2016), drought in the Central and Central Highlands regions and solutions. Department of Water Resources Management.* Ministry of Agriculture and Rural Development.

Khai, H. V., & Yabe, M. (2012). Rice Yield Loss Due to Industrial Water Pollution in Vietnam. *Journal of US-China Public Administration*, *9*(3), 248–256.

Khai, H. V., & Yabe, M. (2013). Impact of Industrial Water Pollution on Rice Production in Vietnam. In International Perspectives on Water Quality Management and Pollutant Control (pp. 61-85). INTECH Publishing.

Rahman, S. (2002). Profit Efficiency Among Bangladeshi Rice Farmers. *Food Policy*, *28*(5-6), 487–503. doi:10.1016/j.foodpol.2003.10.001

Surjit, S. S., & Carlos, A. B. (1981). Estimating Farm-Level Input Demand and Wheat Supply in the Indian Punjab Using a Translog Profit Function. *American Journal of Agricultural Economics*, *63*(2), 237–246. doi:10.2307/1239559

ENDNOTE

1 Breusch-Pagan test for heterscedasticity: $LM = nR^2 \sim \chi^2_K$, where: n is the number of observations; R^2 is the R-Square of $\left|\hat{u}_i\right| = \tilde{\delta}_0 + \tilde{\delta}_1 X_{1i} + \tilde{\delta}_2 X_{2i} + \ldots + \tilde{\delta}_k X_{ki} + \tilde{v}_i$; k is the number of restricted factors.

Chapter 7
From Linear to Circular Tourism:
Environmental Challenge for Tourism

Sebastiano Patti
https://orcid.org/0000-0002-7471-9654
University of Catania, Italy

Antonino Messina
Independent Researcher, Italy

ABSTRACT

There are several relevant studies concerning tourism and environment, some of them studying ecotourism, recreation ecology, adventure tourism, and parks and wilderness management. Many publications on sustainable and responsible tourism described the relationship between environmental and economic growth and considered it important to have to consider them in an integrated approach. Usually, the research highlighted the negative impact of tourism on the environment. However, tourism and environment can be complementary to each other, and sustainable management of tourism may produce positive externalities on the environment. This chapter focuses on the environmental challenges of tourism throughout the passage from linear to circular tourism.

INTRODUCTION

There are several relevant researches concerning tourism and environment, some of them studying ecotourism, recreation ecology, adventure tourism, parks and

DOI: 10.4018/978-1-5225-9562-5.ch007

wilderness management. Many publications on sustainable and responsible tourism described the relationship between environment and economic growth and considered it so important to have to evaluate them in an integrated approach. Usually, the research highlighted the negative impact of tourism on the environment. However, tourism and environment can be complementary, and a sustainable management of tourism may produce positive externalities on the environment.

In addressing the issues of environmental economic policy, some specific concepts must be used. The first issue regards the **long-run perspective**, from which decision making process should be arranged. It is now evident that short-run economic decisions cannot face on the problem of natural resources scarcity. The second issue is strictly connected with the first one and concerns the long-run **availability of natural resources (NR)**. For the economists, price is a "signal" of scarcity, when it goes up it means that commodities are becoming more scarce. Unfortunately, for many NR prices are not correct signals of scarcity. Prices come from the relationship among Countries and they do not take into account "external costs". Prices as well as market mechanism are not reliable to achieve "Pareto optimum". Strong externalities, non-competitive condition and public and common goods do not permit an "optimum" use of natural resources and environment. But the question is: the NR allocation is "optimum"? How is it possible to ameliorate it? If environment is polluted due to the production and consumption activities, the future well-being is the maximum possible? To answer these questions should be a priority for those who manage the environmental economic policy worldwide.

Policy makers rarely worry about whether the rate of utilization of natural resources is good for society and what consequences this will have for future generations. Rather, the interest of governments is to know the value of GDP and its growth rate. Although there is no production without the use of natural resources, not even in the tourist product, there is rarely a link between GDP growth and use of natural resources. There is evidence that GDP is misused. It is used as an indicator of the well-being of the community, but it only indicates the value of production. Since GDP indicates the value of the flow of final goods produced in the year, incorporating a Keynesian view of effective demand. Furthermore, the accounting rules need to be reviewed, with regard to natural and environmental resources. In a scenario in which all Countries pursue the objective of GDP growth, it can be expected that all their choices will lead to halting global growth. In fact, natural resources being a finite quantity, they will not be able to sustain the growth of the population, of the consumption per capita and of the production of waste per capita, indefinitely (Medows and Randers, 2006).

Another important issue is the technical progress. It is considered in a positive perspective, since it is able to solve humanity problems.

Nevertheless, technical progress evolution could be harmful if it follows wrong logics, based on wrong market signals, that is on prices and costs that do not represent the true costs of the society.

Energy production generates carbon dioxide (CO_2 emissions). Carbon dioxide contributes to increasing the greenhouse effect, leading to overheating of the earth's temperature. These effects are present and future costs, which must be considered when making decisions through monetary valuation. It more evident that to calculate these costs, it is necessary, for instance, to know the quantity of CO_2 emitted by a plant that produces energy and that is fueled by coal or diesel and has a certain incorporated technology. Technical progress, unfortunately, does not take into account the resilience of the Earth, nor human health.

Moreover, the indefinite progress is subordinated to an unlimited growth of the economy. The pragmatism of ecomomic growth has been perceived as a prerequisite for the widening of the possibilities of life, developed mostly within the private life of individuals. Governments, on the other hand, have the task of supporting GDP growth. The externalities of this development model have been loaded, for a long time, onto the natural environment. Barry Commoner (1972) synthesized the four fundamental laws of ecology: everything is connected with any other; everything must end somewhere; nature is the only one who knows what it is and there are no free meals. Natural laws were re-evaluated. Into this framework, the Brundtland Report (1987) defined the sustainability concept from which sustainability concerns a development able to satisfy the needs of the present without compromising the possibility of future generations to satisfy their needs.

ENVIRONMENT AND TOURISM: LINKAGES AND COMPLEMENTARITY

The relationship between environment and tourism became important during the last ten years around the world. The environment, for its part, represents the natural landscape for tourism offer organization. Its complementarity is evident in case of particular kind of tourist products as "ecotourism", "green tourism", or tourist activities as "trekking", "walking", "snorkeling" "biking". Today, tourism represents a large global industry and its consumption causes global CO_2 emissions, first of all, because of transport and accommodation facilities. Although tourism produces negative impact on biodiversity and natural landscape, it is also evident that it produces economic benefits on local economies and small business, so that it can be considered like an engine for development, from trade sector to employment. The negative impact is valuable in terms of pollution, environmental and social damages and heritage degradation. Common resources, as water and air, for instance, can be affected by tourism production. Main source of tourism relate air pollution, like automobile, airplanes, marine vehicles that emit greenhouse gases in the air and atmosphere, causing global warming. It is also known that tourism enterprises and visitors generate waste, which produces negative impact on the environment purity. Moreover, tourism uses scarce and non-renewable resources in development tourism facilities and services. The disproportionate use of the environment puts sustainable development in crisis. Crises are natural processes capable of triggering innovation. After all, the resilience concept means “adaptation” plus “innovation”.

However, there are a lot of linkages between tourism and environment, which make it possible to use cultural and environmental heritage without depleting natural resources, but on the contrary by preserving and using them in a sustainable way. At this point, what are these linkages? How can tourism be complementary to the environment and vice versa?

Tourism considers environment as part of its products, for this reason it involves environmental as well as cultural resources. Although tourism can have environmental impacts, it can contribute to conservation as well. To travel to natural areas represents one of the main needs of tourists and tourism operates within rural and urban landscapes, for which it needs to maintain their quality. The tourism linked to the environment, like ecotourism, rises because combine environmental conservation and sustainable travel. Environmental tourism supports the conservation of natural areas, habitats and wildlife, minimizing damage to them. Thus, all of these aspects need a particular strategy like: avoiding physical and visual degradation of the environment, minimizing waste to achieve environmental purity and reducing the use of scarce and non-renewable resources.

Making use of environmental resources, tourism organization should to maintain ecological processes and contribute to preserve natural heritage and biodiversity. Therefore, tourism can be complementary to the environment’s sustainable use, through the respect of host communities cultural authenticity as well as contributing to save their environmental heritage and biodiversity, minimizing air, water and land pollution.

The appreciation of nature can be an important component to make a product: watching wildlife is exciting and also educational (Buckley, 2010a). In addition, there is non consumptive nature-based tourism that include activities based on watching animals and plants as well as enjoying scenery. Clearly, the relationship between tourism and the environment is so strong that the development of one risks causing harm to the other.

Since tourism consists of a network of co-producing actors, the long-term success of business stakeholders depends on integration of resources, assets and services of each one (Luthe et al. 2012).

Figure 1. Resources integration process
(Author elaboration on Luthe et al., 2012 study)

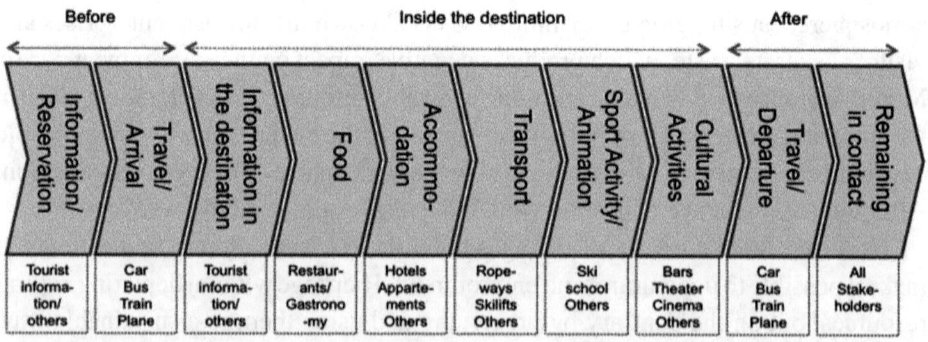

Otherwise it is also true that nature-based tourism is used to enhance economic evaluation of biodiversity (Buckley, 2010b; Kumar, 2010). Ecosystems usually attract tourists, but if they are invaded by animals and plants the consequence should be that they become less attractive.

FROM LINEAR TO CIRCULAR TOURISM

The mobility around the world is one of the main characteristics of tourism. According to the United Nations World Tourism Organization (UNWTO, 2018) tourism is related to the movement of people to stay outside their cities of residence. This process may take place through two different tourism development models: the linear and circular ones. The sustainability concept applied to tourism sector assumes to "transform (production) processes from linear to circular ones" (Fusco Girard and Nocca, 2017; p. 18).

Linear tourism is a model where it is predominant the relationship among taking, making and disposing activities. For that reason, it is known as a disposable model. It contributes to generate five per cent of global CO_2 emissions usually generated by transports and facilities. This model produces negative impact on environment and biodiversity.

It involves five different activities: *take–make–use–dispose–pollute*. The linear production model can be resumed in the following issues: resources, industry, productive process, product, community, end of life, disposal, waste and social cost. It is characterized by competition among parts.

Circular tourism model, instead, represents an alternative solution for the entire life cycle of products and adoption of production and consumption patterns of the closing cycle within the entire economic system. It is based on the consumption and production principles usable to implement sustainable, green, resource effective and environment-friendly technologies. Thus, circular tourism relies on value creation throughout re-use of resources, sharing and collaborative consumption. It represents an important opportunity for tourism businesses to achieve higher sustainability and profitability, first of all related to the provision of accommodation, food and spa services and the related material flows of energy, foodstuffs and water.

Adapting the definition of circular economy of Ellen MacArthur Foundation (2013) to the tourism industry, thus, circular tourism does not regard the pursuit of waste reduction, but aims at organisational and social innovation throughout the value chain in order to 'design-out' waste from the beginning.

Hence, circular tourism offers a new paradigm in which every tourism actor, like tour operator as well as traveler, adopts an eco-compatible approach. The choice of circular tourism let travelers to take a responsible approach at all stages of their stay, from preparation for travel to local experience (Zhang & Tian, 2014).

Therefore, circular tourism is a process with the following activities: *make-use-remake-reuse-recycle*. The model addresses relationship between humans and the environment where they live. Tourism as circular system should be seen as a closed system with no exchanges of matter with the outside environment (Ghisellini et al., 2015).

The transition from linear to circular tourism represents an opportunity to trasform global tourism and make it sustainable, contributing to climate scores, saving resources, creating local jobs and generate competitive advantages.

The industrial evolution led to the transition from the linear to the systemic production model, characterized by collaboration between subjects. In this model resources can be external and territorial and they contribute to produce outputs for foreign trade as well as for the local requirements. All of them can be recovered and saved through a natural system that put all in a new production. The two model differ each other: in the linear model recovering and saving procedures happen twice, while in the systemic production model they happen three times. More precisely, in the last production model recover and save concern the efficiency production phase, in the production for the local requirements and within territorial context. Final goal is the tendency to Zero emissions (Ze).

The circular production model is based on the linkages among supply chain. It is possible to distinguish three phases:

1. produce and assemble
2. product life
3. collect and disassemble

All of them act from the biosphere decomposition to the technosphere recycling.

Figure 2. Linear and circular tourism
(Source: Author elaboration)

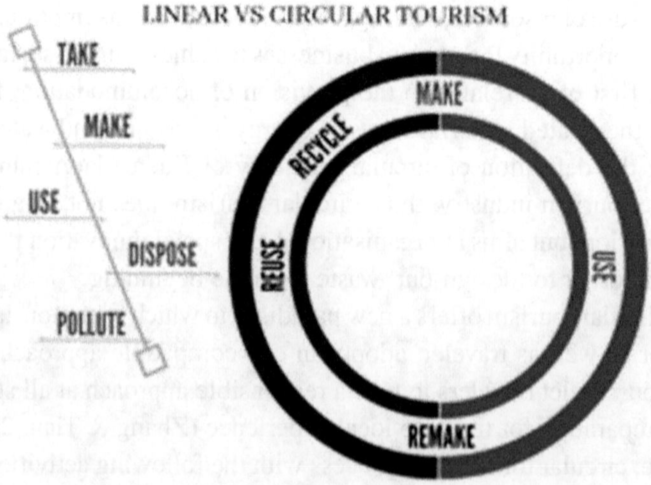

Circular tourism can be explained as a social and economic system where the value of products, materials and resources is maintained in the economy for as long as possible, and the generation of waste minimised.

The circular tourism is linked to the sharing and collaborative consumptions, which represent exchange economic models. Sharing consumption does not include disposable goods and services as well as does not generate waste. Sharing and circularity, therefore, regard goods and services, the former concerns the ownership the latter the life cycle. Both of them contribute to make tourism sustainable.

Although circular economy refers to waste cycle management (Ghisellini et al., 2015), it must also take into consideration energy, water, environmental and cultural issues. An example comes from the use of electric bus and car into the main European cities. Accommodation facilities are introducing particular precautions to reduce CO_2 emissions as well as restaurant are predisposing particular menu with zero Km products.

Hence, comparing linear and circular tourism paradigms, some of their characteristics come out. About economic value proposition, linear tourism is characterized by a growth through intensive use of resources; while circular tourism by innovation of resource design at niche level and competitive right positioning. In linear tourism production, the number of tourist increase as well as the profit per guest; while in circular tourism production there is an opportunity for creating profitable circularised flows and value chains as well as an adaptation to a circular resource system. Moreover, linear tourism consumption is characterized by hedonic and luxury experiences; while within circular tourism consumption, many services, as accommodation facilities as well as restaurants become circular behaviour labs, where the relationship between culture and environment as well as linkages between daily life and environment are observed.

The search for the "new" on the part of consumers, in general, and tourists, in particular, pushes towards the continuous demand for goods and services. Hence, the life cycle of goods is getting shorter, the examples of planned obsolescence in the consumer technology sector (domestic appliances, computers, mobile telephones, etc.) are now provided. The continuous research of something new means that goods and services become immediately old. Consumer needs to change goods and services more and more. For this reason, the contemporary era is characterized by many goods that are disposable and not reusable. In the circular economy model, on the contrary, goods and services regenerate themselves.

A consequence of this consumption system is the contrast between consumption and consumerism. Consumption expresses a part of household's income, spent for final goods and services. All the household consumptions is the aggregate expenditure. Consumerism is an ephemeral need that is continuously satisfied by the purchase of goods and services, which must be consumed and eliminated as quickly as they were produced. At the contrary "circularity consumption" indicates a conscious and ethical consumption, more respectful of the environment with social implications and not only economic ones.

While consumerism is more typical of the linear economy, circular consumption is certainly an expression of the circular economy. This also happens for tourism, circular consumption, which finds its most important example in "experiential" and "relational" tourism, is in line with circular tourism, where consumption takes the form of rational action directed towards a common altruistic purpose.

Therefore, in the case of circular tourism, the post-modern tourist is aware and well informed and wants to share the offer up to even the experience. Otherwise, in the linear tourism there is a relationship of exploitation between economy and environment. Linear tourism is characterized by products for a season. In circular tourism, on the other hand, goods age slowly: they are reusable. Their life cycle is lengthened and nothing is destroyed. The environment is intended as content and not just as a container. There is less waste. Rejection, as a second raw material, represents a resource; thus, rejection has value and is interchangeable, like money.

In the transition from linear to circular tourism, there is a change in the meaning of resource: from "usable" to "re-usable", from "generated" to "re-generated", from "new" to "re-new".

Nowday, there is a technology able to reduce waste and energy in order to make tourism more sustainable. In construction sector, for instance, it is possible to use renewable energy or energy efficient systems like "passive house" contributing to make tourism more sustainable. Zero waste as well as zero energy strategies represent important examples to realize circular economy model worldwide. Moreover, circularity may regard also tourist behaviour and lifestyle. It is clear that circularity and sustainability within tourism are closely linked. It means that redevelopment, recovery and reuse are important issues to make circular and sustainable tourism. Circular tourism should be extended to cities organization, as well as to their economic, social and governance system.

However, also if circular tourism is indicated as a possible way to reconcile economic growth with sustainable development (Ellen MacArthur Foundation, 2012), it is true that circular economy projects are still scarce as well as the assessment methods able to evaluate the circular tourism impacts are very few.

To be regenerative-by-design, circular tourism addresses a redesign of products and services with circularity in mind, improving product reuse, refurbishment and recycling. Therefore, tourist operators have to use products easy to recondition in order to close the loop. Furthermore, circular business model can be used to foster circular tourism. An example is provided by the Product Service System, which is defined as an integrated bundle of product and services able to create customer utility and value: a clear pattern is the pay-per-result contract (Bohem and Thomas, 2013).

CIRCULAR AND LOW CARBON TOURISM: HAND IN HAND

Circular tourism throughout sharing consumption would retain product and material value better than linear tourism. Moreover, circular tourism could contribute to reduce greenhouse gas (GHG) emissions by decreasing demand for materials and energy as minimising waste.

It is known that GHG as well as CO_2 emissions represent a really big problem in climate change issue. The problem has a global dimension, affecting all industrialized and non-industrialized countries. The main UN goal concerns the reduction of GHG emissions by 2050. Following this target, cities worldwide have to seek low carbon solutions to achieve urban sustainability. Circular tourism contribution is not immediately evident in the greenhouse gas emissions accounting system. Sharing car or accommodation consumption, for instance, could save more carbon emissions.

However, before to describe the concept of low carbon tourism, it needs to define what low carbon economy does mean and to do this it is compulsory to go back to the notion of "tourism growth". Tourism growth is not compatible with climate change mitigation requirements (Gössling et al., 2010). Tourism growth influenced resources use and depletion. People around the world were stimulated to travel without any feeling for saving environment.

The concept of "Low-carbon tourism" was first proposed at the Copenhagen conference in 2009 (Zhao et al., 2015). It has great social value as well as economic significance (He and Wang, 2014). Low carbon tourism represents an efficiency model (Li, 2013), based on the coordination between economic development and environmental protection of tourism areas. It is able to establish and promote durable tourism development.

Low-carbon tourism seems to be antithetic to the economic growth, nevertheless it can work hand-in-hand with tourism growth notion. Low carbon tourism represent the opposite side of the tourism development. The way to control future risks for tourism. Low-carbon tourism is the fundamental way to realize the sustainable development of tourism industry, and it is also an inevitable choice (Tang et al., 2011; Yang, 2015). Li (2013) have evaluated the tourism industry from a low-carbon perspective, established a low-carbon tourism service efficiency model, and evaluated the carbon footprint of scenic spots in Sichuan Province, suggesting that the government should coordinate the economic development and environmental protection of tourism areas to promote the stable development of tourism.

The low carbon tourism represents a new type of economic development model as well as a trend for future economic growth. This model refers to reduction of carbon dioxide and greenhouse gases emissions throughout policies definition and changes in people style of life and behaviour to form a mode of economic development of low carbon emission.

The low-carbon model might meet the needs of economic development as well as protect the environment. It should be possible by using carbon neutral technology for green growth and following the principles of low energy consumtpion and high efficiency.

The tourism industry represents an important source of economic development as well as the main sources of environmental degradation. Tourism development, energy consumption and environmental pollution have not too much been investigated in the literature. It is known that tourism growth comes with an increased demand for transportation, accommodation, catering, water supply, and the management of tourist attractions (Gössling, 2002). CO_2 emissions, for instance, represent a portion of the environmental degradation caused by tourism. So as the use of energy for building and maintaining tourism infrastructure can be expected to cause various forms of environmental degradation (Lee and Brahmasrene, 2013). The relationship between tourism and carbon (CO_2) emissions which, contextually, involves energy consumption and tourism development on environmental degradation, should be of great interest. At this purpose, it should be interesting to consider a part of the literature that has tested the validity of the Environmental Kuznets Curve (EKC) hypothesis (Coondoo and Dinda, 2002; Dinda, 2004; Stern, 2004).

In this regard it should be noted that while for some pollutants the EKCs can be found, for others it does not seem to exist. For example, environmental Kuzntes curves do not exist for indices such as per-capita CO_2 emissions.

CIRCULAR ECONOMY AND ENVIRONMENTAL KUZNETS CURVES

Environmental Kuzntes Curves (EKCs) lies the idea that environmental quality deterioration proceeds in parallel with the growth of an economic system only at an early stage of its development. Beyond a certain level, there is a reversal of the trend, and, for further increases of income, a smaller quantity of emissions is obtained. EKCs can be used to show the relationship between tourism growth and environmental degradation.

EKCs allow to investigate, simultaneously, the extent to which environmental pollution responds to changes in income in addition to energy consumption and tourism development. The hypothesis concerns the relationship between tourism development and environmental pollution as well as between income inequality and tourism growth.

Moreover, the EKC hypothesis states that, as part of the development process, environmental degradation increases as a country's economic growth, but begins to decrease when income reaches the so-called 'turning point', which is a non-income threshold, after which environmental degradation may begin to recede. The hypothesis, therefore, can provide support for a policy that emphasizes the growth of tourism, which in many developing economies can act as a growth engine, at the expense of short-term environmental protection. If the hypothesis is true, tourism policies should allow a wide use of the environment for growth purposes.

An important consideration concerns the EKC hypothesis by using the ecological footprint as an environmental indicator and GDP from tourism as the economic indicator. The variable tourism arrivals were also utilized to determine the EKC hypothesis (De Vita et al., 2015). Using ecological footprint to test EKC hypothesis means that, when the income from tourism increases, thus the public appreciation to the environment rises as well by providing more environmental protection and awareness of environmental problems, boost the numbers of legally protected natural areas, and maintain a more sustainable tourism business. This might cause an inverted U-shaped relationship between tourism income and environmental damage, it means the ecological footprint.

However, it should be pointed out that environmental quality and the growth of tourism may not go in the same direction, beyond a certain level of tourism growth. Inverted U curves could turn into "N" curves. This would happen because, beyond certain levels of per capita income, the growth of tourism would be to the detriment of the environment. The expectations that with the growth of per capita income the problems of environmental depletion will be solved automatically are destined not to be realized if they have as their basis the environmental Kuznets curves.

SHARING AND COLLABORATIVE CONSUMPTION FOR A CIRCULAR TOURISM

Collaborative and sharing consumption represent a niche form of consumer behaviour. Collaborative consumption produces economic incentives like cost consciousness, space and effort saving as reasons for joining collaborative business models. Reputation, trust (Botsman and Rogers, 2010), belonging to a community represent the new forms of consumption (Belk, 2010; Schor and Fitzmaurice, 2015). In this context, environmental consciousness became a reason to participate in the collaborative and sharing consumption (Belk, 2014; Leismann et al., 2013). Therefore, trust as well as social interaction are the key components of these consumption behaviour. There are on line platforms, like "peerby" for instance, that matches tourists in temporary need of a specific object with those who have the object and are willing to lend it, free of charge. Tourists can be borrowing of caravans, canoes, bicycles, decreasing the amount of products that they must transport from one destination to another. The are many other examples of sharing consumption developped in the last ten years, within tourism industry, as airb&b, Uber, car2go, which represent examples of a hugely popular and profitable services. They represent community based-models that include a variety of local small initiatives. All of these forms of collaborative and sharing consumption positively contribute to develop circular tourism, since they help to decrease in the use of natural resources, energy and emissions based on more intensive use of existing products and services. The car as well as the accommodation sharing markets lead to an increaseing utilisation of existing products. Collaborative and sharing consumption represent ones of the best options for tourists to shift from linear to circular tourism model.

Otherwise, it is also true that a more intensive use of products and services does not guarantee positive environmental effects, whether these are not efficient. There sould be also negative impacts as unfair price competition against traditional products (EEA, 2016); so as more people might travel thanks to the availability of cheap accommodation leading an increase in emissions from transport. This can determine rebound effects.

However, these examples show that an evaluation of the environmental impact about collaborative consumption is not an easy task (Fremstad, 2015). Therefore, it is definitely necessary to enhance further researches to demonstrate if collaborative and sharing consumption contribute to the circular tourism.

ECONOMIC POLICY OF TOURISM AND ENVIRONMENTAL EFFECTS

Economic policy of tourism towards environment plays second fiddle with respect to other policies. For instance, the threat of nuclear power plants on environment seems to be more important than an accommodation's lack of solar power. On the contrary, tourism generates income for many countries. In this regards, economic policy of tourism can have distortive effects on the environment. Policies of devaluation and liberalization, for instance, may attract foreign investments stimulated by lower prices. But this would produce damage to the environment, causing pollution in the tourist destinations. Excellent planning of policies will never be possible, if among the fundamental macroeconomic variables, policy makers do not consider the environment and the market for "environmental goods". It is clear that, in preparing economic policy reforms for tourism, ignoring the variable "environment" can determine social costs that can offset the expected benefits.

However, tourism can produce positive effects to envrionmental conservation through political as well as social mechanism. These mechanisms differ between countries and depend on government institutions and their economic policy of tourism. Economic policy of tourism established without taking into consideration environmental concerns produces natural resources deploitation. It means that tourism policies must be supported by an environmental consciousness.

Economic Policies of tourism are as enablers for circular business, since they may permit business models to be more circular. For instance, they might encourage producers to design products that do not waste resources, or give incentives, to customers or producers, to change respectively their consumption and production behaviours.

Thus, it is necessary to include environment-friendly practices in tourism policies. After all, it is more evident that tourism policies towards environment represent an important issue in the political processes, because of a variety of reasons, as:

- Sustainable development of tourism represents an intergenerational agreement;
- A clean and healthy environment is a human right;
- Circular tourism is important for social and economic life;
- Environment and tourism relate each other;
- Is to include environment-friendly practices in tourism policies.

THE ENVIRONMENTAL CHALLENGE OF CIRCULAR TOURISM: THE FUTURE OF ENVIRONMENTAL TOURISM

The environmental challenge of circular tourism regards the way to put in order environmental tourism policies. The goal is to establish a sustainable environmental economic policy able to "nudge" towards strategies useful to reduce CO_2 as well as to change tourists' behaviour. It is, therefore, urgent to answer two questions: "What are the polluting tourist behaviors?" and "what the safeguard strategies can be?".

The problem of polluting behavior of tourists can manifest itself in different ways depending on the different needs and sensitivities of individuals. The polluting behaviors concern both the consumption practices of goods and services, and the lack of attention towards the places visited as well as the non-respect of the rules applied in the destination.

Hence, the safeguard strategy has to take into account a broad process of change that affects the behavior of tourists. The presence of tourists who behave differently, requires actions aimed at informing and educating visitors / tourists of the need to change some of their habits.

There are market deterrents, such as price, that push the consumer to change their behavior. For example, the price of energy. if the individual consumer had to pay for energy at a price that also includes the waste of energy, he would be led to avoid waste. In this sense, the green economy, in general, represents a promise of change.

Despite this, it is appropriate to start activities to educate tourists in the sense of respect for the environment, environmental ethics and the civic sense of respect for others. despite this, it is appropriate to start activities to educate tourists in the sense of respect for the environment, environmental ethics and the civic sense of respect for others. Obviously relying on the "ecological" attitude that many people have regarding environmental pollution.

However, the cost of this transformation must be considered. It is known that, thanks to technology, the costs of the transition from the brown economy to the green economy should be sustainable. However, it is necessary to define and initiate global joint initiatives.

Therefore, it is noted that the link between environment and tourism should be ethic, libertarian and ecofriendly and holistic. It is necessary to develop an environmental ethic amongst tourism stakeholders that recognises the value of nature. In this process, ecological virtue is the main component (Holden, 2017).

The challenge, therefore, is the relevance and implications of environmental ethics for tourism. In general, the future in the economy will be characterised by circular design. The same will happen in the tourism industry, where growth will be within the scope of circular tourism vision for a competitive worldwide economy.

To achieve this gaol, it will be necessary to design the vision of a sustainable and circular tourism and then to understand how to achieve it.

Moreover, to adopt circular tourism model, it will be necessary to pursue the following elements: use the sustainable tourism opportunities coming from tourism agencies; organize and supply more sustainable tourism servicies; select environmentally friendly transport alternatives; enhance waste management and energy conservation; improve the feedback between visitors and professionals to ameliorate sustainable tourist supply; use local food products, craft and eco-sustainable measures; develop sharing economy (Green Ideas for Tourism, 2018).

All tourism stakeholders need to better understand what vision they want for the future and what they will have to do to achieve it. The best way should be to consider the following actions:

1. Begin with the end in mind
2. Move backwards from the vision to the present
3. Move step by step towards the vision.

At this point, it is necessary to know the methodologies to design circular tourism as to understand circular flows, to follow the regenerative thinking and to know service flip. Therefore, it needs to define challenge, circular opportunities and circular business model as well as to imagine new partnerships, align organization and release continuous learning loops.

In this framework, the concept of a "Green Economy", promoted by key international organisations, may not deliver the needed transformations required in an increasingly resource-constrained world (Alexander, 2014). The green economy (Bailey & Wilson, 2009) merely presents a 'nudge' and distracts from more fundamental changes. Nudging through the provision of small incentives or particular choice sets has become an important tool of governments policy (Goulden et al., 2014). Proposed choices although comply with economic structures and institutions fail to address underlying root problem.

FUTURE RESEARCH DIRECTIONS

The transition from the traditional linear model to the circular one represents one of the economic issues under discussion worldwide. This implies that maximum value should be extracted from available resources. In this regard, there are several questions concerning how to measure the degree of "circularity" of the economy at the level of enterprises, districts and nations as well as tourism destination.

Further research is needed to understand how to know that the maximum value has been extracted from the resource. It is known that the same resources can be used in different areas, some of which are more preferable from an economic point of view than others. Secondly, technologies are developing very fast, which does not allow to create a reference version of the life cycle for any resource due to the appearance of new, more effective ways to use it. Last but not the least, there is a need to know what role human resources play in the circular tourism and whether this role differs between linear and circular economy.

CONCLUSION

Environment and tourism relie each other towards an eco-friendly and sustainable development. In this framework, the transition from linear to circular tourism becomes necessary and unavoidable.

The worldwide debate considered only some marginal problems, distracting from fundamental changes. The transition needs to consider a new valuation of natural resources as well as a new approach of consumption. It is important to define a new re-education process, through which people around the world are trained in a new style of consumption. It means a new style of life. Every lifestyle starts from an education process. Children can, probably, be involved in the adult re-education process. Consuming less does not necessarily mean reducing production and, therefore, profit. It can simply mean rationalizing the supply and managing production costs better.

Circular tourism should be useful to promote sustainability. This kind of tourism helps to develop an integrated perspective of the economy able to solve problems dwindling natural as well as economic resources. It is clear that a way may be to treat economic waste as a useful economic resource. It would be interesting to implement circular optimal growth path as well as to introduce an open circular economy model where Countries develop the recycling technology. Circular tourism can come into existence as long as Countries reuse and recycle more waste for production and consumption.

REFERENCES

Alexander, S. (2014). Post-growth economics: A paradigm shift in progress. *Arena Journal*, *41/42*, 93–122.

Bailey, I., & Wilson, G. A. (2009). Theorising transitional pathways in response to climate change: Technocentrism, ecocentrism, and the carbon economy. *Environment & Planning A*, *41*(10), 2324–2341. doi:10.1068/a40342

Belk, R. (2010). Sharing. *The Journal of Consumer Research*, *36*(5), 715–734. doi:10.1086/612649

Belk, R. (2014). You are what you can access: Sharing and collaborative consumption online. *Journal of Business Research*, *67*(8), 1595–1600. doi:10.1016/j.jbusres.2013.10.001

Boehm, M., & Thomas, O. (2013). Looking beyond the rim of one's teacup: A multidisciplinary literature review of Product-Service Systems in Information Systems, Business Management, and Engineering & Design. *Journal of Cleaner Production*, *51*, 245–260. doi:10.1016/j.jclepro.2013.01.019

Botsman, R., & Rogers, R. (2010). *What's mine is yours: The rise of collaborative consumption* (1st ed.). New York: HarperBusiness.

Brundtland, G. H. (1987). *Report of the World Commission on Environment and Development: Our Common Future*. Oxford Paperbacks, Report of, 400.

Buckley, R. C. (2010a). *Adventure Tourism Management*. Oxford, UK: Elsevier.

Buckley, R. C. (2010b). *Conservation Tourism*. Wallingford, UK: CABI Publ. doi:10.1079/9781845936655.0000

Commoner, B. (1986). *Il cerchio da chiudere*. Milano: Garzanti.

Coondoo, D., & Dinda, S. (2002). Causality between income and emission: A country group-specific econometric analysis. *Ecological Economics*, *40*(3), 351–367. doi:10.1016/S0921-8009(01)00280-4

De Vita, G., Karticioglu, S., Altinay, L., Fethi, S., & Mercan, M. (2015). Revisiting the Environmental Kuznets Curve Hypothesis in a Tourism Development Context. *Environmental Science and Pollution Research International*, *12*. doi:10.100711356-015-4861-4 PMID:26081781

Dinda, S. (2004). Environmental Kuznets Curve Hypothesis: A Survey. *Ecological Economics*, *49*(4), 431–455. doi:10.1016/j.ecolecon.2004.02.011

Dredge, D., & Jamal, T. (2015). Progress in tourism planning and policy: A post-structural perspective on knowledge production. *Tourism Management*, *51*, 285–297. doi:10.1016/j.tourman.2015.06.002

EEA. (2016). *Circular economy in Europe: Developing the knowledge base*. EEA Report No 2/2016. European Environment Agency.

Ellen MacArthur Foundation. (2012). *Towards the Circular Economy Vol. 1: an economic and business rationale for an accelerated transition*. Retrieved from www.ellenmacarthurfoundation.org/publications

Ellen MacArthur Foundation. (2013). *Towards the Circular Economy: Opportunities for the consumer goods sector*. Ellen MacArthur Foundation. Retrieved from www.ellenmacarthurfoundation.org/publications

Fremstad, A. (2015). *Online platforms for exchanging and sharing goods*. Portland, OR: Ecotrust.

Fusco, G. L., & Nocca, F. (2017). From linear to circular tourism. *Aestimum (Firenze)*, *70*, 51–74.

Ghisellini, P., Cialani, C., & Ulgiati, S. (2015). A review on circular economy: The expected transition to a balanced interplay of environmental and economic systems. *Journal of Cleaner Production*, 1–22.

Gössling, S. (2002). Global environmental consequences of tourism. *Global Environmental Change*, *12*(4), 283–302. doi:10.1016/S0959-3780(02)00044-4

Gössling, S., Hall, C. M., Peeters, P., & Scott, D. (2010). The future of tourism: Can tourism growth and climate policy be reconciled? A mitigation perspective. *Tourism Recreation Research*, *35*(2), 119–130. doi:10.1080/02508281.2010.11081628

Goulden, M., Ryley, T., & Dingwall, R. (2014). Beyond 'predict and provide': UK transport, the growth paradigm and climate change. *Transport Policy*, *32*, 139–147. doi:10.1016/j.tranpol.2014.01.006

Green Ideas for Tourism. (2018). *Green Ideas for Tourism for Europe*. Retrieved from http://www.greentourism.eu/

He, J. B., & Wang, Z. (2014). Research on Low Carbon Transformation of Tourism Industry in China. *Applied Mechanics and Materials*, *651-653*, 1470–1473. doi:10.4028/www.scientific.net/AMM.651-653.1470

Holden, A. (2018). Environmental ethics for tourism- the state of the art. *Tourism Review*, *74*(3), 694–703. doi:10.1108/TR-03-2017-0066

Kumar, P. (2010). *The Economics of Ecosystems and Biodiversity: Ecological and Economic Foundations*. London: Earthscan.

Lee, J. W., & Brahmasrene, T. (2013). Investigating the Influence of Tourism on Economic Growth and Carbon Emissions: Evidence from Panel Analysis of the European Union. *Tourism Management*, *38*, 69–76. doi:10.1016/j.tourman.2013.02.016

Leismann, K., Schmitt, M., Rohn, H., & Baedeker, C. (2013). Collaborative consumption: Towards a resource-saving consumption culture. *Resources*, *2*(3), 184–203. doi:10.3390/resources2030184

Li, Z. Y. (2013). The use of an efficiency evaluation method in the tourism service industry based on a low-carbon economy perspective. *Luyou Xuekan*, *28*(10), 71–80.

Luthe, T., Wyss, R., & Schuckert, M. (2012). Network governance and regional resilience to climate change: Empirical evidence from mountain tourism communities. *Regional Environmental Change*, *12*(4), 839–854. doi:10.100710113-012-0294-5

Medows, D., & Randers, J. (2006). *I nuovi limiti allo sviluppo*. Milano: Oscar Mondadori.

Schor, J. B., & Fitzmaurice, C. J. (2015). Collaborating and connecting: The emergence of the sharing economy. In L. A. Reisch & J. Thøgersen (Eds.), *Handbook of research on sustainable consumption*. Cheltenham, UK: Edward Elgar Publishing. doi:10.4337/9781783471270.00039

Stern, D. I. (2004). The Rise and Fall of the Environmental Kuznets Curve. *World Development*, *32*(8), 1419–1439. doi:10.1016/j.worlddev.2004.03.004

Tang, Z., Shi, C. B., & Liu, Z. (2011). Sustainable Development of Tourism Industry in China under the Low-carbon Economy. *Energy Procedia*, *5*, 1303–1307. doi:10.1016/j.egypro.2011.03.226

Yang, Y. (2015). Implementation Strategy of Low-carbon Tourism. *The Open Cybernetics & Systemics Journal*, *9*(1), 2003–2007. doi:10.2174/1874110X01509012003

Zhang, Y., & Tian, L. (2014). The Sustainable Development of Circular Economy under the Perspective of Ecological Tourism. *Advanced Materials Research*, *1010–1012*, 2090–2093. doi:10.4028/www.scientific.net/AMR.1010-1012.2090

Zhao, L. M., Chen, Z. Z., & Liu, J. Y. (2015). Evolutionary game theory between local government and tourism enterprises in the context of a low-carbon economy. *Luyou Xuekan*, *30*(1), 72–82.

KEY TERMS AND DEFINITIONS

Environmental Kuznets Curve: The environmental Kuznets curve suggests that economic development initially leads to a deterioration in the environment, but after a certain level of economic growth, a society begins to improve its relationship with the environment and levels of environmental degradation reduces.

Long-Run Perspective: The long run is a theoretical concept where all markets are in equilibrium and all prices and quantities have fully adjusted and are in equilibrium.

Section 3

Environment, Consumer Behaviour, and Urban Governance

Chapter 8
Consumer Behavior:
Motivational Factors for the Decision to Purchase Organic Products in the Municipality of Guadalajara, Jalisco

José G. Vargas-Hernández
University Center for Economic and Managerial Sciences, University of Guadalajara, Mexico

Jovanna Nathalie Cervantes-Guzmán
University Center for Economic and Managerial Sciences, University of Guadalajara, Mexico

ABSTRACT

The objective of this study is to develop a model of the behavior of the ecological consumer in order to know the motivations that influence the decision to purchase organic products in citizens from 25 to 45 years of the municipality of Guadalajara. The methodology used in the research is qualitative. It was carried out through the non-experimental design, with respect to the data collection tool, in-depth interviews were carried out. The results obtained with respect to the factors that influence the purchase decision of the products are accepted the general hypothesis. One of the limitations that the study faced was a limited literature regarding studies related to it in the case of the city of Guadalajara.

DOI: 10.4018/978-1-5225-9562-5.ch008

INTRODUCTION

The society is currently aware and gives greater importance to the care of the environment, therefore the objective of this study is to develop a model of the behavior of the ecological consumer in order to know the motivations that influence the consumption of organic products.

The first part of this study focuses on the problem statement, the objectives, research questions are presented and hypotheses are proposed to continue with the second part of the study where the concepts related to the subject are concentrated. In this way, the concepts of ecological product will be revised so that the term used throughout the investigation is understood. Another concept that is necessary to explain is an ecological consumer that, like the previous one, is mentioned repeatedly throughout the study.

In the third part of the research, the motivational factors that influence the decision to purchase organic products are presented, which are concern for health and the environment, social influences, marketing mix (4p's) and consumer knowledge about environmental problems. In the fourth part, the methodology used in the research is presented, followed by the results and analysis of the results obtained from the research. To conclude with the main limitations and guidelines for future research.

BACKGROUND

Statement of the Problem

In recent years, environmental problems have intensified, especially those related to non-pollution, climate change and ecological awareness in the consumption of products. Currently, at the national and international level, there are four large environmental groups founded in the 60s and 70s that are the current basis of the militant institutional environmental movement. These are basically Greenpeace, WWF-ADENA, Ecologists in Action, and Seo / Birdlife. (Bravo, 2010).

Due to ecological and marketing research that took place at an early stage in the sixties, environmental movements emerged (Hendarwan, 2002). they sought a new lifestyle and global alternatives to the industrial and consumer society, thus seeking to achieve the transformation of ecology. And it is because of this social movement that materializes the new market segment constituted by ecological consumers, individuals more concerned about the environmental consequences of what they consume, and be sensitive to the negative effects that the impact of human activities have on the environment and the health of people (Santesmases, 2004).

According to Fernández, Cea, Santander & Nuñez, (2013) the main reason for purchasing organic products is that consumers consider them to be healthier because their products are subjected to methods that guarantee the care of environment. On the other hand, Tregear, Dent & McGregor, (1994) tells that the environmental factor explains only a small part of organic food purchases, because consumers have a more egocentric behavior, where concern for oneself and, consequently, concern for their health plays a much more important role in the purchase of these products.

Meanwhile the survey conducted by National Geographic; GlobeScan, (2012) showed that consumers with "ecological conscience" are a niche that grows fast in Mexico, creating a trend, but what factors motivates them to buy this type of products? it is just a novelty or the consumers really consider that the consumption of ecological products and / or services help with the care of the environment. Green consumption in Mexico has been a subject little investigated academically, since the few jobs that exist are market studies, such as the Green Study of (TNS Research International, (2010) which mentions that almost 50% of Mexicans prefer consume products that are friendly to the environment.

Therefore, it is necessary that more research be done especially in Mexico to decipher the behavior of consumers who prefer organic products. The subject is of interest for various audiences because there is a possible business opportunity for the creation of companies, products and / or services with green features that help differentiate in an increasingly competitive market and of course for associations, movements and people that seek to promote sustainable lifestyles in the population. For these reasons, the object of study is to know the motivations that influence the decision to purchase organic products in citizens from 25 to 45 years of the municipality of Guadalajara.

Justification

To understand the importance of studying the motivational variables of purchase, one must first reflect on the concept, according to Myers, (2005) Quoted in Arana, Meilán, Gordillo, & Carro, J., (2010). Motivation forms together with the emotion the non-cognitive part (practical, irrational, warm) of the human mind. Etymologically, the word motivation comes from the Latin moveo, movere, movi, motum (what moves or has the virtue to move) and is interested in knowing the reason for the behavior. It is the need or desire that directs and energizes the behavior toward a goal.

When explaining ecological behavior, motivational variables can contribute to the understanding of this behavior and explain why it is often found that individuals do not show high stability in their actions and, therefore, it is difficult to make an exact prediction of behavior (Thogersen, 2004). In this research, a review and interpretation is carried out in relation to the behavior of the ecological consumer attending to this research object, the motivational variables that predict an ecological behavior in the consumers between the ages of 25 and 45 years of the municipality of Guadalajara, Jalisco are identified. Being very useful to know the changes that are currently in the buying behavior.

MAIN FOCUS OF THE CHAPTER

Research Objectives

General Objective

Develop a model of the behavior of the ecological consumer in order to know the motivations that influence the decision to purchase organic products in the 25 to 45-year-old citizens of Guadalajara.

Specific Objectives

1. Determine what is the motivation that influences the decision to purchase organic products in citizens from 25 to 45 years of the municipality of Guadalajara.
2. Identify the degree of knowledge that citizens of 25 to 45 years of the municipality of Guadalajara have about organic products
3. Analyze what actions reflect consumers of organic products from 25 to 45 years of the municipality of Guadalajara in terms of environmental concerns.

General Research Question

Which are the motivations that influence in the decision of purchase of ecological products in the citizens of 25 to 45 years of the municipality of Guadalajara?

Specific Research Questions

1. What is the motivation that influences the decision to purchase organic products among citizens between 25 and 45 years of age in the municipality of Guadalajara?
2. What is the degree of knowledge that citizens of 25 to 45 years of the municipality of Guadalajara have about organic products?
3. What actions do consumers of organic products from 25 to 45 years of age reflect in the municipality of Guadalajara regarding environmental concerns?

Hypothesis

General

H: The environmental motivation is not the predominant at the time of preferring organic products.

Specific Hypotheses

- H1: The concern for health and the environment is a motivational factor that influences the decision to purchase organic products.
- H2: Social influences are a motivational factor that influences the decision to purchase organic products.
- H3: The Marketing mix (4p's) is a motivational factor that influences the decision to purchase organic products.
- H4: The consumer's knowledge about environmental problems is a motivational factor that influences the decision to purchase organic products.

Matrix of Operationalization of Variables

See Table 1.

CONCEPTUAL FRAMEWORK

Product

Taking Bonta and Farber (1994) as a reference, they describe the term product as having certain peculiarities to satisfy the needs or desires of the consumer. In the same way, the American Marketing Association (A.M.A., 2017) states that the concept of product from a marketing perspective refers to a set of attributes (characteristics, functions, benefits and uses) that give the ability to be exchanged or used. Usually, it is a combination of tangible and intangible aspects. Thus, a product can be an idea, a physical entity (a good), a service or any combination of the three. The product exists for purposes of exchange and for the satisfaction of individual and organizational objectives.

While Kotler and Armstrong, (2012) offer another more detailed concept: The product concept holds that consumers will favor products that offer the highest quality, the best performance and the most innovative features. Under this concept, the marketing strategy focuses on making continuous improvements to the product.

Table 1. Matrix of operationalization of variables

Theme	**Consumer behavior: Motivational Factors for the decision to purchase organic products in the municipality of Guadalajara, Jalisco**
General objective	**Develop a model of the behavior of the ecological consumer in order to know the motivations that influence the decision to purchase organic products in the citizens of 25 to 45 years of the municipality of Guadalajara.**
Specific objectives	**Determine what is the motivation that influences the decision to purchase organic products in citizens from 25 to 45 years of the municipality of Guadalajara. Identify the degree of knowledge that citizens of 25 to 45 years of the municipality of Guadalajara have about organic products. Analyze what actions consumers of organic products from 25 to 45 years of Guadalajara reflect regarding environmental concerns.**
General question	**Which are the motivations that influence in the decision of purchase of ecological products in the citizens of 25 to 45 years of the municipality of Guadalajara?**
Specific questions	**What is the motivation that influences the decision to purchase organic products for citizens between 25 and 45 years of age in the municipality of Guadalajara? What is the degree of knowledge that citizens of 25 to 45 years of the municipality of Guadalajara have about organic products? What actions do consumers of organic products from 25 to 45 years of Guadalajara reflect regarding environmental concerns?**
General hypothesis	**H: The environmental motivation is not the predominant at the time of preferring organic products.**
Specific hypothesis	**H1: The concern for health and the environment is a motivational factor that influences the decision to purchase organic products H2: Social influences are a motivational factor that influences the decision to purchase organic products. H3: The Marketing mix (4p's) is a motivational factor that influences the decision to purchase organic products H4: The consumer's knowledge about environmental problems is a motivational factor influencing the decision to purchase organic products.**
Variables	**Dependent: Consumer behavior. Independent: Motivational Factors.**
Indicators	**Ecological consumer behavior. Concern for health and the environment. Social influence. Marketing Mix (4p's) Consumer knowledge about environmental problems**
Methodology	**Qualitative**

Quality and product improvement are important parts of most marketing strategies.

However, concentrating only on the products of the company can also lead to marketing short-sightedness.

Ecological Products

It is important to mention that for the purposes of this work, that it is understood ecological product. According to (Minetti, 2002), in different countries they are called by different names. Foods called organic in the United States and other countries are called "organic" (Singer & Mason, 2009). Also are used interchangeably the terms "biological product" or "organic product" as synonyms (López Eguilaz & Remírez Esparza, 1998). To define the concept of this type of product, Calomarde (2000) says that it is ecological when the product fulfills the same function as a conventional one and causes a lower environmental impact considering its life cycle.

The International Federation of Organic Agriculture Movements (IFOAM, 2009), states that this type of food compared to conventional, show:

1. Lower amount of water, storing a higher density of nutrients.
2. Greater amount of iron, magnesium, vitamin C and antioxidants.
3. Better balance with essential amino acids.

While the animals raised with this system, they present:

1. Better health in general.
2. Reduced risk of contracting or carrying diseases.
3. Less amount of fat.

The Ecological Consumer

Orozco (2003), defines the concept of ecological consumer as one who is willing to change their behavior patterns for others more respectful of the environment. On the other hand, Carrete, et al. (2013) establish five groups of consumers according to their degree of ecological activity:

1. Eco Indifferent are those that focus on reduction activities, with little interest in recycling or buying organic products.
2. Eco-followers of trends buy organic products
3. Eco-savers focus on the reduction and reuse and not so much in the purchase of products.
4. Anti-ecological they are not interested in anything related to reuse, reduction, or recycling or purchase of organic products.

5. Eco-integral, are the most committed to the ecological, reduction, recycling, purchase of organic products and reused.

Profile of Ecological Consumers

Mostafa (2006) determines gender differences in relation to knowledge, pro-environmental concerns and attitudes about green purchases. Their results suggest that men show greater knowledge in environmental issues. The Revista Vinculado, (2005) confirms that in Mexico, as in Latin American and European countries, the people with the greatest willingness to buy are women, who belong to small families, with higher expenses in food and belonging to middle income segments. However, the segment of higher consumption is in the high income and high educational levels as well as coincides with Martínez (2006) which indicates that the usual consumer of organic products has a high level of education and a high purchasing power.

A study carried out by Fraj Andrés & Martínez Salinas, (2002) define in a general way that the ecological consumer has the following characteristics:

1. They are young people with a medium or higher level of education.
2. In relation to their values and lifestyle they have a high entrepreneurial capacity, they like to be fashionable, lead a healthy life and collaborate in the improvement of the environment
3. Their attitude can be called ecological because they are very concerned about environmental pollution.
4. They show a greater knowledge about environmental issues.

THEORETICAL FRAMEWORK

Ecological Marketing

Green marketing consists of all the activities designed to generate and facilitate any exchange the intention of satisfying human needs and desires, in such a way that the satisfaction of these needs and desires occurs, with minimal harmful impact on the natural environment (Rani, Aravind, & Prasad, 2014). From a social point of view, ecological marketing is about educating, informing and changing behaviors that damage the environment (Rivera Camino, 2001).

Eco-marketing has become a means by which environmental issues can be addressed and the company's products can be commercialized (Rani, Aravind, & Prasad, 2014), which is why companies have needed to design and implement environmental programs. Ecological marketing to reach consumer segments sensitive

Figure 1. Ecological marketing
Source: Vicente Molino (2001)

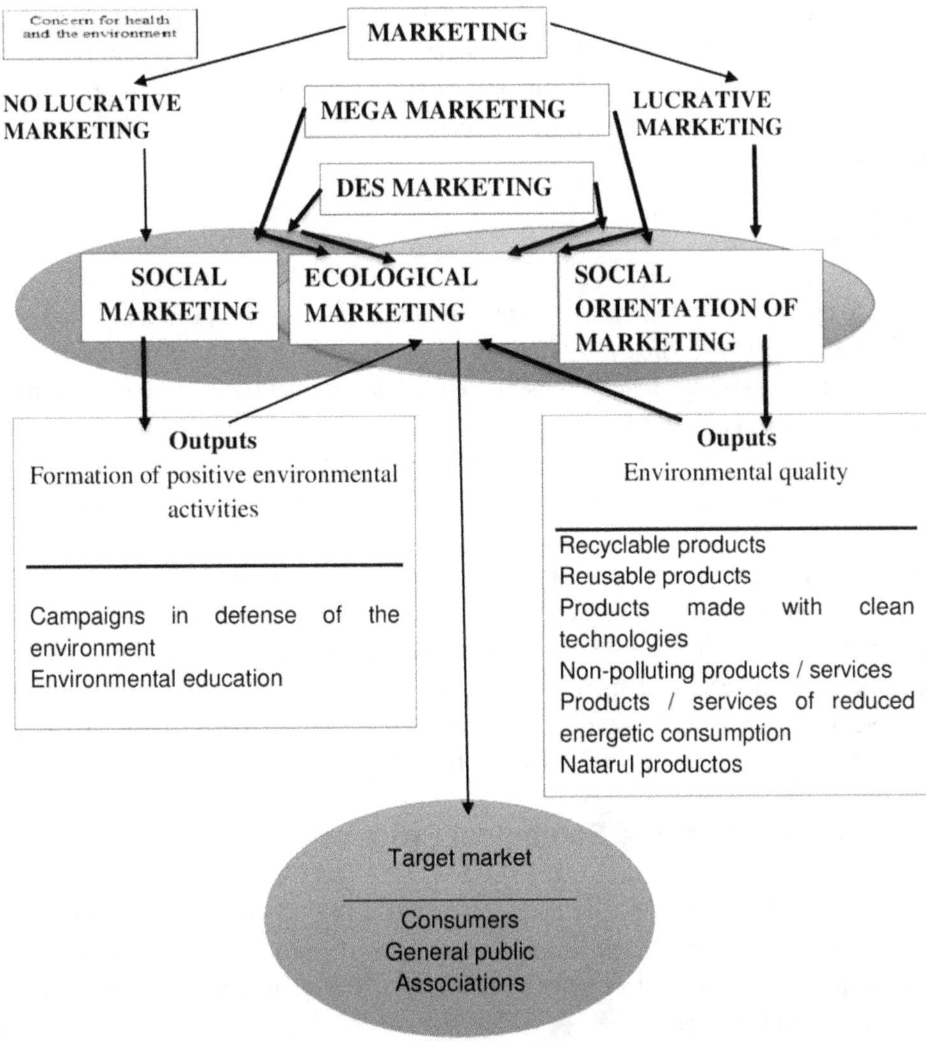

to problems and educate them in their transformation to sustainable consumption patterns (Calomarde, 2000).

The Production and Purchase of Organic Products in Mexico

The Research Institute of Ecological Agriculture (FiBL) and IFOAM (2018) show data from the study "The world of ecological agriculture 2016" where 210,000 of organic producers were registered in Mexico, ranking third in the world. The organic products that are most produced in Mexico are coffee, aromatic and medicinal herbs, vegetables, cocoa and wild grapes. As for the sale of organic foods in self-service stores, they have increased 20 percent annually and in specialty stores, the increase was 10 percent. (SAGARPA, 2013). In Mexico, they can be found in a matter of fresh foods: fruits, vegetables, milk, milk, cheese, egg, chicken, buffalo and processed: juices, sweets, grains, flours, wines, liqueurs, honeys, syrups (Impulso Orgánico Mexicano AC, 2014).

Life Cycle

The life cycle is used to assess the environmental burden of a product, process or activity throughout its life cycle (Capuz Rizo & Gómez Navarro, 2004). The author Calomarde (2000) says that there is no ecological product by itself, but according to its environmental behavior throughout its life cycle, from the analysis of the raw materials that comprise it, its production processes as a whole, its use, the waste generated by its distribution and transport and, finally, its reuse or disposal.

Therefore, the production of an ecological product is based on obtaining greater human well-being and at the same time reducing environmental risks (United Nations Industrial Development Organization [UNIDO], 2011). The raw materials and materials used in the production processes constitute a flow of materials that includes raw materials of natural origin. (Cervera-Ferri & Ureña, 2017). In the Arroyo, Chamorro and Miranda, (1999) present the stages that a product must go through in its life cycle and this reduces its ecological footprint.

Characteristics of the Ecological Product

The ecological products have certain peculiarities in their elaboration which does not harm the environment and the animals besides that the properties of these products are totally natural (Buenstorf and Cordes, 2008). The ecological attributes can be classified into two types:

1. Specific attributes of the product: duration, its facility to be recycled / reused, the type, the amount of materials used in the product and its packaging.
2. Specific attributes of the process: energy consumption, water or the generation of waste (Hernández & López, 2012).

The Purchase of Organic Products

The purchase of organic products can be defined as a practice of environmental awareness that reduces sources of waste and promotes recycling and reclamation of

Figure 2. Stages of the product life cycle
Source: Arroyo et al. (1999)

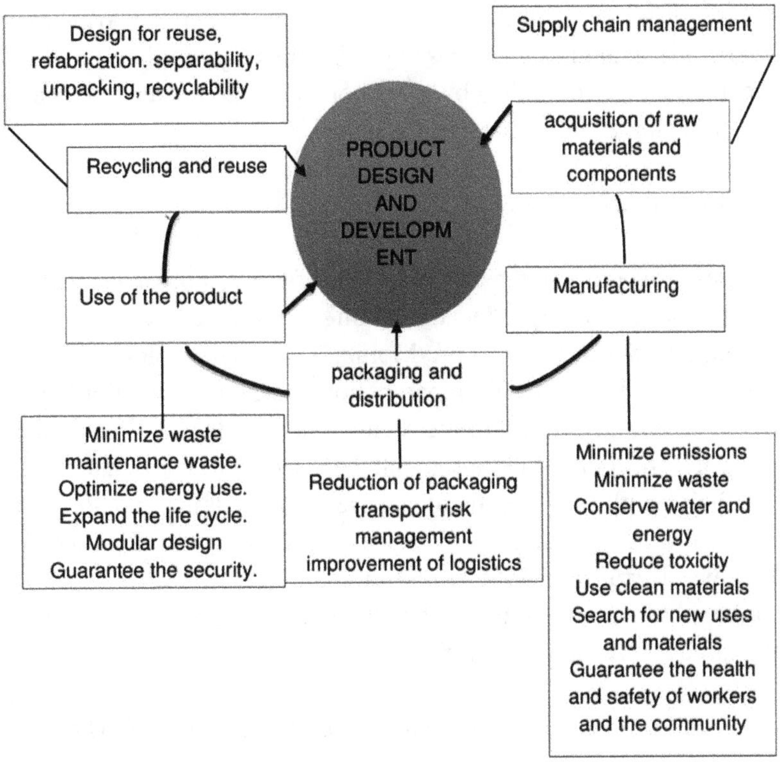

purchased materials, without adversely affecting the requirements for the execution of such materials (Min & Galle, 2001). A study conducted by Trujillo León & Vera Martínez, (2011) "Green consumption in Mexico: knowledge, attitude and behavior", people are willing to make more responsible purchases, but 41% consider that the prices of green products are higher than traditional products.

Consumer Behavior

Consumer behavior reflects the decisions of consumers regarding the acquisition, consumption and disposal of goods, services, activities, experiences (Hoyer et al., 2010). There are several theories that try to explain the behavior of the consumer, for this work only the following are briefly explained:

The psychoanalytic theory of Sigmund Freud cited by Kotler and Armstrong (2012), suggests that purchasing decisions are influenced by subconscious motives that even the consumer does not understand. According to Veblen (1899) in his theory of idle class the main reason that guides the behavior of people in their need for integration in their social group. The theory of classical conditioning, demonstrated by the physiologist Ivan Pavlov where Kotler and Armstrong (2012) explain that advertising has to be based on this theory according to which buyers learn to identify a certain product by a symbol repeatedly linked to it. The learning process is through the stimulus-response model.

Ecological Behavior

The ecological consumer has behaviors with different approaches that can range from the purchase of organic products, recycling, voting, activism or others (Izagirre-Olaizola, Fernández-Sainz, & Vicente-Molina, 2013). The ecological consumer is a conscious and sensitive buyer of the repercussions that his consumption habits impose on the sustainable development of the region where he lives. Values the quality of life in terms of respect for the environment, the responsible use of natural resources, the care of their health and the general welfare of their community. Recognizes that this attitude towards life can have additional economic costs and is willing to face them (Martínez Turrubiates & Martín Prieto, 2009).

Consumers have different attitudes that can better explain consumer behavior on organic products (Calomarde, 2000):

1. Ecological conscience. It represents the ecological beliefs and knowledge that are part of the consumer. These can be increased thanks to the information you receive and remember about the benefits of a certain type of consumption.
2. Eco posture. Affective attitude toward organic products. This position is influenced by the culture, education and information that the consumer receives.
3. Eco activity. It is related to personality based on the consumer's tendency to act ecologically.

Purchase Motivation

Motivation forms together with emotion the non-cognitive part of the human mind. Etymologically the word motivation comes from the Latin moveo, moveré, movi, motum (what moves or has the virtue to move) and is interested in knowing the reason for the behavior. It is the need or the desire that directs and energizes the behavior toward a goal (Myers, 2005; Cited in Arana, et al., 2010).

When a consumer is sufficiently motivated to acquire the product, has the ability and the opportunity to do so, he / she will be sure to expose themselves, perceive and pay attention to the information that they consider relevant for their decision (Hoyer, MacInnis, & Pieters, 2010). Another term of motivation suggests that people are driven to act by different types of factors, experiences and highly varied consequences or in other words, people have not only different amounts of motives but also different types of motives (Ryan & Deci, 2000).

Motivational Factors of Ecological Purchase

The factors that intervene in the ecological behavior are internal and external. The first are those sources of information about an ecological product or service that influence the values, ideas, attitudes, intentions, opinions of each person. Externally, they are advertising, information, social groups, family and friends, among others (Shiffman & Kanuk, 2001) (Fraj Andrés & Martínez Salinas, 2002). In this research, four factors studied by several authors are presented:

Concern for Health and the Environment

The ecological consumer manifests his concern for the environment in his buying behavior (Min & Galle, 2001). derived from this concern, another concern appears, the environmental health that is related to all the physical, chemical and biological external factors of a person. That is, it encompasses environmental factors that could affect health. (World Health Organization, [WHO] 2018). According to research on the consumer of organic products, in Mexico, Latin America and Europe, the main reason to buy organic products is related to health (Linked Magazine, 2005).

A study conducted by the Cuidadano Observatory of quality of life: Jalisco as we go, (2017) in the state of Jalisco a percentage of 34% of the population of the lower social strata reported having had a serious health problem the final semester of 2016.

Food

In the state of Jalisco, people's health is affected by several factors (some are congenital); Certain habits such as food can also influence him. (Cuidadano Observatory of quality of life: Jalisco as we go, 2017). The change in the diet of consumers has changed, mainly for health reasons (Del Greco, 2010). Islas García & Sánchez Plascencia, (2013) state that: Healthy consumption has a direct impact not only on the individual sphere, but also on the social sphere and above all on the environment.

Social Influences

To reduce the search and evaluation effort or reduce uncertainty, consumers seek opinions from other people, especially when the perceived risk of the decision increases (Lamb, Hair, & McDaniel 2011). Through coexistence with other people is that consumers form attitudes that influence their lives. (Schiffman, Kanuk, & Wisenblit, 2010). The consumer seeks and issues his opinions based on the information he receives from friends, family, friends, and media that interest him (Rojas, 2012).

Family

For the Mexican it is very important to have family approval and feel accepted. He is very concerned about "what they will say", a situation that is accentuated in more closed societies such as in the province, and manifests itself even more in the lower social classes, since it is not uncommon to find cases in which a family cohabits with its families and close relatives (Galindo, 2010). Lamb, et al. (2011) state that the influencers in the family are the members whose opinions are valued, but who makes the decision to buy or cannot be another member. While Galindo, (2010) states that in Mexican families, the process, from the decision and until the completion of the purchase is the responsibility of the housewife. Although she is the one who makes the decisions, her tastes and needs are always subordinated, in the first place, to family demands and secondly to spending.

In Mexico, each generation of families are transmitters of values and cultural norms, so children learn by observing their parents' consumption patterns, so they will tend to buy in a similar pattern (Lamb, et al., 2011).

Influencer

The use of celebrities in communication increases the credibility of the messages, increases the recall and recognition of the advertised brands, improves the attitude towards the organization that sells the product, and even increases the likelihood of purchase (Agrawal & Kamakura, 1995). Nine of the ten most important influencers come from the digital environment and influence 60% in the decision of the brands that users buy (Expansión, 2017).

Marketing Mix

Kotler & Armstrong, (2012) claim that the marketing mix as the set of controllable tactical marketing tools that the company combines to produce a desired response in the target market. The marketing mix includes everything the company can do to influence the demand for your product. The marketing mix consists of four elements (known as the four p's): product, price, place and promotion (Schiffman, Kanuk, & Wisenblit, 2010).

Price

Kotler & Armstrong, (2012) point out that the consumer can establish a purchase intention based on issues such as their expectations of disposable income, the price to be paid and the benefits to be obtained. However, unexpected events would change their purchase intention. There is a limitation when buying organic products which Caamal Cauich, Pat Fernandez, Ascencio, & Pérez Fernández, (2007) explain that the high price of organic products it is partly due to production costs, which are higher compared to the costs of conventional foods.

A study conducted in 60 countries showed that 66% of the global respondents, being consumers from all types of regions and income levels, acknowledged their willingness to pay more for sustainable products (Nielsen, 2016).

Promotion

The promotion involves activities that communicate the advantages of the product and persuade the target customers to buy it (Kotler & Armstrong, 2012). Lamb, et. al., (2011) states that the promotional strategy uses elements or tools, which may include advertising, public relations, sales promotion and personal sales. Advertising affects the daily life of consumers, informs them about products and services and influences their attitudes, beliefs and, finally, their purchases (Lamb, et al., 2011).

The attitude towards ecological awareness publicity depends on the involvement of the consumer (Zinkhan & Carlson, 1995). It has been shown in various studies that to be credible this publicity consumer must be highly involved while those who feel little involved do not trust in said announcements (D'Souza & Taghian, 2005). Green advertising is about informing customers about the environmental benefits of the products, and its objective is to influence consumers' buying behavior by encouraging them to buy organic products and direct their attention to the positive consequences for them and the environment (Rahbar & Wahid, 2011).

A study conducted by Nielsen, (2016) shows that television ads that highlight a company's commitment to positive social and / or environmental impact influence the purchasing process for 34% of global respondents.

Consumer Awareness of Environmental Problems

The knowledge of the consumer is considered as one of the factors that influence several stages of the decision process (Laroche, Bergeron, & Barbaro-Forleo, 2001).

Several studies found that individuals with greater knowledge of environmental issues were willing to pay more for products considered ecological (Amyx, et al., 1994, cited by Laroche, et al., 2001).

Ecological Awareness

This term is defined as the knowledge and experiences that people actively use in their relationship with the environment (Febles, 2004 cited in Alea, 2006). The degree to which people are aware of environmental problems and support efforts to resolve them or manifest a willingness to personally contribute to the solution (Dunlap & Jones, 2002, cited by Romero, s.f.).

Environmental education is a learning process which needs to transform social practices through the habitus which provides human behavior with patterns of perception, thought and action that shape subjectivity (Barbosa Sánchez, 2008). In Mexico, the Secretary of the Environment and Natural Resources (SEMARNAT) is in charge of raising awareness among the population in general about the importance of the global environment and its problems. (Pérez Abuin, 2016)

Environmental education lies in providing a particular knowledge about the interaction of the human being with its biological and social environment (Barbosa Sánchez, 2008)

It is worth mentioning that in Mexico, environmental education is very poor at all levels (Montaño Salas, 2012).

Proposed Structural Model

Based on the theoretical framework, the study seeks to define the relationships between the motivations that influence the decision to purchase organic products, the model presented below was adapted for citizens from 25 to 45 years of the municipality of Guadalajara from a study called "Important Motivators for Buying Green Products" made in Malaysia and which was prepared by Kianpour, Anvari, Jusoh, & Fauzi Othman, (2014).

METHODOLOGY

In this chapter the methodology used for the development of the study is explained. Based on the needs of the study, qualitative research was used, it was carried out through non-experimental design, with respect to the data collection tool they were carried out through in-depth interviews. The methodology of the work is described in more detail below.

Figure 3. Proposed structural model
Source: Authors' own elaboration

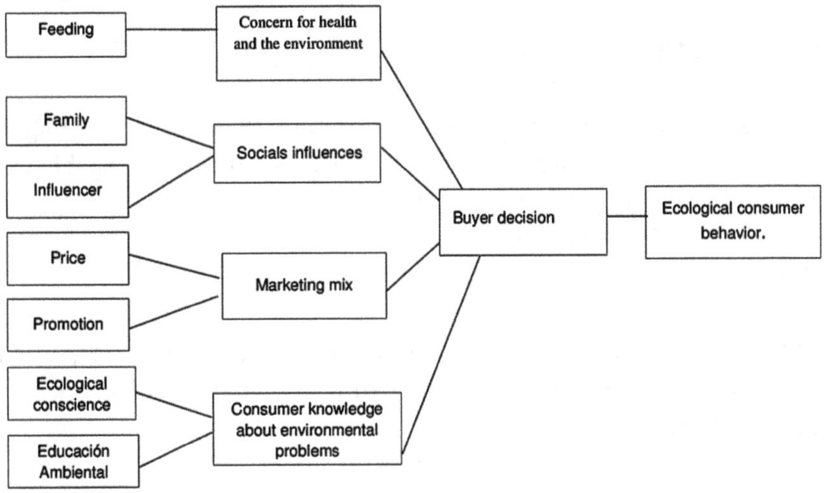

Research Focus

The development of this research is of a qualitative nature. It uses data collection without numerical measurement to discover or refine research questions in the interpretation process (Sampieri, Fernández Collado, & Baptista Lucio, 2010). Based on in-depth interviews with consumers who have already shown preference for organic and / or organic products in the municipality of Guadalajara, Jalisco.

Research Design

This research was carried out through the non-experimental design. According to Sampieri, et al., (2010) non-experimental designs are studies that are carried out without the deliberate manipulation of variables and in which only the phenomena are observed in their natural environment and then analyzed. Non-experimental designs can be classified as transactional and longitudinal, for this study we chose the transectional classification that is" collect data in a single moment, in a single time (Sampieri, et al., 2010).

The study being descriptive and exploratory the first one investigates the incidence of the modalities, categories or levels of one or more variables in a population (Sampieri, et al., 2010). The exploratory is ideal for the present investigation. According to Sampieri, et. al., (2010), the exploratory studies serve to familiarize with relatively unknown phenomena, obtain information about the possibility of carrying out a more complete investigation.

Sampling Design

The investigation was carried out by means of a non-probabilistic sampling, so the type of sampling is for convenience. Which is used simply with available cases to which have access (Sampieri, et al., 2010).

Sample Size

The unit of analysis indicates who will be measured, whether the participants or cases to whom in the last instance we will apply the measurement instrument (Sampieri et al., 2010).

- Elements: People from 25 to 45 years old from the municipality of Guadalajara Jalisco, who frequent stores, eco-bazaars and organic markets.
- Scope: Municipality of Guadalajara, Jalisco.
- Time: March 9, 2018 to March 11, 2018.

Data Collection

To carry out the data collection, first a procedure plan was elaborated in which, first, the variables to be measured were established to later build the collection instrument and finally establish the dates to carry it out. The data collection was made on March 9 and 11, 2018, visiting the stores, eco-bazaars and organic markets, to collect the information was done by means of a questionnaire being applied by an interviewer.

Data Collection Instrument

The data collection instrument that was used was through an in-depth interview applied through a questionnaire consisting of questions structured in an open manner. To measure the variables included in the proposed model have been measured individually assigning a series of items for each, obtaining a total of thirteen items.

ANALYSIS OF RESEARCH RESULTS

An analysis of the qualitative data obtained is carried out. As a first step the data has been organized and classified with the most relevant of the interview. Data were analyzed directly from the collection tool as Sampieri et al. (2010) says in the qualitative research data collection and analysis. They usually occur at the same time. Next, representative maps of the results obtained are presented.

Results of the Factors of Concern for Health and the Environment

Next, Figure 4 shows the categories (patterns or responses) most frequently mentioned, health care being the most repetitive concept when it comes to asking the questions assigned to this item and ensuring that while taking care of their health. At the same time, they take care of the planet, in addition to agreeing that conventional products are harmful. So it is concluded that the H1: The concern for health and the environment is a motivational factor that influences the decision to purchase organic products is accepted.

Results of The Social Influences Factors

With respect to social influences, it was obtained that consumers follow a line of recommendations from friends and health professionals, leaving aside the recommendations and opinions of the family. Figure 5 shows the categories (patterns or responses) with the highest frequency of mention. The H2: Social influences are

Figure 4. Responses more frequently
Source: Authors' own elaboration

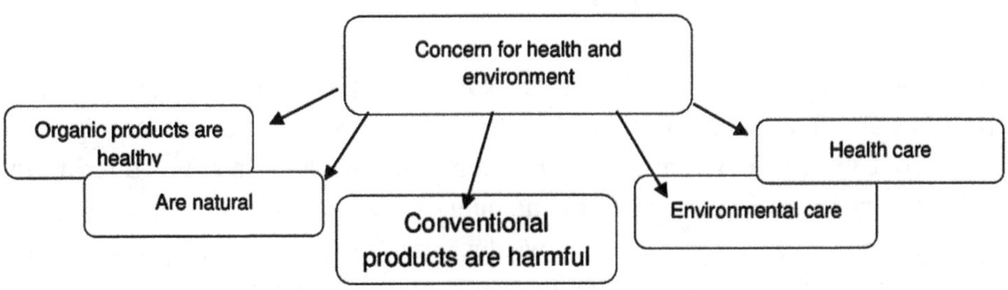

Figure 5. Results of social influence factors
Source: Authors' own elaboration

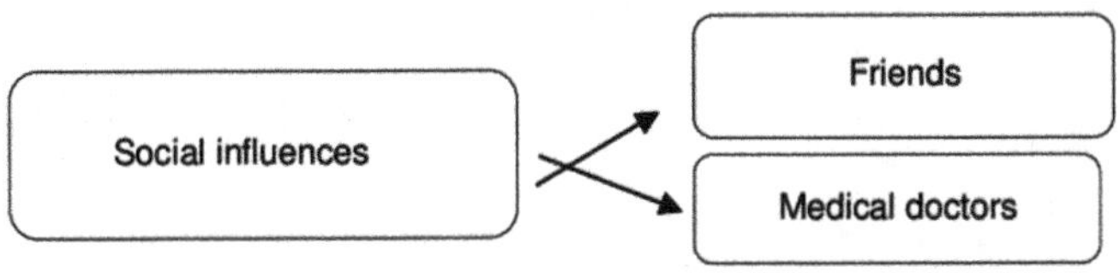

Figure 6. Results of the factors of the marketing mix
Source: Authors' own elaboration

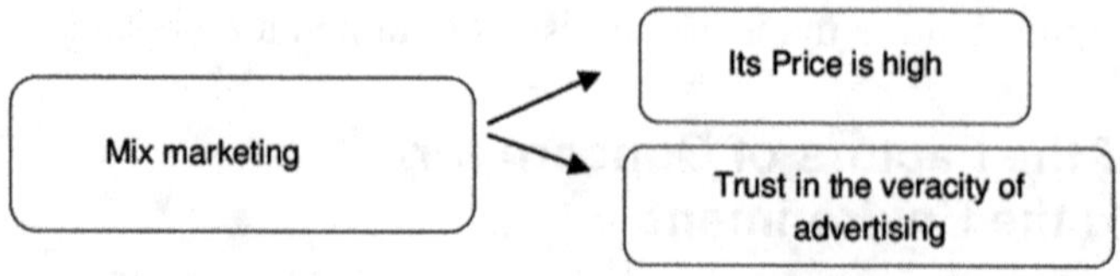

a motivational factor that influences the decision to purchase organic products, it is accepted.

Results of Marketing Mixing Factors

The categories (patterns or responses) are shown with the highest frequency of mention. For the interviewees, the perception of the price attribute, is valued by consumers as a relevant attribute because they all agreed that they are expensive, so it is considered that it can be a reason to influence when buying the product. On the other hand, they have been exposed to the advertising of these products, they trust in the veracity of the commercial, but most deny having acquired the product only because they have seen the advertising of the product. Based on the results obtained, the H3 is accepted: The Marketing mix (4p's) is a motivational factor that influences the decision to purchase organic products.

Results of the Consumer Knowledge Factors on Environmental Problems

The people interviewed stated that they know the problems that currently exist regarding environmental problems and claim to take action to do something about it and contribute to environmental care, being the recycling and not littering the street the actions most performed by the interviewees.

So the H4: The consumer's knowledge about environmental problems is a motivational factor that influences the decision to purchase organic products is fully accepted. In figure 7, the categories (patterns or responses) are shown with the highest frequency of mention.

Figure 7. Results of consumer knowledge factors on environmental problems
Source: Authors' own elaboration

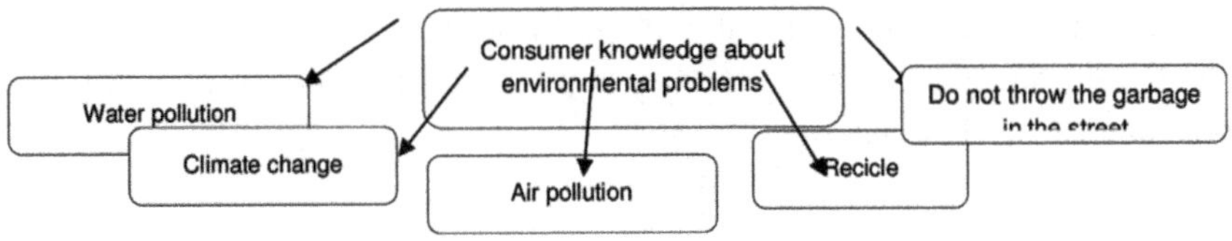

CONCLUSION

There is a great lack of information in terms related to the behavior of the ecological consumer. However, this study allows to know more about the motivations that influence the decision of ecological purchase and the situation in which this market is currently in the municipality of Guadalajara, Jalisco.

At the conclusion of the study, the objectives set for the research are achieved. In relation to the first objective, a structural model is proposed, based on the analyzed theory. Regarding the specific objectives, the first one has been able to conclude that the motivation that most influences the decision to purchase organic products among citizens between 25 and 45 years of age in Guadalajara is the concern for health and the environment. In relation to the second specific objective, it is possible to identify that the citizens of the municipality of Guadalajara are aware of the environmental problems that exist today. In relation to the third specific objective, it has been observed that the citizens of Guadalajara have been forced to modify their habits of life and take action measures such as recycling, care of water and responsible use of resources to contribute to environmental care.

Regarding the general hypothesis raised at the beginning of this study which says that the environmental motivation is not the predominant at the time of preferring organic products, so based on the results obtained it is possible to say that the hypothesis is fully accepted. It should be noted that this research study is one of the first to offer information on ecological behavior in the municipality of Guadalajara. So it is suggested to continue researching in this type of topic since the ecological market is growing and it is important to know about it also that it can be applied in the other municipalities of Jalisco.

RESEARCH LIMITATIONS

The main limitation in this study is the time that was established for conducting the study. On the other hand, the selection of the sample is another limitation, since it has not been sufficiently representative of the population because the method of data collection used was the in-depth interview, however, allows to obtain information of great interest to design future studies on the subject.

Finally, the study faced a limited literature regarding studies related to it in the case of the city of Guadalajara.

SOLUTIONS AND RECOMMENDATIONS

This analysis on Consumer behavior: Motivational factors for the decision to purchase organic products in the municipality of Guadalajara, Jalisco, have important implications for the formulation and implementation of marketing strategies and practices of companies. Undoubtedly, entrepreneurs have to make greater efforts to position themselves and place themselves in the organic products market in Guadalajara.

The importance of increasing sustainable consumption based on organic products, among other benefits, brings a reduction in environmental impact, generating satisfaction in consumers concerned about their personal health and a greater awareness of environmental and ecological sustainability, in order to preserve natural resources and the environment for future generations. The motivational factors of consumers exert a great influence on the decision-making processes of buying organic products for sustainable consumption. Sometimes, the behavior of consumers in the decision to buy organic products motivated by the improvement of consumer health, has greater significance than the purchase decision motivated by a greater ecological awareness.

The limited knowledge that consumers and buyers of organic products have is expressed in their few purchasing decisions, so it is recommended to put a special emphasis on the design of pricing strategies but also communication strategies, advertising and promotion. The companies that produce, distribute and sell organic products have to make great efforts to strengthen communication, advertising, promotion and public relations programs to improve the perception and knowledge of the benefits of organic products and their ecological and sustainable orientation.

In order to influence the behavior of the consumer and buyer in their decision-making processes, it is important that this communication process between companies and consumers and buyers is based on the expression of the relationship between the consumption of organic products and the environment. At the same time that it promotes an ecological lifestyle, a corporate image of environmental responsibility and sustainability is presented, in such a way that they convince and influence the acquisition and consumption of organic products.

The development of organic agriculture in Mexico has been driven by foreign agents who, through Mexican producers, produce certain organic products. Mexico responds to the external demand of global markets for organic products with the development of organic production systems, especially in organic tropical and winter products. The development of the national market of organic products is the opportunity for Mexican producers who have advanced with their own resources and with the support of international experience, but with little support and participation from the State.

Organic products are those that do not use synthetic chemical inputs, but use resources of natural origin that are quickly biodegradable, low impact or that can be recycled, including the label, in packaging, packaging and packaging. The consumption of foods based on organic products moves away from trends such as veganism and vegetarianism, food habits that are incongruous, because they are not always made with organic products and are still exposed to altered food. Marketing is aligned in this trend with the concept of "green consumption", a term that does not have an exact definition but that is used in the purchase process and other actions that it takes to care for the environment.

Organic production is based on specific and precise production standards that aim to achieve a social, ecological and economically sustainable agroecosystem, through special practices such as the use of compost and green fertilizers, biological control, natural repellents from plants, association and rotation of crops, etc. This form of production considers the ecological aspect and includes in its philosophy and practice the improvement of the living conditions of its practitioners, in such a way that it aspires to an integral sustainability of the production system, economic, social and ecological. Organic, ecological or biological agriculture that produces organic products is defined as a production system that uses natural inputs and rejects chemical synthesis inputs such as fertilizers, fungicides, pesticides and insecticides, as well as genetically modified organisms.

Sustainable consumption based on organic products is one that mainly considers factors of environmental and health relevance in the decision to purchase. Current forms of production have caused harmful damage to people's health, since the food they eat contains pesticides that contaminate not only the product but also the environment. This is one of the reasons why the consumption of organic products increases for sustainable consumption. Many of the human diseases are the result of the consumption of products with pesticides, herbicides, fungicides and genetically modified organisms.

The environmental destruction has a direct impact on the crisis in the field for the production of organic products. Bad agricultural practices contribute to further degrade the ecosystems and the quality of life of people with altered food that they consume every day.

In this research on consumer behavior and the process of buying organic products, mainly in the metropolitan area of Guadalajara, and more specifically in the municipalities of Guadalajara, Zapopan and Tlaquepaque, the importance of raising awareness in responsible consumption is analyzed. and solidarity, and its repercussions to boost the local economy. It is considered that the raw material possessed by this central region in the state of Jalisco has been wasted and opportunities have been granted to foreigners to enter the market with altered food.

Organic foods, in addition to giving confidence because they do not use agrochemicals or pollute, are also related to the care of nature and because everything is done in a sustainable way. The emotional affinity towards nature is a concept that includes several inclinations and values towards nature such as love or desire to conserve it and to consume organic products. The construction of emotional ties to nature can serve as a motivation to protect it through the sustainable consumption of organic products.

The organic consumption of organic products is related to the context centered on ecological lifestyles. The ecological purchase of organic products is related to a context of development of ecological life forms that incorporate other environmental actions into a holistic conceptualization of ecological lifestyles. The ecological conscience is the reflective knowledge of the problems and environmental aspects that can be reflected in a sustainable consumption of organic products. Ecological awareness is strongly associated with psychological variables, as well as attitudes.

In consumer behavior, psychological behavior manifests as a set of independent multiple factors, although there is evidence that they could relate to each other.

With respect to consumer behavior in the purchase of organic products, they are more willing to pay for a higher price, especially those with higher income levels. The environmental concern is related more to the social class indicated with the variables education, income and occupational prestige. In this regard, the associations between income and environmental concern are very ambiguous and do not support the hypothesis of positive association.

Therefore, other variables acquire importance in the decision-making processes, such as the presentation of the product and the previous information about the specifications of the satisfactory. The uncertainty about the quality of organic products increases due to consumer distrust of the complex system of production, distribution and food marketing. The complexity of this food system only allows organic products to be known at the places of purchase by the buyer.

The internal factors of both the behavior of the consumer and the buyer who have to make decisions about the consumption of organic products are the influences that come from the needs and that interpret the external stimuli according to the personal characteristics and the psychological structure. The personal characteristics correspond to the observable sociodemographic variables that, although by themselves do not necessarily generate a sustainable consumption based on organic products, but for other conditions that have direct and notorious effects. These conditions only explain a small percentage of the variation in the ecological behavior of people. This limited capacity to explain ecological behavior is mainly due to the fact that the environment is already a socially accepted norm.

The behavior of the consumer and buyer of organic products focuses on decision-making processes based on health factors and demographic aspects. Some of the factors of consumer behavior that can influence the decision-making processes of buying an organic product are the values, beliefs, motivations, attitudes and demographic and educational variables. The marketing factors are the price, product, distribution and communication.

Schooling has a positive and significant effect on sustainable consumption. In the relationship between education and the inclination to carry out environmental actions, those with a higher education level are more willing to act pro environmentally. Age correlates positively with environmental concern. With respect to the gender of the average consumer who participates in some of the ecological activities, women are more consistent and intense in their prevention.

The strategy of information and communication of organic products are identified with the emotional component that involves saving the environment and environment appreciated for their beauty and the pleasure that their enjoyment provides. The strategy of communication and promotional activities, advertising and public relations of organic products can express the relationship between the characteristics, benefits and benefits of the satisfactory, product or service, and nature and the environment, present a corporate image of ecological and environmental responsibility or can promote an ecological lifestyle. The advertising strategy and the organic promotion of organic products make reference to nature and the environment, to reach the health sector as in the case of organic food and green products that are free of toxics, as well as general well-being as in the cases of botany and homeopathy.

A great opportunity for Mexican producers of organic, biological or ecological agriculture is the development of the national market of organic products. The national production of food and other organic products destined for local consumption must adjust its surcharge to market conditions in such a way that the products are accessible to a greater number of consumers. Organic products reach a premium price of 20 to 40 percent compared to their normal price in the municipalities of Guadalajara, Zapopan and Tlaquepaque.

There is very little specification of organic products in relation to meeting the needs, fulfilling the wishes and avoiding the fears of consumers, as well as barriers to the perception of the scope of the environmental impact of these products.

Human beings have basic individual and collective needs to satisfy from survival to the so-called superfluous. When people manifest their ecological concern in an environment of respect for the environment, they are motivated by the satisfaction of more universal needs. A segment of consumers expresses concerns about the growing degradation of the environment through their behavior in their decisions in the purchasing processes. What these consumers are looking for is to make an ecological purchase that allows them to consume organic products that have a lesser impact on the degradation of the environment.

The concept of sustainable consumer behavior based on organic products refers to the consumption and use of goods and services that satisfy basic needs and also improve the quality of life. The consumption of organic products reduces the environmental impact in the production processes. The critical factor in sustainable consumption based on organic products is the amount of resources and energy used. On the other hand, consumer behavior focused on sustainable consumption tends to reduce the use of natural resources, toxic and polluting materials, waste emissions during the life cycle, in such a way that the needs of the future generations.

In general, there are discrepancies in the decision-making processes in the behavior of the consumer and the buyer both in the ecological concern and in the purchase actions from the demand for organic products. The demand for organic products expands especially in the markets of the most developed countries in tandem with the development of organic agriculture. These discrepancies may be greater when analyzing marketing strategies for sustainable organic products. It is evident that the producers, distributors and marketers of organic products require a greater effort in the strategies of ecological communication and green marketing to motivate the processes of decision and purchase of the consumers.

The studies relate the advantages of the implementation of public policies and environmental regulations by governments to encourage consumer behavior in making decisions based on sustainable consumption and organic products. As a priority for development, state institutions exercise government functions to formulate and implement policies related to the consumption of organic products, as well as to establish regulatory frameworks that regulate the behavior and decision-making processes in function of the preservation of the environment and the ecology of the systems, the health and feeding of the population, as well as other benefits.

The Mexican State must become more involved with domestic producers of organic products, taking advantage of international experience, in such a way that it formulates and implements a policy that encourages the efforts of producers and motivates consumption.

The regulations on the production, distribution and consumption of organic products have to go beyond economic growth based on consumption, to consider inclusion and social equality and environmental sustainability in order to truly contribute to improving the welfare of consumers. The fact that synthetic inputs are not used in production is not sufficient for the product to be recognized as organic. It has to go through a process of inspection, verification and subsequent certification. For exports, it must be certified by an agency of the importing country. For organic products to be recognized in the market they require the validation of certification bodies: organisms with international recognition, but foreign to both producers and consumers.

FUTURE RESEARCH DIRECTIONS

Further research on the consumer behavior and their relationships with motivational factors for the decision to purchase organic products in the municipality of Guadalajara, Jalisco, is necessary to have a clearer understanding of the phenomenon in contrast with the traditional and modern production. Moreover, the practical implications to production, distribution and marketing should be study.

DISCUSSION QUESTIONS

This research has intended to answer to the questions:

- Which are the motivations that influence in the decision of purchase of ecological products in the citizens of 25 to 45 years of the municipality of Guadalajara?
- What is the motivation that influences the decision to purchase organic products among citizens between 25 and 45 years of age in the municipality of Guadalajara?
- What is the degree of knowledge that citizens of 25 to 45 years of the municipality of Guadalajara have about organic products?
- What actions do consumers of organic products from 25 to 45 years of age reflect in the municipality of Guadalajara regarding environmental concerns?
- However, while conducting the research new questions have emerged:
- Is the term "organic products" more marketing oriented to target upper economic segments of consumers?
- Is the term "agro-ecological products" more marketing oriented to target middle and lower economic segments of consumers?
- What are the differences in the motivational factors of consumer behavior of organic products and agro-ecological products?
- The motivational factors of consumer behavior of organic products and agro-ecological products are different in consumers of the municipality of Guadalajara that in the other municipalities of the Metropolitan Area?

REFERENCES

Agrawal, J., & Kamakura, W. (1995). The economic worth of celebrity endorsers: An event study analysis. *Journal of Marketing*, *59*(3), 56–62. doi:10.1177/002224299505900305

Alea García, A. (2006). Diagnóstico y potenciación de la educación ambiental en jóvenes universitarios. *Odiseo, Revista electrónica de Pedagogía, 3*(6).

American Marketing Association. (2017). *Ama.org*. Obtenido en febrero de 2018, de https://www.ama.org/Pages/default.aspx

Arana, J., Meilán, J., Gordillo, F., & Carro, J. (2010). Estrategias motivacionales y de aprendizaje para fomentar el consumo responsable desde la Escuela. *Revista electrónica de Motivación y Emoción, 13*(35-36), 19-39.

Arroyo, A., Chamorro, A., & Miranda, F. J. (1999). *Diseño para el medio ambiente: Hacia una integración entre innovación y medio ambiente*. Libro de ponencias del XIII Congreso Nacional de AEDEM.

Barbosa Sánchez, A. (2008). Hacia una cultura ambiental con equidad de género. In *U. d. Chiapas, Educación Ambiental para la sustentabilidad en México* (1st ed.). Chiapas: UNICACH.

Bonta, P., & Farber, M. (1994). 199 preguntas sobre marketing y publicidad. Bogotá: Norma.

Bravo, G. F. (2010). *Partidos verdes y movimientos ecologistas*. Recuperado de www.revistas.unam.mx/index.php/matices/article/download/25725/24217

Buenstorf, G., & Cordes, C. (2008). Can sustainable consumption be learned? A model of cultural evolution. *Ecological Economics*, *67*(4), 646–657. doi:10.1016/j.ecolecon.2008.01.028

Caamal Cauich, I., Pat Fernández, V. G., Ascencio, F. J., & Pérez Fernández, A. (2007). Producción, comercialización y consumo de productos orgánicos en Alemania. *Textual (Chapingo)*, 133–153.

Calomarde, J. (2000). *Marketing Ecológico*. Madrid: Pirámide ESIC.

Capuz Rizo, S., & Gómez Navarro, T. (2004). *Ecodiseño: Ingeniería del ciclo de vida para el desarrollo de productos sostenibles*. Alfaomega.

Carrete Lucero, L., González, E. M., Centeno Velázquez, E., Castaño González, R., & Félix, R. (2013). ¿Qué características tienen los consumidores verdes en México? Un enfoque sobre segmentación demográfica fundamentada en las 3R's y la compra de productos ecológicos. *Estudios Gerenciales, 30*(132), 287-300. Recuperado de http://static1.squarespace.com/static/56228080e4b04bb42a1523da/t/56b39785cf80a1b5f4184f1d/1454610372295/TG2013_Carrete_etal.pdf

Cervera-Ferri, J. L., & Ureña, M. L. (2017). *Indicadores de producción verde: Una guía para avanzar hacia el desarrollo sostenible.* Santiago: CEPAL.

D'Souza, C., & Taghian, M. (2005). Green advertising effects on attitude and choice of advertising themes. *Asia Pacific Journal of Marketing and Logistics, 17*(3), 51–66. doi:10.1108/13555850510672386

Del Greco, N. I. (2010). Estudio sobre tendencias de consumo de alimentos. Primera parte-Generalidades y casos. *Datos relevantes para la toma de decisiones en la Agroindustria de Alimentos y Bebidas.*

Diehr, P., & Beresford, S. A. (2003). The relation of dietary patterns to future survival, health, and cardiovascular events in older adults. *Journal of Clinical Epidemiology, 56*(12), 1224–1235. doi:10.1016/S0895-4356(03)00202-6 PMID:14680674

Expansión. (2017). Influencers 2017. *Expansión.* Obtenido de https://www.pressreader.com/mexico/expansion-m%C3%A9xico/20171115/283128544143988

Fernández, C., Cea Valencia, J., Santander, P., & Nuñez, K. (2013). Consumo verde en Chile: estudio exploratorio sobre consumidor de productos ecológicos. *Global Conference on Business and Finance Proceedings.* Obtenido de https://www.researchgate.net/profile/Cristobal_Fernandez/publication/260364788_Consumo_Verde_en_Chile_Estudio_exploratorio_sobre_consumidor_de_productos_organicos/links/0f317530e614c76869000000/Consumo-Verde-en-Chile-Estudio-exploratorio-sobre-consumidor-

Fraj Andrés, E., & Martínez Salinas, E. (2002). *Comportamiento del consumidor ecológico.* Madrid: ESIC.

Galindo, A. (2010). Psicología del Consumidor Mexicano. *Revista del Instituto Tecnológico de México,* (48), 1-4.

Hendarwan, E. (2002). Seeing green. *Global Cosmetic Industry, 170*(5), 16–18.

Hernández, Y., & López, D. (2012). El marketing ecológico y su integración en la planificación estratégica. *Revista de Estudios Interdisciplinarios en Ciencias Sociales, 14*(2), 223-231.

Hopfenbeck, W. (1993). *The green management revolution: Lessons in environmental excellence*. Prentice Hall.

Hoyer, W., MacInnis, D., & Pieters, R. (2010). Comportamiento del consumidor (5th ed.). Cengage Learning.

IFOAM Federación Internacional de Movimientos de Agricultura Orgánica. (2009). *La Agricultura Orgánica y la Salud Humana*. Obtenido de http://infohub.ifoam.bio/sites/default/files/page/files/oa_humanhealth_es.pdf

Impulso Orgánico Mexicano, A. C. (2014). *Orgánicos en México*. Obtenido de Impulso Orgánico Mexicano A.C.: https://www.impulsoorganicomexicano.com/productos-orgnicos-en-mxico

Islas García, C., & Sánchez Plascencia, M. A. (2013). Consumo saludable: hacia nuevos hábitos de consumo. *Procuraduría Federal del Consumidor*. Obtenido de https://www.profeco.gob.mx/educ_div/educ_y_org_cons/documentos/Consumo%20saludable%20ci.pdf

Izagirre-Olaizola, J., Fernández-Sainz, A., & Vicente-Molina, M.-A. (2013). Antecedentes y barreras a la compra de productos ecológicos. *Universia Business Review*, (38), 108-127.

Kianpour, K., Anvari, R., Jusoh, A., & Fauzi Othman, M. (2014). Important motivators for buying green products. *Intangible Capital*, *10*(5), 873–896. doi:10.3926/ic.470

Kotler, P., & Armstrong, G. (2012). *Marketing* (14th ed.). Pearson.

Lamb, C., Hair, J., & McDaniel, C. (2011). *Marketing*. Cengage Learning.

Laroche, M., Bergeron, J., & Barbaro-Forleo, G. (2001). Targeting consumers who are. *Journal of Consumer Marketing*, *18*(6), 503–520. doi:10.1108/EUM0000000006155

López Eguilaz, M. J., & Remírez Esparza, L. (1998). *Marketing ecológico y sector industrial*. Madrid: UNED.

Martínez Ramón, M. (2006). El mercado de los productos ecológicos en EE.UU. *Instituto español del comercio exterior*. Obtenido de http://www.exportapymes.com/documentos/productos/Ie2409_eeuu_ecologicos.pdf

Martínez Turrubiates, A., & Martín Prieto, F. (2009). *Las megatendencias sociales actuales y su impacto en la identificación de oportunidades estratégicas de negocios* (1st ed.). Monterrey: Instituto Tecnológico y de Estudios Superiores de Monterrey. Obtenido de http://studylib.es/doc/7253097/las-megatendencias-sociales-actuales-y-su-impacto

Min, H., & Galle, W. (2001). Green Purchasing practices of US firms. *Interntions Journal of Operaations & Production Management, 21*(9).

Minetti, A. C. (2002). *Marketing de alimentos ecológicos* (1st ed.). Madrid: Pirámide.

Montaño Salas, F. E. (2012). La educación ambiental en México ante la crisis ambiental. *Revista Vinculando*. Obtenido de http://vinculando.org/ecologia/la-educacion-ambiental-en-mexico-ante-la-crisis-ambiental.html#Educacion_Ambiental_en_Mexico

Mostafa, M. M. (2007). Gender differences in Egyptian consumers' green purchase behaviour: The effects of environmental knowledge, concern and attitude. *International Journal of Consumer Studies, 31*(3), 220–229. doi:10.1111/j.1470-6431.2006.00523.x

National Geographic; GlobeScan. (2012). *Greendex 2012: Consumer Choice and the Environment a worldwide tracking Survey*. Obtenido de http://images.nationalgeographic.com/wpf/media-content/file/NGS_2012_Final_Global_report_Jul20-cb1343059672.pdf

Nielsen. (2016). Nuevas percepciones en las expectativas de consumo. *Ganar-Ganar*, 38-43.

Observatorio Cuidadano de calidad de vida: Jalisco como vamos. (2017). ¿Como nos vemos los tapatíos? *Encuesta de percepción cuidadana sobre la calidad de vida 2016*. Obtenido de http://www.jaliscocomovamos.org/encuesta2016

ONUDI (Organización de las Naciones Unidas para el Desarrollo Industrial). (2011), *Iniciativa de industria verde para el desarrollo industrial sostenible. Viena*. Obtenido de http://www.greenindustryplatform.org/wp-content/uploads/2014/06/green-industry_ES_highres.pdf

Organizacion Mundial de la Salud. (2018). *Organizacion Mundial de la Salud*. Obtenido de http://www.who.int/topics/environmental_health/es/

Orozco Abundis, M. A., Cortes Lamas, A. I., González, M., & Gracia Villar, S. (2003). *Mercadotecnia ecológica: actitud del consumidor ante los productos ecológicos*. Obtenido de http://www.aeipro.com/files/congresos/2003pamplona/ciip03_1041_1050.2224.pdf

Pérez Abuin, J. A. (2016). *Revista de Educacion y Cultura*. Obtenido de http://www.educacionyculturaaz.com/noticias/educacion-ambiental-en-mexico

Rahbar, E., & Wahid, N. A. (2011). Investigación del efecto de las herramientas de marketing verde 'en el comportamiento de compra de los consumidores. *Serie de estrategia empresarial, 12*(2), 73-83. doi:10.1108/17515631111114877

Rani, A., Aravind, J., & Prasad, T. (2014). Green Marketing and its impact. *European Centre for Research Training and Development UK, 2*(8), 45-48. Obtenido de http://www.eajournals.org/wp-content/uploads/Green-Marketing-and-Its-Impact1.pdf

KEY TERMS AND DEFINITIONS

Buying Behavior: Conduct of the consumers relative to the de facto purchase of a product, as well as to the site and the frequency of such purchases.

Consumer Behavior: Consumer behavior is that part of the behavior of people and the decisions that this implies when they are acquiring goods or using services to meet their needs.

Decision Purchase: Important decision process that lies behind the act of buying a product or service, consisting of different stages through which the buyer passes to decide which product or service is best suited to their needs and provides a greater value. If the purchasing decision is satisfactory and provides value to the consumer and, in addition, relational marketing tools are used for the loyalty of the latter, the reiteration of the purchase to the same supplier is highly probable.

Ecological Purchases: "Ecological purchases" suppose the systematic application of compatible criteria with the environment to all the acquisitions and daily operations. In short, it is about meeting the needs of the company with the most appropriate products and favorable to the environment.

Guadalajara: The name of the capital of Jalisco, Mexico. Guadalajara is a city and Mexican municipality, capital and most populated city of the state of Jalisco. It is located in western Mexico, in the center of Jalisco.

Motivation Factors: The set of needs that explain the behavior of people are what we call motivating factors or motives: organic motivators, social motivators and psychological motivators. The motivation is those stimuli that move a person, to perform certain actions, which require an effort to achieve in objective.

Organic Products: Called organic food, organic food, or biological food to agricultural or agro-industrial product that is produced under a set of procedures called "ecological." In general, ecological methods avoid the use of synthetic products, such as pesticides, herbicides and artificial fertilizers.

APPENDIX

Guide to the Interview That Was Applied

Good day / afternoon. I am a graduate student in Marketing, from the University of Guadalajara. The interview I do is about a survey, to know Motivational Factors that influence the decision to buy organic products. All the data you provide will be treated responsibly for educational purposes.

Name:
Age: ____________ Genre: ____________
Civil status:____________________________
Level of studies: ________________________
Municipality: _____________________________

1. What are organic products for you?
2. What kind of organic products do you buy?

(Organic agricultural products, Hygiene products, keeping the home, Biodegradable materials, Sustainable fashion, Products for physical and emotional well-being)

3. Since when do you consume organic products?
4. Why have you decided to buy organic products?

Consumer knowledge about environmental problems

5. Do you know the main environmental problems that affect the planet?

Mention 3

6. What kind of action do you take to care for the environment?

Concern for health and the environment

7. What are the benefits of buying organic products?
8. What do you think of the phrase? "The purchase of organic products contributes to the improvement of the Environment"
9. Why consume organic products instead of conventional ones?

10. Social influences
11. Has any member of your family, friends or other person influenced your purchase decision to any extent? Specify

Marketing mix

12. What is your opinion about the prices of organic products?
13. Do you trust the veracity of the advertising of organic products?
14. Have you bought an organic product because you saw its advertising? In what medium? what a product?

Chapter 9
Urban Governance, Democratic Decentralization, and Natural Resources

José G. Vargas-Hernández
University Center for Economic and Managerial Sciences, University of Guadalajara, Mexico

ABSTRACT

This study aims to analyze the implications of democratic or political and administrative or fiscal decentralization in the downward accountability, participatory and deliberative democracy to shape the urban governance of natural resources, facilities, infrastructure, etc. The methodological and theoretical approach of the analysis is framed by the institutional theory and analyses the power relationships and interactions between national and local governments, authorities, agencies, politicians, and other actors within the urban democratic governance system, downward accountability, participative and deliberative democracy, etc. Finally, in the conclusion it is argued that some institutionalized democratic mechanisms and management practices can be implemented in the political or democratic and administrative or fiscal decentralization to improve democratic urban governance of natural resources and environmental and urban green areas.

INTRODUCTION

Democracy decentralization reforms in most of developing countries provide the framework for analyzing the development of democratic local authority and democratic local governance. Centralized states and systems have failed to provide basic services

DOI: 10.4018/978-1-5225-9562-5.ch009

due to inefficient infrastructure, lack of transparency and accountability and high levels of corruption. The Latin America´s state formation was the result of a struggle between metropolitan, regional and local economic elites and oligarchies (Del Río, 2004; Faletti, 2004; Selee, 2004) until the period if 1980s and 1990s when appeared a strong process of democratic decentralization.

Since the mid-1980s, decentralization reforms and policies, democratic or political and administrative have been developed and legislated in most of the developing countries aimed to improve efficiency and equity (Crook and Manor, 1999; World Bank, 2000; Ndegwa, 2002; Mawhood, 1983; Crook and Manor, 1998). In the early and mid-1990s, democratic decentralized urban management practice incorporated some participative mechanisms to engage citizens in decision making and policy formulation. The 1990s witnessed a wave of liberal democratic decentralization process across the world. This process is associated with structural adjustment reforms and policies supported by a neoliberal expression of a modernization theory (Samoff, 1990). The Modernization theories are more concerned with socioeconomic prerequisites of local democracy.

Political reforms promoted democratic decentralization processes characterized by the transfer of power and resources to local governments and representative authorities, democratically elected and accountable to their constituents (Crook and Manor, 1998; Agrawal and Ribot, 1999). Democratic reforms of the State are motivated by the desire to foster democratic local institutions aimed to meet the needs of a diverse citizenry (Vedeld, 2003). Institutional economic and political reforms shape the democratic capabilities of the state and civil society.

Democratic decentralization reforms are implemented to promote the empowerment of local governments and authorities expecting to contribute to local democracy despite the difficulties to establish local democratic authorities (Ribot, Agrawal &Larson 2006; Agrawal &Ribot 1999; Grindle 2007). Democratic decentralization plays a crucial role in accompanying the democratic reforms (Manor, 1999). Under the framework of democratic reforms, the design and implementation of democratic decentralization have to take into account the powers and the means to transfer from central and national institutions of government to local government institutions. Reforms must establish the basic institutional arrangements of democratic decentralization, and paying attention to be fully implemented.

Democratic decentralization reforms, policies and projects transfer functions, powers and resources to elected local governments, authorities and agencies affecting democracy. Initiatives in policy instrument reforms aimed to develop and practice of principles and strategies of democratic decentralization create opportunities for more equitable distribution of benefits. Local urban economic, social, ecological and cultural dynamic must be taking into account when adjusting policy to the particularities of democratic decentralization of each local space.

The public justifications for choices of democratic decentralization processes and local government institutions may vary widely the design and implementation under the framework of democratic decentralization reforms and the outcomes could be not the expected but a weak functioning of powerless decentralized local institutions (Hara 2008). Implementation of democratic reforms have demonstrated that local authorities, governments and urban governance pose challenges for advancing policy equity and efficiency by increasing political representation of vulnerable individuals, groups, neighborhoods and local communities. Democratic decentralization reforms taking place may prove difficult to determine if they improve the conditions of equity, efficiency and alleviates poverty.

POLITICAL OR DEMOCRATIC DECENTRALIZATION

Democratic decentralization offers a compelling argument about why local governments and politics matter in the creation and development of democratic and participatory urban governance institutions. Political or democratic decentralization refers to the transfer of powers and authority to representative and downwardly accountable elected local governments.

Decentralization refers to any act of national central government or agency formally transfers or cedes powers and resources to local institutions, agencies and actors at lower levels in a territorial and administrative, bureaucratic and political hierarchies. Democratic decentralization process transfers political power, functions and resources from central government to lower and local levels within the political-administrative hierarchy of the state (Mawhood 1983). Democratic decentralization processes transfer power to local institutions. Democratic decentralization must have specific objectives to achieve through rules to establish incentives for transferring appropriate powers to local accountable authorities (Agrawal & Ribot 1999; Kulipossa 2004; Larson 2003).

Ribot (2004) defines democratic decentralization as the transfer of powers from central governments to elected, representative and accountable local community governments in the name of local citizens. Democratic decentralization processes have reemerged to challenge local governments (van Rouveroy van Nieuwaal et al, 1999; Geschiere and Boone, 2003; Ntsebeza, 2002, 2005). Democratic decentralization involves transfers of powers to representative elected local community government under whose authority are the citizens' who live in the jurisdiction. Democratic decentralization involves the transfer of powers from centralized authorities to democratically elected local governments.

Democratic decentralization and political decentralization transfer powers and resources to representative authorities accountable to local populations. Representative forms of local government are required for the democratic processes without marginalizing the vulnerable groups of population (Agrawal &Gupta 2005; Crook &Manor 1998; Crook &Sverrisson 2001). An engendered system of democratic decentralization in which vulnerable people and interests can be addressed to strengthen political and administrative participation in decision making processes al local level. Democratic decentralization entails the forging of strategic compromises that firmly secure the interests of the most disadvantaged groups with outcomes regularly reviewed (Mandondo and Mapedza 2003).

Democratic decentralization can serve the underprivileged and vulnerable groups to redress entrenched inequity focusing on biased hierarchy is a needed complement of local democracy in any local authority (Mansuri &Rao 2003:11-14; Heller et al. 2007:629; Crook &Sverrisson 2001). Decentralization is neither representation without powers nor powers without representation.

Democratic decentralization aims to increase public local participation in decision-making, supported by a strong downward accountability to local governments, agencies and constituencies. Decisions related to democratic decentralization must involve a political broad-based dialogue with a commitment to be efficient, effective and equity. Local government development is fostered by democratic decentralization, popular participation including vulnerable constituencies and constitutional commitment.

Democratic decentralization entails that central authorities entrust significant powers to representative local authorities, individual or collective bodies. All citizens give form to a community which is under the jurisdiction of local government. Local authorities to be representative requires powers to be democratic decentralized and to strengthen their local deconcentrated functions and not avoiding democratic institutions (Ribot & Oyono 2006; Ribot *et al.* 2008). Democratic decentralization of local governments facilitates the design and development of local institutions with capabilities of enhancing democratic deliberation.

Democratic decentralization is an institutionalized form of popular political participation. Democratization is linked on political participation in a democratic society and essential element in individual self-development. However, in some countries, political participation takes place at the central level while the local officials are the field operations functionaries of deconcentrated central monasteries and agencies.

FISCAL OR ADMINISTRATIVE DECENTRALIZATION

Fiscal decentralization is a democratic and administrative decentralization which refers to the transfer of fiscal powers and resources for revenue generation Democratic decentralization is a means of national central governments and agencies to transfer fiscal and administrative burden to local governments, agencies and actors (Nsibambi, 1998).

Where democratic decentralization is being practiced, the relationship with administrative decentralization may not be hold true (Tacconi, 2007). There are several forms of decentralization, which can be administrative, deconcentration and democratic or political decentralization. Deconcentration is a weaker form of administrative decentralization with not well established downward accountability as it is in the democratic or political decentralization. Administrative decentralization is delegating authority and supervising administrative areas to local governments and agencies from national central governments requiring strong lines of accountability (Ribot, 2003; Ribot and Larson, 2005).

Downward Accountability

Downward accountability is the essence of democratic institutions. Downward accountability of local governments and authorities require direct and democratically elected political representatives (Agrawal & Ribot, 1999; Crook & Manor, 1998). Democratic institutions must be representative and accountable to the people who may be empowered to respond. Local as well as central accountability benefit from democratic decentralized governments improving their functioning. Democratic decentralization aims to increase public local participation in decision-making, supported by a strong downward accountability to local governments, agencies and constituencies.

The development of the downward accountability is essential for the democratic processes taking into consideration that excessive oversight undermines local autonomy and democracy (Bigombe 2003). Downward accountability and grassroots democratic participation are essential mechanisms to strengthen democratic decentralization. Democratic electoral institutions and accountability mechanisms such as disciplinary action are needed (Kassibo 2003). Downward accountability is built into the functions of democratic decentralization processes of local governments and agencies with responsibility to national central government.

Weak state institutions can undermine the effectiveness of a democratic systems and accountability of local polities in regulatory authority, democratic planning, taxing or spending. Democratic national and local governments tend to have a positive interaction with political decentralization assuming that democratic elections improve the accountability of decentralized authorities (Mookherjee 2001). Legitimate democratic representation must be directed towards financial management institutions in order to guarantee the accountability of managers to state and local authorities and communities (Oyono and Efoua, 2006; Ribot, 2007).

Competitive local elections for local authorities encourage political parties and social movements to reach out to previously ignored and vulnerable groups (Cleary, 2004; Harriss et al., 2005; Hirschman, 1970). New social movements, and individuals use communication media to educate, organize and expand the action of democratic politics. Democratic government stimulates accountability overall, improving its performance. Democratic institutions are representative and accountable to the people empowered to respond. Democratic decentralization must recognize, operate and strengthen democratic institutions as well as distributional and procedural equity which can be obtained through public participation and downward transparency and accountability.

Local authorities holding democratic representation are responsive to the needs expectations and aspirations of their local population and citizens. Democratic representation of local authorities is driven by accountability and responsiveness to the concerned population of the communities being governed.

Democratic decentralization is not always implemented correctly in terms such as representation and accountability of authorities, management of resources and decision making power. Public sphere has been questioned as a form of deliberative democracy through internet practice for failing support the status quo of social and political systems and accountability of power.

Participatory and Deliberative Democracy

Democratic theory has developed the notions of citizen participation or participatory democracy under the assumption that democracy is government by, of, and for the people The participatory democracy of the Greeks is contrasted by Habermas (1996) with the radical democratic movements, the representative, parliamentary bourgeois democracy and the attempts at reducing citizen participation in the welfare state. The participatory democracy requires that citizens must be politically informed, active, organized, participative, debate, discuss, argue and deliberate to become a political force within the lifeworld and civil society to transform the public sphere of polity. Participatory democracy legitimizes governments' policies and allows followers engagements in decision making processes.

Strategic formulation and implementation of participatory democratic institutions affect government and citizen's behaviors as in line with democratic outcomes. Participatory democratic institutions contribute to the deepening of democracy when the interests and activities of local government and civil society organizations complement to favor the new political and social rights for citizens. An elected democrat local government and civil society share interests to work together in a legitimate decision-making process to elaborate and develop participatory budgeting programs by fostering the growth of social capital within the "participatory publics".

Participatory budgeting helps local governments to identify themselves as democratic and participatory with strong ties to the participatory public civil society organizations.

Participants in participatory budgeting have the opportunity to make decisions in local government spending, taxing, and other state investments, raising the profile of government and civil society leaders in neighborhoods and local communities. Successful participatory democratic programs can have positive effects on democracy deepening and improving the quality of local democratic processes participatory budgeting outcomes has contributed to advancing participatory democratic experience by fostering the growth of social capital through local democratic processes.

Local participatory democracy is a learning arena for democracy (Grindle 2007:7-13a) and skills of deliberation. Local government leaders can be linked to participatory public civil society organizations and have strong ties to support deliberative and democratic processes.

The theoretical analysis and studies on local participatory democracy is growing exponentially based on normative democratic theory (Habermas 1996; Cohen and Arato 1992; Sen 1999; Evans 2002) and recognizing the deficits of representative democracy.

Local participatory democracy is also an effective school for democracy teaching people the rules structuring conflict resolution and to be more effective at rewarding and punishing the political behavior of local officials. Local government officials more likely to delegate authority can be linked to democratic and participatory public civil society organizations. Schooling and media play a critical role in forming citizens to make them capable of participating in democracy (Kellner 1990 and 1998). The media assuming democratic functions must be vigilant in checking excessive and corrupt powers and informing adequately the citizenry.

Democratic decentralization is an institutional participatory processes used to increase public participation in local decision-making from which can be derived great benefits. Local authorities create and develop significant discretion to deliver benefits. Local authorities may have a narrow institutional space of discretion that they do not represent the local population and have a little effect on participatory local management arrangements. In a country with a strong central control, the imperative of participatory planning must be legally inscribed in laws of local development.

All citizens and citizen groups involved in participatory parity, regardless of identity, must have equal and the same opportunities to participate in democratic institutions (Fraser 2000:115). Transfers of powers through democratic decentralization is occurring under different processes of privatization, civil society and NGOs, empowerment and participatory approaches, community-driven development, social funds, and other organizational, institutional and authority forms which have different distributional and democratic outcomes (Pritchett and Woolcock, 2004; Ribot, 2004).

Urban democracy literature is more concerned with the "right to the city" than a participatory or deliberative democracy approaches from the perspective of neo-liberalization, which also is problematic (Dryzek, 1996, p. 6). Deliberative democracy (Habermas 1995), is based on principles of social inclusion, argumentation and deliberation processes in the formation of democratic decisions. Privatization schemes do not follow the logic of democratic decentralization because they are taking public resources away from democratic local institutions and transferring them to private owners who are self-regulating, self-serving and often non-sanctionable. Participatory approaches and transfers to customary and private bodies rarely constitute democratic decentralization processes.

The participatory democratic theory assumes that local space is more democratic than other space scales. The associative democrats support the argument that devolution of power to localities invigorates democracy (Cohen and Rogers,1995; Matthews, 1989 and Cunningham, 2001, p. 136). Diverse democratic forms of decentralization are being analyzed and practiced around the world including the participatory approaches consisting of consultation, mobilization and involvement of people. These forms can be a democratic decentralization with power transfers and the contractual participation such as co-management.

Participatory democratic practices are necessary for the implementation of routinizing democratic decentralization through widening political local spaces for citizenship participation to legitimate a democratic local government in such a way that the expectations of citizens from local authorities sustain the democratic practices. Strengthen decentralized democratic processes and practices assumes granting local authorities, agencies and political actors, greater decision-making power, democratic representation and making them accountable local entities To remedy the so called democratic deficit central governments of nation states grant new powers to local governments making them more accountable to citizens and communities by designing structures, mechanisms and procedures for direct involvement in decision making, planning and budgeting. Besides of devolving resources to local governments, it is promoted the participatory democracy.

Citizens and citizen group through a process of participatory parity must have equal opportunity to participate in decision making. Movements such as #Occupy, egalitarian, radical democratic grassroots that has contributed to the development of an alternative democratic self-organization model through open and participatory assemblies shifting public discourse, influencing political discussions, corporate financial interests and shaping policy debates on economic stagnation and growing inequality.

Media technologies are serving the basis for a participatory democratic communication politics. Communication media and technology can be democratized to give support to democratic media politics and thus to democratic transformation.

Public interest communication multiplies information and discussion for a more informed citizenry geared toward democratic participation for the common good. Habermas's analysis makes rigid and imperative the distinction between lifeworld and system understood as economy – state, removing this one from democratic transformation. Also, the analysis limits participatory democracy to the lifeworld undergoing new threats from the system such as the colonization by technologies of information and communication.

Democratically local governments can be captured by economic and political elites whose involvements in the political arena distort priorities limiting the participatory democratic processes. Power relations surrounding and filling new spaces for democratic decentralization engagements are critical for an analysis and assessment of the participatory democratic development and their transformative potential. The long-term democratic effects of tutelage should allow access to the local authorities giving voice to civil society and citizens without producing clientelism.

Local governments unwilling to delegate authority to citizens cannot have full participatory programs with democratic content. Research is required to measure the impact that democratic and participatory programs have on citizens, urban local communities and civil society organizations Local government willing to delegate authority and practice participatory democracy as a strategy to reach out to interested constituents and develop deep links to participatory public civil society organizations.

URBAN GOVERNANCE

The macro-level institutional context is having an interactive effect with local political democracy and government shaping the urban democratic governance. The creation and development of an urban green areas network under the framework of democratic decentralization is a possibility of entering to the field of local urban governance and contributing to expanding their scale and scope with some democratic content. This innovation is being labeled in different forms: participatory urban governance, deliberative democracy, empowered deliberative democracy (Fung and Wright 2001:7).

Participatory urban governance institutions as a democratic innovation, are attracting citizens associated with radical political parties broadly concerned with the political commitment of radical democracy and achievement of social good.

Political theories of democratic urban governance have developed a whole range of assumptions supported by the actualization of the reality of modern citizenship in plural expressions of democratic forms. There are no *a priori* reasons that local forms of governance are more democratic and decentralized authority, which in fact, in some contexts may be quite pernicious. Democracy as a form of urban governance is shifting from transition to deepening the democratic rule (Linz & Stepan, 1996), the democratic quality of institutions and urban governance with more political direct participation than only electoral participation, and by promoting and improving the overall capabilities of citizens in new forms of engagement with public decision making (Dre`ze & Sen, 1995). Therefore, democracy is strengthening and countering the influence of powerful hegemonic interests (Avritzer, 2002).

Local government and politicians in times of electoral competition are more likely to promote participatory urban governance institutions in order to appeal ignored and vulnerable groups to participate in decision-making and policy formulation processes. Vulnerable people and groups are inhibited from participation on democratic consolidation processes with technocratic structures and procedures that engender governance. The dynamics of participatory democratic urban governance in countries where it is used, is subject to all sorts of imperfections, abuses and manipulations. Privileged urban enclaves are created and developed against the concept of democratic urban spaces with economic, social and cultural divisions, which in some cases are the result of bad governance, insecurity and unsafety.

New democratic experiments transform direct forms of citizen engagement with more participative urban governance of people in political decentralized spaces through the strength of liberal democratic institutions. Democratic local urban governance points to accountability, participation and empowerment.

Empowered participatory urban governance (Fung and Wright 2003) in political democratic practice is grounded on the dynamics of culture, power and politics which are critical elements of deliberative democratic spaces. The ideological preference for participatory urban governance lends legitimacy to a radical political culture that breaks with authoritarian past of governments. The elements of the new political culture in participatory urban governance institutions favors normative and democratic practices in which everyone has a right to express his opinion and arguments, join in the debates, object and negotiate any terms that is considered to be democratic, right and fair.

Democratic urban governance is the result of the civil rights in a congruent relation with political entitlements, legitimacy and accountability as a dimension of collective responsibility. These processes are taking place instead of participatory democracy involving participation related to rights of citizenship and to democratic urban governance, deepening democratic forms of responsive government expressions, transparency, accountability, responsiveness, democratic state intervention, etc.

Local democratic urban governance may use other mechanisms like co-management, CBNRM and other participatory approaches sometimes difficult to distinguish from democratic decentralization (Tacconi et al 2006, p15, Nemarundwe, 2004, p285). Democratic ecological, environmental and urban sustainable development governance has as fundaments the political and managerial representation and discretion of local public authorities and governments.

Representative democratic politics and participatory urban governance have similar styles of political behavior matched by networks, ideological commitments and political projects spanning these spaces (Fox 1996).

Citizens engagement in democratic and participative forms of urban governance face serious limitations in societies where the inequalities are deeply rooted. The failure of the reforms for democratic urban governance have critical consequences for local sustainable development.

THEORETICAL AND METHODOLOGICAL APPROACH

Democratic decentralization as a theoretical approach framed by the institutional theory, analyses the power relationships and interactions between national and local governments, authorities, agencies, politicians, and other actors within the urban democratic governance system, downward accountability, participative and deliberative democracy, etc. The contribution of local actors and agents in the making, granting and taking of the institutional space in local urban governance challenge democratic deliberation processes beyond the social movements and the electoral politics. Consolidation of democratic institutions that forge a nation and consolidation of the political power and territorial integrity are the foundations of the democratic governance and rule.

Institutional theory framework of democratic decentralization provides the basis of political democratic rationality to enhance resource sustainable development to build political spaces for citizens instead of the market rationality in competitive spaces of consumers. Democratic decentralization theory sustains that its spirit is the empowerment of local institutions. The institutional analysis approach is more context specificity oriented and more theoretically compatible with the study of democratic decentralization.

A comprehensive review of the political economy approach of democratic decentralization is provided by Manor (1999). The logic of democratic and administrative decentralization process is inclusive and public and because the proximity to the benefited population, it reduces transaction costs and internalize costs of externalities, provides better accountability of local government, authorities and decision makers integrating them across the local needs and aspirations of population and matching with resources (Agrawal and Ribot 1999).

Local governments receiving authority over resource management need downward accountability to have effective democratic decentralization.

Studies of democratic decentralization have focused on service delivery efficiency and equity at local government level (Crook &Manor 1998; Bardhan & Mookerhee 2006; Tulchin & Selee 2004; Oxhorn, Tulchin &Selee 2004; Ribot & Larson 2004). However, recent analysis on democratic decentralization are focusing more on democracy outcomes and the effects on local democracy (Ribot 1999; 2003; 2004; Grindle 2007; Ribot, Chhatre &Lankina 2008; Harriss, Stokke &Törnquist, 2004).

Local democracy is contingent on democratic local government and institutions have to offer to local citizens. Each region and town requires different alternatives and approaches to build more effective democratic decentralization institutions which can work close to the people. Harriss, Stokke &Törnquist (2004:6) argue that "… the test for democracy is not about the existence of formal democratic rights and institutions, but whether they have real meaning for people." Local government should recognize and respect the fundamental democratic rights of citizens and civil social organizations (CSOs). However, CSOs should have enough capacity to engage the local government on their own terms.

DEMOCRATIC DECENTRALIZATION AND URBAN GOVERNANCE

Devolution to urban and rural municipalities in the aftermath of the democratic decision-making transitions of the1990s standing as governance generated significant benefits for the communities. Democratic decentralization can support the practice and experience of local governance based on the benefits to the community. Democratic decentralization of power and resources through external interventions in the form of capital converted into authority, reshaped through institutions and practice of norms, has effects on national and local democracy and democratic urban governance. However, democratic local urban governance is not necessarily a consequence of decentralization policies.

This democratic decentralization process takes different forms in different public spaces depending of the urban governance design of states.

The neo-liberal democratic decentralization policy called right to the city and urban citizenship, moves urban community governance away from participatory and deliberative democratic decision-making. Democratic and accountable local urban governance is able to implement devolved responsibilities from central government. However, at the local and regional levels, policy and urban governance interventions do not necessarily are decentralized and democratic.

Between the assumptions about participation, accountability and democratic decentralization embedded in participatory urban governance and deliberative democracy, there is a tension that needs to be more explored for the understandings and practice of the new actors in these new democratic spaces (Cornwall 2004). Increasingly democratic decentralization practices are more sustainable for long and bring more democratic participation of citizens on decision making over natural resources and urban green areas governance to local governments.

The urban space-taking by citizens and communities stressing their role of moving democratic subjects may be supported by the institutions of local governance. Still today, a civil society approach to local institutional democratic decentralization and governance may result to benefit the economic and political elites but excluding the marginal and poor populations from democratic decision making and ignoring their demands.

The principles of democratic decentralization and subsidiarity apply to the governance of urban green ecosystem services. Deliberative democratic decision-making can transform the mechanisms of state power as a form of authoritarian urban governance into permanently more mobilized deliberative democratic grassroots forms.

Decentralization processes in environmental and natural resources sectors has not well developed and much have to occur on actors receiving limited transfer of powers due to divergence of local state institutions and governance. Democratic reforms on decentralization of resources to local authorities have some limitations regarding the prospects for sustainable management, local environmental governance, and benefits redistribution. Most of the times, influential local elites are reinforced. Ribot assumes that democratic environmental decentralization may be feasible with accountable urban local communities.

DEMOCRATIC DECENTRALIZATION IN NATURAL RESOURCES

The concept of democratic decentralization in the area of natural resources is being questioned by some conservation advocates who propose the notion of democratic conservation. There is a marked trend towards greater community engagement in urban green areas management. Community conservation of environmental and green areas initiatives are growing in large number in urban settlements taking place, most of the times, outside the formal confines of democratic decentralization projects. Urban green innovation planning authority needs to develop democratic participative decision-making processes on issues of environmental and sustainable development.

Local people's entitlements and rights to make democratic decisions about their environmental and natural green resources are not always recognized, prompting displacements from protected green areas in the name of conservation principles for surviving and striving democratic decentralization and conservation of environmental and green urban areas may create and develop conditions for innovation of power democratic exercise to benefit the citizenship, urban communities and neighborhood. Urban communities must explore more equitable forms of space allocations to ensure public access, use and enjoyment of urban public spaces and streets.

Community-based natural resource management (CBNRM) is related to democratic decentralization which is considered as an institutionalized and scaled-up for. Democratic decentralization of natural resource management (NRM) is distinct to CBNRM in the inclusion of all citizens in decision making processes based on representative authorities of local governments while CBNRM represent specific sectors of population (Alden Wily, undated; Ribot, 2002).

Institutionalized representation of local government and authorities in the form of democratic decentralization hold political and management responsibilities over local natural resources as an institutionalized form of CBNRM. Representative authorities of local governments and agencies through democratic decentralization processes in the form of CBNRM receive transfers of powers and resources in the name of citizens. A decentralized small community at local level in the context of a city tends to be weaker in power and in democratic decision making, thus local action entails a fragmented vision and loss of coherence.

Several analyses do not question the core assumptions of democratic decentralization considered as an institutionalized form of Community-based natural resource management (CBNRM) with engagement of people on conservation of benefits (Tacconi *et al.*, 2006 and Hailey 1938). Democratic decentralization and community-based natural resource management (CBNRM) are different (Ribot 2004).

The participatory ideology considers than communities can legitimate manage natural resources over democratically elected local governments and authorities involved in related issues. In this case, democratic decentralization cannot deliver the promised benefits to the community. Several analyses do not question the core assumptions of democratic decentralization considered as an institutionalized form of Community-based natural resource management (CBNRM) with engagement of people on conservation of benefits (Tacconi *et al.*, 2006 and Hailey 1938). Strong elected local authorities can have some options to choose to work through participatory democracy, community-driven development (CDD), stakeholder or Community-based natural resource management (CBNRM) approaches.

Democratic decentralization is a mechanism of reintegrating and placing priorities in terms of needs and aspirations de the community. This allows local representative governments and authorities to place natural resource management (NRM) and urban green areas innovation and NRM among other basic needs of their communities. Some contextual factors of urban green areas innovation are more supportive of local democratic decentralized authorities without developing negative trade-offs on the political and ecological fronts between local elites. These contextual factors that shape the outcomes of democratic decentralization, are according to (Olivier de Sardan 2004, p3) the socio-political aspects including the role of local aristocracies.

Supporting democratic urban green areas innovation, development, conservation and management initiatives require allocating meaningful resources for community, local government, citizens and other stakeholder's capacity-building to encourage open and participative deliberation over environmental and natural resource management and fostering a shift from regulation to support functions. Local democratic government institutions can transfer meaningful discretionary powers to communities and neighborhoods over the management of natural resources in urban green areas.

Devolution to local communities in the form of democratic decentralization as Community-based natural resource management (CBNRM) brings some benefits, sometimes as utilitarian incentives (Tacconi, 2007). Lummis (1997, p. 18) contends that democracy depends on the local spaces where the people live. However, some analysts argue that local-scale institutional arrangements do not always result in more participatory democratic decision making outcomes. The capacity of subordinate groups in a consolidated formal democracy has an effective role in shaping public policy. Factors such as the macro-economic policy articulated with issues of accessibility and affordability to natural resources engenders democratic decentralization, mainly affecting to vulnerable groups of population.

Local government is inherently based on political interests, power relations, hierarchies and authority achieved by political competition and rivalry and solved by electoral votes rather than by democratic representation on detrimental of environmental, ecological and natural resources. The proliferation of user committees in political decentralization of natural resources, criticized by Manor (2005) as having shortcomings, it is questionable that facilitates democratic transformations of the local government institutions and electoral democracy they lack representative and democratic credentials and are vulnerable to elite manipulation.

An institutionalized representation of authorities in democratic decentralization in the form of Community-based natural resource management (CBNRM) has managerial responsibilities over natural resources. Democratic decentralization can establish as recipients of decentralized powers and natural resources management to the elected local authorities and governments (Ribot, 2008; Alden Wily, undated). However, democratic participation and deliberation as a way of life in urban settlements has been very limited not allowing naturally the gathering together all people. Local actors can be chosen by agents willing to intervene and accomplish democratic decentralization and de-concentration initiatives and processes to transfer powers and resources to local governments such as Community-based natural resource management (CBNRM).

Democratic decentralization of natural resource management either transfer too little power or transfer this power to non-representative local authorities (Ribot, 2004; Larson and Ribot, 2007). Democratic decentralization may not contribute for the good of local livelihoods (Blaikie, 2006; Tacconi et al, 2006). The democratizing discourse is associated with natural resource decentralizations and transferring significant powers to democratic local bodies (Ribot,2004; Ribot and Larson,2005). Democratic decentralization processes of natural resources have failed to empower democratic local governments. Assuming that locally entrenched economic, political, social and cultural factors, democratic decentralization to local government does not always result in fair representation of citizens and direct access to environmental and natural resources.

DISCUSSION

Different patterns of associational democracy can improve the quality of democratic urban governance. Institutionalized democratic mechanisms and management practices can be implemented for democratic urban governance of environmental and urban green areas. The efforts of the state should aim to design and build local democratic institutions to foster democratic decentralization of resources and more participatory democratic governance. National central authorities play a relevant role in democratic-political and administrative decentralization to ensure that local governments and democratic institutions address the expectation, needs and aspirations of local people. Opportunities for legislation, formulation and implementation of democratic decentralization processes have to be created and developed aimed to promote local democratic environmental governance.

The basic assumption of the decentralization effectiveness, political or administrative, is that local government, authorities and public decision makers are physically close to those citizens to whom are better able to respond to meet their local needs, to work on their behalf and to be accountable to all local population. Democratic decentralization, either political or administrative, empowers local institutions, authors and actors with potentially institutional outcomes. Democratic decentralization empowers the local communities while administrative decentralization increases central state government monitoring authorities and governments at the local level.

Increased democratic participation may bring a broader cross-section of the population into political and administrative decision making issues, participatory processes are not often necessarily neither representative nor binding (Mosse 2001).

Interventions of democratic and administrative decentralization can develop and work together with other local developments outside the official authorities but recognizing, strengthening and legitimating them. Some capabilities required to support the implementation of democratic and administrative decentralization are administrative and financial management, problem solving, decision making, capacity for democratic leadership and other technical skills.

Local actors in natural resource sector decentralizations must hold powers in democratic form and be accountable to their population. Holding non-democratic power are contingent to powers without accountability or accountability without powers (Ribot 2004). Local actors may be more active as democratic subjects in different actions of local agency leading to qualify as more efficient than democratic and administrative decentralization processes.

Political and administrative decentralization in Mexico was opposed by strong traditional bureaucratic actors, the tendency towards more centralized oriented planning and intersectoral coordination. All these factors lead to falling short of devolution purposes and with serious consequence for the equity and efficiency of services becoming more a measure to increase central control than a democratic principle or a response to political pressure from below (Gonzalez-Block and others1989).

Olowu et al (2001, p1) sustains that decentralization copes "*...with two major political problems. The first stems from the fact that the political and administrative leaders are not ready to share the monopoly of power they inherited from the colonial period... The second political dilemma is the confiscation of power by local elites. In many cases, the local elite, rather than the most vulnerable groups, capture decentralized powers... In the absence of more ambitious institutional, political and economic reforms, democratic decentralization will be a contradiction because improvements in financial allocation can only take place if the local government is accountable to its citizens and has the capacity to carry out its functions.*

Civil society democratic participation alongside considerable increases in representation of vulnerable groups can make important contributions to political and administrative decentralization development of local communities.

More complex concepts of environmental and urban green areas governance, decentralized democracy and conservation are required to build participatory governance and promote democratic and accountable vertical links at differing levels of governance and across actors are the challenges, from local to global reform and vice versa (Mohan and Stokke 263 Democratic and administrative decentralization of urban environmental and sustainable development programs must be supported by policies and practices.

Democratic decentralization to be fed by technical dimensions to have an impact on sustainable local green development requires responsive government authorities and strong commitment from organized civil society to vulnerable groups involvement. Decentralization process increases the capacity of citizens to elect responsive authorities and select public officials holding both of them accountable for their political and administrative performance.

REFERENCES

Agrawal, A., & Gupta, K. (2005). Decentralization and Participation: The Governance of Common Pool Resources in Nepal's Terai. *World Development, 33*(7), 1101–1114. doi:10.1016/j.worlddev.2005.04.009

Agrawal, A., & Ribot, J. C. (1999). Accountability in decentralization: A framework with South Asian and African cases. *Journal of Developing Areas, 33*, 473–502.

Alden Wily, L. (n.d.). *Making Woodland Management More Democratic: Cases from Eastern and Southern Africa*. Academic Press.

Avritzer, L. (2002). *Democracy and the Public Space in Latin America*. Princeton, NJ: Princeton University Press.

Bardhan, P., & Mookherjee, D. (2004). *Decentralization in West Bengal: origins, functioning and impact*. Paper presented at Conference on Democracy and human development: A global inquiry, Boston University.

Bigombe, P. (2003). *The Decentralized Forestry Taxation System in Cameroon: Local Management and State Logic*. Environmental Governance in Africa Working Papers no 10. WRI.

Blaikie, P. (2006). Is small really beautiful? Community-based natural resource management in Malawi and Botswana. *World Development, 34*(11), 1942–1957. doi:10.1016/j.worlddev.2005.11.023

Cleary, M. (2004). *Electoral competition and democracy in Mexico* (Unpublished doctoral dissertation). University of Chicago.

Cohen, J., & Rogers, J. (1995). *Associations and Democracy*. London: Verso.

Cohen, J. L., & Arato, A. (1992). *Civil Society and Political Theory*. Cambridge, MA: MIT Press.

Cornwall, A. (2004). New Democratic Spaces: The Politics and Dynamics of Institutionalised Participation. *IDS Bulletin, 34*(2), 1–10.

Crook, R. C., & Manor, J. (1998). *Democracy and Decentralization in Southeast Asia and West Africa: Participation, accountability, and performance*. Cambridge, UK: Cambridge University Press.

Crook, R. C., & Sverrisson, A. S. (2001). *Decentralization and poverty-alleviation in developing countries: A comparative analysis, or is West Bengal unique?* Working paper no. 130. Institute of Development Studies, Brighton.

Cunningham, F. (2001). *Theories of Democracy*. New York: Routledge.

Del Río, L. S. (2004). Decentralization and democratic governance in Mexico. In J. S. Tulchin & A. Selee (Eds.), *Decentralization and Democratic Governance in Latin America, Woodrow Wilson Center Report on the Americas no 2* (pp. 167–186). Washington, DC: Woodrow Wilson Center.

Dre'ze, J., & Sen, A. K. (1995). *India: Economic development and social opportunity*. Delhi: Oxford University Press.

Dryzek, J. (1996). *Democracy in Capitalist Times*. Oxford, UK: Oxford University Press.

Evans, P. B. (Ed.). (2002). *Livable Cities? Urban Struggles for Livelihood and Sustainability*. University of California Press.

Faletti, T. (2004). Federalism and decentralization in Argentina: Historical background and new intergovernmental relations. In J. S. Tulchin & A. Selee (Eds.), *Decentralization and Democratic Governance in Latin America, Woodrow Wilson Center Report on the Americas no 2* (pp. 67–100). Washington, DC: Woodrow Wilson Center.

Fox, J. (1996). How does civil society thicken? The political construction of social capital in rural Mexico. *World Development, 24*(6), 1089–1103. doi:10.1016/0305-750X(96)00025-3

Fraser, N. (2000). Rethinking Recognition. *New Left Review, 3*(3), 107-20.

Fung, A., & Wright, E.O. (Eds.). (2003). Deepening Democracy: Institutional Innovation in Empowered Participatory Governance. London: Verso.

Fung, A., & Wright, E. O. (2001). Deepening Democracy: Innovations in Empowered Participatory Governance. *Politics & Society, 29*(1), 5–41. doi:10.1177/0032329201029001002

Geschiere, P., & Boone, C. (2003). *Crisis of Citizenship: New Modes in the Struggles over Belonging and Exclusion in Africa and Elsewhere*. Research concept sketch for SSRC-programme.

Gonzalez-Block, M., Leyva, R., Ata, O. Z., Loewe, R., & Alagón, J. (1989). Health services decentralization in Mexico: Formulation, implementation and results of policy. *Health Policy and Planning*, *4*(4), 301–315. doi:10.1093/heapol/4.4.301

Grindle, M. S. (2007). *Going Local*. Princeton, NJ: Princeton University Press.

Habermas, J. (1995). Reconciliation through the public use of reason: Remarks on John Rawls's political liberalism. *The Journal of Philosophy*, *92*(3), 109–131.

Habermas, J. (1996). *Between Facts and Norms: Contributions to a Discourse Theory of Law and Democracy*. Cambridge, UK: Polity Press. doi:10.7551/mitpress/1564.001.0001

Hailey, L. (1938). *An African Survey: A Study of Problems Arising in Africa South of the Sahara*. London: Oxford University Press.

Harriss, J., Stokke, K., & Törnquist, O. (Eds.). (2004). *Politicising Democracy: the New Local Politics of Democratisation*. New York: Palgrave Macmillan.

Harriss, J., Stokke, K., & Törnquist, O. (Eds.). (2005). *Politicizing democracy: The new local politics of democratization*. New York: Palgrave Macmillan. doi:10.1057/9780230502802

Heller, P., Harilal, K. N., & Chaudhuri, S. (2007). Building Local Democracy: Evaluating the Impact of Decentralization in Kerala, India. *World Development*, *35*(4), 626–648. doi:10.1016/j.worlddev.2006.07.001

Hirschman, A. (1970). *Exit, voice, and loyalty. Responses to the decline in firms, organizations, and states*. Cambridge, MA: Harvard University Press.

Kassibo, B. (2004). *Historical and Political Foundations for Participatory Management and Democratic Decentralization in Mali: A Synthesis of Two Case Studies*. Environmental Governance in Africa Working Papers no16. WRI.

Kellner, D. (1990). *Television and the Crisis of Democracy*. Boulder, CO: Westview Press.

Kellner, D. (1998). Multiple Literacies and Critical Pedagogy in a Multicultural Society. *Educational Theory*, *48*(1), 103–122. doi:10.1111/j.1741-5446.1998.00103.x

Kulipossa, F. P. (2004). Decentralisation and democracy in developing countries: An overview. *Development in Practice*, *14*(6), 768–779. doi:10.1080/0961452042000284003

Larson, A. M. (2003). *Decision-Making under Decentralization: Local Governments in Natural Resource Management. Draft*. Academic Press.

Larson, A. M., & Ribot, J. C. (2007). The poverty of forestry policy: Double standards on an uneven playing field. *Sustainability Science*, *2*(2), 189–204. doi:10.100711625-007-0030-0

Linz, J. J., & Stepan, A. C. (1996). *Problems of democratic transition and consolidation: Southern Europe, South America, and post-communist Europe*. Baltimore, MD: Johns Hopkins University Press.

Lummis, C. (1997). *Radical Democracy*. Ithaca, NY: Cornell University Press.

Mandondo, A., & Mapedza, E. (2003). *Allocation of Governmental Authority and Responsibility in Tiered Governance Systems: The Case of Environment-Related Laws in Zimbabwe*. Environmental Governance in Africa.

Manor, J. (1999). *The Political Economy of Democratic Decentralization*. Washington, DC: World Bank. doi:10.1596/0-8213-4470-6

Manor, J. (2005). User Committees: A potentially damaging second wave of decentralization? In J. C. Ribot & A. M. Larson (Eds.), *Decentralization of Natural Resources: Experiences in Africa, Asia and Latin America*. London: Frank Cass.

Mansuri, G., & Rao, V. (2003). *Evaluating community-driven development: A review of the evidence*. First draft report. Development Research Group, World Bank.

Matthews, J. (1989). *Age of Democracy: The Political Economy of Post-Fordism*. New York: Oxford University Press.

Mawhood, P. (1983). *Local Government in the Third World*. Chi.

Mohan, G., & Stokke, K. (2000). Participatory development and empowerment: The dangers of localism. *Third World Quarterly*, *21*(2), 247–26. doi:10.1080/01436590050004346

Mookherjee, D. (2001). *Combating the crisis in government accountability: a review of recent international experience*. Discussion Paper No. 117. Boston University Institute for Economic Development.

Mosse, D. (2001). "People's Knowledge", Participation and Patronage: Operations and Representations in Rural Development. In Participation: The New Tyranny? London: Zed Book.

Ndegwa, S. (2002). *Decentralization in Africa: A Stocktaking Survey*. Africa Regional Working Paper Series no 40. World Bank.

Nemarundwe, N. (2004). Social characters and organisation for access to woodlands: Institutional implications for devolving responsibilities for resource management to the local level in Chivi District, Zimbabwe. *Society & Natural Resources, 17*(4), 279–291. doi:10.1080/08941920490278629

Nsibambi, A. (Ed.). (1998). *Decentralisation and Civil Society in Uganda: The Quest for Good Governance*. Kampala: Fountain Publishers.

Ntsebeza, L. (2002). *Decentralization and natural resource management in rural South Africa: Problems and prospects*. Paper submitted to the Conference on Decentralization and the Environment, Bellagio, Italy.

Ntsebeza, L. (2005). Democratic Decentralisation and Traditional Authority: Dilemmas of Land Administration in Rural South Africa. In J. C. Ribot & A. Larson (Eds.), *Decentralization of Natural Resources: Experiences in Africa, Asia and Latin America*. London: Frank Cass.

Olivier de Sardian, J.-P. (2004). *Local powers awaiting decentralisation (Niger)*. Paper presented at the Decentralisation in Practice: Power, Livelihoods and Cultural Meaning in West Africa Workshop, Uppsala, Sweden.

Olowu, D., Wunsch, J. S., & Ayee, J. R. A. (2004). *Local Governance in Africa: The Challenges of Democratic Decentralization*. Boulder, CO: Lynne Rennier Publishers.

Oxhorn, P., Tulchin, J., & Selee, A. (Eds.). (2004). Decentralization, Democratic Governance, and Civil Society in Comparative Perspective: Africa, Asia, and Latin America. Baltimore, MD: The Woodrow Wilson Center Press; The Johns Hopkins University Press.

Oyono, P. R., & Efoua, S. (2006). Qui represente qui? Choix organisationnels, identites sociales et formation d'une elite forestiere au Cameroon. *Africa Development. Afrique et Developpement, 31*, 147–182.

Prichett, L., & Woolcock, M. (2004). Solutions When the Solution is the Problem: Arraying the Disarray in Development. *World Development, 32*(2), 191–212. doi:10.1016/j.worlddev.2003.08.009

Ribot, J. (2007). *Dans l'Attente de la Démocratie: La Politique des Choix dans la Décentralisation de la Gestion des Ressources Naturelles*. Washington, DC: World Resources Institute.

Ribot, J. C. (1999). Decentralization, participation and accountability in Sahelian forestry: Legal instruments of political–administrative control. *Africa, 69*(1), 23–65. doi:10.2307/1161076 PMID:19130688

Ribot, J. C. (2002). *African Decentralization: Local Actors, Powers, and Accountability*. Working Paper no 18. UNRISD and IDRC.

Ribot, J. C. (2003). Democratic decentralization of natural resources: Institutional choice and discretionary power transfers in sub-Saharan Africa. *Public Administration and Development, 23*(1), 53–65. doi:10.1002/pad.259

Ribot, J. C. (2004). *Waiting for Democracy: The Politics of Choice in Natural Resource Decentralization*. Washington, DC: WRI.

Ribot, J. C. (2006). *Analyse de la filière charbon de bois au Sénégal: Recommendations. Policy Brief based on the research program Pour une gestion décentralisée et démocratique des ressources forestières au Sénégal, September*. Washington, DC: WRI.

Ribot, J. C., Agrawal, A., & Larson, A. M. (2006). Recentralizing While Decentralizing: How National Governments Reappropriate Forest Resources. World Development, 34(11), 1864-86.

Ribot, J. C. (2008). *Authority Over Forests: Negotiating Democratic Decentralization in Senegal*. Working Paper no 36. WRI.

Ribot, J. C., Chhatre, A., & Lankina, T. (2008). *Institutional choice and recognition in the formation and consolidation of local democracy*. Washington, DC: World Resources.

Ribot, J. C., Chhatre, A., & Lankina, T. (2008). Institutional Choice and Recognition in the Formation and Consolidation of Local Democracy. *Conservation & Society, 6*(1).

Ribot, J. C., & Larson, A. (2004). Democratic decentralization through a natural resource lens: An introduction. *European Journal of Development Research, 16*(1), 1–25. doi:10.1080/09578810410001688707

Ribot, J. C., & Larson, A. M. (Eds.). (2005). *Democratic Decentralisation through a Natural Resourcem Lens*. London: Routledge.

Ribot, J. C., & Oyono, R. (2006). Decentralization in Africa: An overview. *Africa Development. Afrique et Developpement, 31*, 1–19.

Samoff, J. (1990). Decentralization: The politics of interventionism. *Development and Change, 21*(3), 513–530. doi:10.1111/j.1467-7660.1990.tb00387.x

Selee, A. (2004). Exploring the link between decentralization and democratic governance. In J. S. Tulchin & A. Selee (Eds.), *Decentralization and Democratic Governance in Latin America, Woodrow Wilson Center Report on the Americas no 12* (pp. 3–36). Washington, DC: Woodrow Wilson Center.

Sen, A. K. (1999). *Development as Freedom* (1st ed.). New York: Knopf.

Tacconi, L. (2007). Decentralization, forests and livelihoods: Theory and narrative. *Global Environmental Change*, *17*(3-4), 338–348. doi:10.1016/j.gloenvcha.2007.01.002

Tacconi, L., Siagian, Y., & Syam, R. (2006). *On the Theory of Decentralization, Forests and Livelihoods*. Environmental Management and Development Occasional Papers no 9. Asia Pacific School of Economics and Governments, Australian National University.

Tulchin, J. S., & Selee, A. (Eds.). (2004). *Decentralization and Democratic Governance in Latin America*. Washington, DC: Woodrow Wilson International Center for Scholars.

Van Rouveroy, E. R. B., van Nieuwaal, A., & van Dijk, R. (Eds.). (1999). African Chieftaincy in a New Sociopolitical Landscape. Lit Verlag.

Vedeld, T. (2003). Democratic decentralisation and poverty reduction: Exploring the linkages. *Forum for Development Studies*, *2*(2), 159–203. doi:10.1080/08039410.2003.9666243

World Bank. (2000). *World Development Report1999/2000: Entering the 21st century: The changing development landscape*. Oxford, UK: Oxford University Press.

KEY TERMS AND DEFINITIONS

Accountability: Individuals and organizations (public, private, and civil society) have a responsibility for the proper fulfillment of their functions.

Administrative Decentralization: Action to transfer authority and decision-making capacity in public sector organizations with their own legal personality and assets, as well as organic and technical autonomy, as in the case of decentralized organizations.

Deliberative Democracy: It is a normative model that complements the notion of representative democracy to the use by adopting a collective procedure of political decision making with the active participation of all those potentially affected by such decisions, based on the principle of deliberation, which implies the argumentation and public discussion of the various proposals.

Democratic Decentralization: It is a transfer of power from the central government to various authorities that are not subordinated at the hierarchical level.

Natural Resources: they are those goods that can be obtained from nature without mediating the intervention of the hand of man. These have a positive influence on the economy by helping their development and meeting the needs of the population.

Participatory Democracy: Participatory democracy is a system of political organization that gives citizens a greater, more active and more direct capacity for intervention and influence in public decision making.

Urban Governance: It is the articulation between institutions, organizations, communities and people for the management, development, design, and planning of the city.

Related Readings

To continue IGI Global's long-standing tradition of advancing innovation through emerging research, please find below a compiled list of recommended IGI Global book chapters and journal articles in the areas of green cities, environmental management, and sustainable urban development. These related readings will provide additional information and guidance to further enrich your knowledge and assist you with your own research.

Ahuja, K., & Khosla, A. (2019). A Framework to Develop a Zero-Carbon Emission Sustainable Cognitive City. In K. Ahuja & A. Khosla (Eds.), *Driving the Development, Management, and Sustainability of Cognitive Cities* (pp. 1–26). Hershey, PA: IGI Global. doi:10.4018/978-1-5225-8085-0.ch001

Akkucuk, U. (2016). SCOR Model and the Green Supply Chain. In U. Akkucuk (Ed.), *Handbook of Research on Waste Management Techniques for Sustainability* (pp. 108–124). Hershey, PA: IGI Global. doi:10.4018/978-1-4666-9723-2.ch006

Albuquerque, C. M. (2017). Cities Really Smart and Inclusive: Possibilities and Limits for Social Inclusion and Participation. In L. Carvalho (Ed.), *Handbook of Research on Entrepreneurial Development and Innovation Within Smart Cities* (pp. 229–247). Hershey, PA: IGI Global. doi:10.4018/978-1-5225-1978-2.ch011

Angelucci, F., Di Girolamo, C., & Zazzero, E. (2018). New Designing Codes for Urban Infrastructures: A Hypothesis of a Transdisciplinary Approach. In G. Carlone, N. Martinelli, & F. Rotondo (Eds.), *Designing Grid Cities for Optimized Urban Development and Planning* (pp. 209–237). Hershey, PA: IGI Global. doi:10.4018/978-1-5225-3613-0.ch012

Avdimiotis, S., & Tilikidou, I. (2017). Smart Tourism Development: The Case of Halkidiki. In L. Carvalho (Ed.), *Handbook of Research on Entrepreneurial Development and Innovation Within Smart Cities* (pp. 491–513). Hershey, PA: IGI Global. doi:10.4018/978-1-5225-1978-2.ch021

Ayvaz, B., & Görener, A. (2016). Reverse Logistics in the Electronics Waste Industry. In U. Akkucuk (Ed.), *Handbook of Research on Waste Management Techniques for Sustainability* (pp. 155–171). Hershey, PA: IGI Global. doi:10.4018/978-1-4666-9723-2.ch008

Bagnato, V. P. (2018). Technology and Urban Structure: The Grid City Between Technological Innovation and New Public Space System. In G. Carlone, N. Martinelli, & F. Rotondo (Eds.), *Designing Grid Cities for Optimized Urban Development and Planning* (pp. 238–253). Hershey, PA: IGI Global. doi:10.4018/978-1-5225-3613-0.ch013

Bala, I., & Singh, G. (2019). Green Communication for Cognitive Cities. In K. Ahuja & A. Khosla (Eds.), *Driving the Development, Management, and Sustainability of Cognitive Cities* (pp. 87–110). Hershey, PA: IGI Global. doi:10.4018/978-1-5225-8085-0.ch004

Bernardino, S., & Santos, J. F. (2017). Building Smarter Cities through Social Entrepreneurship. In L. Carvalho (Ed.), *Handbook of Research on Entrepreneurial Development and Innovation Within Smart Cities* (pp. 327–362). Hershey, PA: IGI Global. doi:10.4018/978-1-5225-1978-2.ch015

Bernardo, M. D. (2017). Smart City Governance: From E-Government to Smart Governance. In L. Carvalho (Ed.), *Handbook of Research on Entrepreneurial Development and Innovation Within Smart Cities* (pp. 290–326). Hershey, PA: IGI Global. doi:10.4018/978-1-5225-1978-2.ch014

Bhatia, P., & Singh, P. (2019). Technological and Gamified Solutions for Pollution Control in Cognitive Cities. In K. Ahuja & A. Khosla (Eds.), *Driving the Development, Management, and Sustainability of Cognitive Cities* (pp. 234–249). Hershey, PA: IGI Global. doi:10.4018/978-1-5225-8085-0.ch010

Bhatt, R. (2017). Zero Tillage for Mitigating Global Warming Consequences and Improving Livelihoods in South Asia. In W. Ganpat & W. Isaac (Eds.), *Environmental Sustainability and Climate Change Adaptation Strategies* (pp. 126–161). Hershey, PA: IGI Global. doi:10.4018/978-1-5225-1607-1.ch005

Bolívar, M. P. (2018). Governance in Smart Cities: A Comparison of Practitioners' Perceptions and Prior Research. *International Journal of E-Planning Research, 7*(2), 1–19. doi:10.4018/IJEPR.2018040101

Bostanci, S. H., & Albayrak, A. N. (2017). The Role of Eco-Municipalities in Climate Change for a Sustainable Future. In W. Ganpat & W. Isaac (Eds.), *Environmental Sustainability and Climate Change Adaptation Strategies* (pp. 213–231). Hershey, PA: IGI Global. doi:10.4018/978-1-5225-1607-1.ch008

Brkljačić, T., Majetić, F., & Tarabić, B. N. (2017). Smart Environment: Cyber Parks (Connecting Nature and Technology). In L. Carvalho (Ed.), *Handbook of Research on Entrepreneurial Development and Innovation Within Smart Cities* (pp. 150–172). Hershey, PA: IGI Global. doi:10.4018/978-1-5225-1978-2.ch008

Cai, Y. Z., Wu, F., Li, J., Wang, J., & Huang, M. (2019). Application of UAV Technology to Planning Study on Chinese Villages in Guanzhong. In J. Vargas-Hernández & J. Zdunek-Wielgołaska (Eds.), *Bioeconomical Solutions and Investments in Sustainable City Development* (pp. 180–195). Hershey, PA: IGI Global. doi:10.4018/978-1-5225-7958-8.ch008

Calisto, M. D., & Gonçalves, A. (2017). Smart Citizens, Wise Decisions: Sustainability-Driven Tourism Entrepreneurs. In L. Carvalho (Ed.), *Handbook of Research on Entrepreneurial Development and Innovation Within Smart Cities* (pp. 20–43). Hershey, PA: IGI Global. doi:10.4018/978-1-5225-1978-2.ch002

Capelo, C. (2017). Exploring the Dynamics of an Energy Service Venture. In L. Carvalho (Ed.), *Handbook of Research on Entrepreneurial Development and Innovation Within Smart Cities* (pp. 269–289). Hershey, PA: IGI Global. doi:10.4018/978-1-5225-1978-2.ch013

Caridi, G. (2018). Calabria 1783: The Orthogonal Grid as a Physical and Ideological Device of Reconstruction. In G. Carlone, N. Martinelli, & F. Rotondo (Eds.), *Designing Grid Cities for Optimized Urban Development and Planning* (pp. 176–187). Hershey, PA: IGI Global. doi:10.4018/978-1-5225-3613-0.ch010

Carlone, G. (2018). Cities and Extension Plans in the Kingdom of the Two Sicilies: Borgo Murattiano of Bari (1812-1859). In G. Carlone, N. Martinelli, & F. Rotondo (Eds.), *Designing Grid Cities for Optimized Urban Development and Planning* (pp. 1–18). Hershey, PA: IGI Global. doi:10.4018/978-1-5225-3613-0.ch001

Carvalho, L. C. (2017). Entrepreneurial Ecosystems: Lisbon as a Smart Start-Up City. In L. Carvalho (Ed.), *Handbook of Research on Entrepreneurial Development and Innovation Within Smart Cities* (pp. 1–19). Hershey, PA: IGI Global. doi:10.4018/978-1-5225-1978-2.ch001

Castagnolo, V. (2018). Analyzing, Classifying, Safeguarding: Drawing for the Borgo Murattiano Neighbourhood of Bari. In G. Carlone, N. Martinelli, & F. Rotondo (Eds.), *Designing Grid Cities for Optimized Urban Development and Planning* (pp. 93–108). Hershey, PA: IGI Global. doi:10.4018/978-1-5225-3613-0.ch006

Castilla-Polo, F., Gallardo-Vázquez, D., Sánchez-Hernández, M. I., & Ruiz-Rodríguez, M. D. (2017). Cooperatives as Responsible and Innovative Entrepreneurial Ecosystems in Smart Territories: The Olive Oil Industry in the South of Spain. In L. Carvalho (Ed.), *Handbook of Research on Entrepreneurial Development and Innovation Within Smart Cities* (pp. 459–490). Hershey, PA: IGI Global. doi:10.4018/978-1-5225-1978-2.ch020

Charalabidis, Y., & Theocharopoulou, C. (2019). A Participative Method for Prioritizing Smart City Interventions in Medium-Sized Municipalities. *International Journal of Public Administration in the Digital Age*, *6*(1), 41–63. doi:10.4018/IJPADA.2019010103

Chatsiwa, J., Mujere, N., & Maiyana, A. B. (2016). Municipal Solid Waste Management. In U. Akkucuk (Ed.), *Handbook of Research on Waste Management Techniques for Sustainability* (pp. 19–43). Hershey, PA: IGI Global. doi:10.4018/978-1-4666-9723-2.ch002

Chawla, R., Singhal, P., & Garg, A. K. (2019). Impact of Dust for Solar PV in Indian Scenario: Experimental Analysis. In K. Ahuja & A. Khosla (Eds.), *Driving the Development, Management, and Sustainability of Cognitive Cities* (pp. 111–138). Hershey, PA: IGI Global. doi:10.4018/978-1-5225-8085-0.ch005

Cılız, N., Yıldırım, H., & Temizel, Ş. (2016). Structure Development for Effective Medical Waste and Hazardous Waste Management System. In U. Akkucuk (Ed.), *Handbook of Research on Waste Management Techniques for Sustainability* (pp. 303–327). Hershey, PA: IGI Global. doi:10.4018/978-1-4666-9723-2.ch016

Collignon de Alba, C., Haberleithner, J., & López, M. M. (2017). Creative Industries in the Smart City: Overview of a Liability in Emerging Economies. In L. Carvalho (Ed.), *Handbook of Research on Entrepreneurial Development and Innovation Within Smart Cities* (pp. 107–126). Hershey, PA: IGI Global. doi:10.4018/978-1-5225-1978-2.ch006

Corum, A. (2016). Remanufacturing, an Added Value Product Recovery Strategy. In U. Akkucuk (Ed.), *Handbook of Research on Waste Management Techniques for Sustainability* (pp. 347–367). Hershey, PA: IGI Global. doi:10.4018/978-1-4666-9723-2.ch018

Crosas, C. (2018). Latin American Cities: Modern Grids From 1850s. In G. Carlone, N. Martinelli, & F. Rotondo (Eds.), *Designing Grid Cities for Optimized Urban Development and Planning* (pp. 39–51). Hershey, PA: IGI Global. doi:10.4018/978-1-5225-3613-0.ch003

D'Onofrio, S., Habenstein, A., & Portmann, E. (2019). Ontological Design for Cognitive Cities: The New Principle for Future Urban Management. In K. Ahuja & A. Khosla (Eds.), *Driving the Development, Management, and Sustainability of Cognitive Cities* (pp. 183–211). Hershey, PA: IGI Global. doi:10.4018/978-1-5225-8085-0.ch008

Dalzero, S. (2018). The Time of the Finished World Has Begun: A New Map of the World – National Borders Partially or Fully Fenced-Off. In G. Carlone, N. Martinelli, & F. Rotondo (Eds.), *Designing Grid Cities for Optimized Urban Development and Planning* (pp. 254–275). Hershey, PA: IGI Global. doi:10.4018/978-1-5225-3613-0.ch014

Damurski, L. (2016). Recent Progress in Online Communication Tools for Urban Planning: A Comparative Study of Polish and German Municipalities. *International Journal of E-Planning Research*, *5*(1), 39–54. doi:10.4018/IJEPR.2016010103

Damurski, L. (2016). Smart City, Integrated Planning, and Multilevel Governance: A Conceptual Framework for e-Planning in Europe. *International Journal of E-Planning Research*, *5*(4), 41–53. doi:10.4018/IJEPR.2016100103

Das, K. K., & Sharma, N. K. (2016). Post Disaster Housing Management for Sustainable Urban Development: A Review. *International Journal of Geotechnical Earthquake Engineering*, *7*(1), 1–18. doi:10.4018/IJGEE.2016010101

Das, S., & Nayyar, A. (2019). Innovative Ideas to Manage Urban Traffic Congestion in Cognitive Cities. In K. Ahuja & A. Khosla (Eds.), *Driving the Development, Management, and Sustainability of Cognitive Cities* (pp. 139–162). Hershey, PA: IGI Global. doi:10.4018/978-1-5225-8085-0.ch006

Deakin, M., & Reid, A. (2017). The Embedded Intelligence of Smart Cities: Urban Life, Citizenship, and Community. *International Journal of Public Administration in the Digital Age*, *4*(4), 62–74. doi:10.4018/IJPADA.2017100105

Djukic, A., Stupar, A., & Antonic, B. M. (2018). The Orthogonal Urban Matrix of the Towns in Vojvodina, Northern Serbia: Genesis and Transformation. In G. Carlone, N. Martinelli, & F. Rotondo (Eds.), *Designing Grid Cities for Optimized Urban Development and Planning* (pp. 128–156). Hershey, PA: IGI Global. doi:10.4018/978-1-5225-3613-0.ch008

Dolunay, O. (2016). A Paradigm Shift: Empowering Farmers to Eliminate the Waste in the Form of Fresh Water and Energy through the Implementation of 4R+T. In U. Akkucuk (Ed.), *Handbook of Research on Waste Management Techniques for Sustainability* (pp. 368–379). Hershey, PA: IGI Global. doi:10.4018/978-1-4666-9723-2.ch019

Dowling, C. M., Walsh, S. D., Purcell, S. M., Hynes, W. M., & Rhodes, M. L. (2017). Operationalising Sustainability within Smart Cities: Towards an Online Sustainability Indicator Tool. *International Journal of E-Planning Research, 6*(4), 1–17. doi:10.4018/IJEPR.2017100101

Ekman, U. (2018). Smart City Planning: Complexity. *International Journal of E-Planning Research, 7*(3), 1–21. doi:10.4018/IJEPR.2018070101

Erdogan, S. (2016). The Effect of Working Capital Management on Firm's Profitability: Evidence from Istanbul Stock Exchange. In U. Akkucuk (Ed.), *Handbook of Research on Waste Management Techniques for Sustainability* (pp. 244–261). Hershey, PA: IGI Global. doi:10.4018/978-1-4666-9723-2.ch013

Eudoxie, G., & Roopnarine, R. (2017). Climate Change Adaptation and Disaster Risk Management in the Caribbean. In W. Ganpat & W. Isaac (Eds.), *Environmental Sustainability and Climate Change Adaptation Strategies* (pp. 97–125). Hershey, PA: IGI Global. doi:10.4018/978-1-5225-1607-1.ch004

Fasolino, I. (2018). Rules for a New Town After a Disaster: The Gridded Schemes in the Plans. In G. Carlone, N. Martinelli, & F. Rotondo (Eds.), *Designing Grid Cities for Optimized Urban Development and Planning* (pp. 157–175). Hershey, PA: IGI Global. doi:10.4018/978-1-5225-3613-0.ch009

Fernandes, C. M., & Dias de Sousa, I. (2017). Digital Swarms: Social Interaction and Emergent Phenomena in Personal Communications Networks. In L. Carvalho (Ed.), *Handbook of Research on Entrepreneurial Development and Innovation Within Smart Cities* (pp. 44–59). Hershey, PA: IGI Global. doi:10.4018/978-1-5225-1978-2.ch003

Fernandes, V., Moreira, A., & Daniel, A. I. (2017). A Qualitative Analysis of Social Entrepreneurship Involving Social Innovation and Intervention. In L. Carvalho (Ed.), *Handbook of Research on Entrepreneurial Development and Innovation Within Smart Cities* (pp. 417–438). Hershey, PA: IGI Global. doi:10.4018/978-1-5225-1978-2.ch018

Gabriel, B. F., Valente, R. A., Dias-de-Oliveira, J., Neto, V. F., & Andrade-Campos, A. (2017). Methodologies for Engineering Learning and Teaching (MELT): An Overview of Engineering Education in Europe and a Novel Concept for Young Students. In L. Carvalho (Ed.), *Handbook of Research on Entrepreneurial Development and Innovation Within Smart Cities* (pp. 363–391). Hershey, PA: IGI Global. doi:10.4018/978-1-5225-1978-2.ch016

Garrick, T. A., & Liburd, O. E. (2017). Impact of Climate Change on a Key Agricultural Pest: Thrips. In W. Ganpat & W. Isaac (Eds.), *Environmental Sustainability and Climate Change Adaptation Strategies* (pp. 232–254). Hershey, PA: IGI Global. doi:10.4018/978-1-5225-1607-1.ch009

Gencer, Y. G. (2016). Mystery of Recycling: Glass and Aluminum Examples. In U. Akkucuk (Ed.), *Handbook of Research on Waste Management Techniques for Sustainability* (pp. 172–191). Hershey, PA: IGI Global. doi:10.4018/978-1-4666-9723-2.ch009

Gencer, Y. G., & Akkucuk, U. (2016). Reverse Logistics: Automobile Recalls and Other Conditions. In U. Akkucuk (Ed.), *Handbook of Research on Waste Management Techniques for Sustainability* (pp. 125–154). Hershey, PA: IGI Global. doi:10.4018/978-1-4666-9723-2.ch007

Gonçalves, J. M., Martins, T. G., & Vilhena da Cunha, I. B. (2017). Local Creative Ecosystems as a Strategy for the Development of Low-Density Urban Spaces. In L. Carvalho (Ed.), *Handbook of Research on Entrepreneurial Development and Innovation Within Smart Cities* (pp. 127–149). Hershey, PA: IGI Global. doi:10.4018/978-1-5225-1978-2.ch007

Goundar, S., & Appana, S. (2017). Mainstreaming Development Policies for Climate Change in Fiji: A Policy Gap Analysis and the Role of ICTs. In W. Ganpat & W. Isaac (Eds.), *Environmental Sustainability and Climate Change Adaptation Strategies* (pp. 1–31). Hershey, PA: IGI Global. doi:10.4018/978-1-5225-1607-1.ch001

Grochulska-Salak, M. (2019). Urban Farming in Sustainable City Development. In J. Vargas-Hernández & J. Zdunek-Wielgołaska (Eds.), *Bioeconomical Solutions and Investments in Sustainable City Development* (pp. 43–64). Hershey, PA: IGI Global. doi:10.4018/978-1-5225-7958-8.ch003

Gruszecka, K. (2019). Ecological Centre of Warsaw as a Development Path. In J. Vargas-Hernández & J. Zdunek-Wielgołaska (Eds.), *Bioeconomical Solutions and Investments in Sustainable City Development* (pp. 117–150). Hershey, PA: IGI Global. doi:10.4018/978-1-5225-7958-8.ch006

Hesapci-Sanaktekin, O., & Aslanbay, Y. (2016). The Networked Self: Collectivism Redefined in Civic Engagements through Social Media Causes. In U. Akkucuk (Ed.), *Handbook of Research on Waste Management Techniques for Sustainability* (pp. 262–276). Hershey, PA: IGI Global. doi:10.4018/978-1-4666-9723-2.ch014

Ikeda, M. (2019). Developing a Sustainable Eco-City in Pre-Olympic Tokyo: Potential of New Methods and Their Limits in an Urban Era. In J. Vargas-Hernández & J. Zdunek-Wielgołaska (Eds.), *Bioeconomical Solutions and Investments in Sustainable City Development* (pp. 196–223). Hershey, PA: IGI Global. doi:10.4018/978-1-5225-7958-8.ch009

İşcan, E. (2019). Strategies of Sustainable Bioeconomy in the Industry 4.0 Framework for Inclusive and Social Prosperity. In J. Vargas-Hernández & J. Zdunek-Wielgołaska (Eds.), *Bioeconomical Solutions and Investments in Sustainable City Development* (pp. 21–42). Hershey, PA: IGI Global. doi:10.4018/978-1-5225-7958-8.ch002

J., J., Samui, P., & Dixon, B. (2016). Determination of Rate of Medical Waste Generation Using RVM, MARS and MPMR. In U. Akkucuk (Ed.), *Handbook of Research on Waste Management Techniques for Sustainability* (pp. 1-18). Hershey, PA: IGI Global. doi:10.4018/978-1-4666-9723-2.ch001

Jiménez, R., Rodríguez, P. L., & Fernández, R. R. (2019). Green Spaces of the Metropolitan Area of Guadalajara. In J. Vargas-Hernández & J. Zdunek-Wielgołaska (Eds.), *Bioeconomical Solutions and Investments in Sustainable City Development* (pp. 151–179). Hershey, PA: IGI Global. doi:10.4018/978-1-5225-7958-8.ch007

Kais, S. M. (2017). Climate Change: Vulnerability and Resilience in Commercial Shrimp Aquaculture in Bangladesh. In W. Ganpat & W. Isaac (Eds.), *Environmental Sustainability and Climate Change Adaptation Strategies* (pp. 162–187). Hershey, PA: IGI Global. doi:10.4018/978-1-5225-1607-1.ch006

Khan, B. (2019). Bio-Economy: Visions, Strategies, and Policies. In J. Vargas-Hernández & J. Zdunek-Wielgołaska (Eds.), *Bioeconomical Solutions and Investments in Sustainable City Development* (pp. 1–20). Hershey, PA: IGI Global. doi:10.4018/978-1-5225-7958-8.ch001

Khanna, B. K. (2017). Indian National Strategy for Climate Change Adaptation and Mitigation. In W. Ganpat & W. Isaac (Eds.), *Environmental Sustainability and Climate Change Adaptation Strategies* (pp. 32–63). Hershey, PA: IGI Global. doi:10.4018/978-1-5225-1607-1.ch002

Khanna, B. K. (2017). Vulnerability of the Lakshadweep Coral Islands in India and Strategies for Mitigating Climate Change Impacts. In W. Ganpat & W. Isaac (Eds.), *Environmental Sustainability and Climate Change Adaptation Strategies* (pp. 64–96). Hershey, PA: IGI Global. doi:10.4018/978-1-5225-1607-1.ch003

Kocasoy, G. (2016). Economic Instruments for Sustainable Environmental Management. In U. Akkucuk (Ed.), *Handbook of Research on Waste Management Techniques for Sustainability* (pp. 192–211). Hershey, PA: IGI Global. doi:10.4018/978-1-4666-9723-2.ch010

Lallo, C. H., Smalling, S., Facey, A., & Hughes, M. (2017). The Impact of Climate Change on Small Ruminant Performance in Caribbean Communities. In W. Ganpat & W. Isaac (Eds.), *Environmental Sustainability and Climate Change Adaptation Strategies* (pp. 296–321). Hershey, PA: IGI Global. doi:10.4018/978-1-5225-1607-1.ch011

Li, Z., Wang, Y., & Chen, Q. (2017). Real-Time Monitoring of Intercity Passenger Flows Based on Big Data: A Decision Support Tool for Urban Sustainability. *International Journal of Strategic Decision Sciences, 8*(4), 120–128. doi:10.4018/IJSDS.2017100106

Loi, N. K., Huyen, N. T., Tu, L. H., Tram, V. N., Liem, N. D., Dat, N. L., ... Minh, D. N. (2017). Sustainable Land Use and Watershed Management in Response to Climate Change Impacts: Case Study in Srepok Watershed, Central Highland of Vietnam. In W. Ganpat & W. Isaac (Eds.), *Environmental Sustainability and Climate Change Adaptation Strategies* (pp. 255–295). Hershey, PA: IGI Global. doi:10.4018/978-1-5225-1607-1.ch010

López-Arranz, M. A. (2017). The Role Corporate Social Responsibility Has in the Smart City Project in Spain. In L. Carvalho (Ed.), *Handbook of Research on Entrepreneurial Development and Innovation Within Smart Cities* (pp. 439–458). Hershey, PA: IGI Global. doi:10.4018/978-1-5225-1978-2.ch019

Lucas, M. R., Rego, C., Vieira, C., & Vieira, I. (2017). Proximity and Cooperation for Innovative Regional Development: The Case of the Science and Technology Park of Alentejo. In L. Carvalho (Ed.), *Handbook of Research on Entrepreneurial Development and Innovation Within Smart Cities* (pp. 199–228). Hershey, PA: IGI Global. doi:10.4018/978-1-5225-1978-2.ch010

Magrinho, A., Neves, J., & Silva, J. R. (2017). The Triple Helix Model: Evidence in the Internationalization of the Health Industry. In L. Carvalho (Ed.), *Handbook of Research on Entrepreneurial Development and Innovation Within Smart Cities* (pp. 60–79). Hershey, PA: IGI Global. doi:10.4018/978-1-5225-1978-2.ch004

Maiorano, A. C. (2018). Urban Fronts in Murattiano Neighbourhood of Bari: A Selective Survey of the Built Environment. In G. Carlone, N. Martinelli, & F. Rotondo (Eds.), *Designing Grid Cities for Optimized Urban Development and Planning* (pp. 78–92). Hershey, PA: IGI Global. doi:10.4018/978-1-5225-3613-0.ch005

Martinelli, N., & Mangialardi, G. (2018). Cities With Grid Layout: Ubiquitousness and Flexibility of an Urban Model. In G. Carlone, N. Martinelli, & F. Rotondo (Eds.), *Designing Grid Cities for Optimized Urban Development and Planning* (pp. 188–208). Hershey, PA: IGI Global. doi:10.4018/978-1-5225-3613-0.ch011

Mizutani, S., Liao, K., & Sasaki, T. G. (2019). Forest-River-Ocean Nexus-Based Education for Community Development: Aiming at Resilient Sustainable Society. In J. Vargas-Hernández & J. Zdunek-Wielgołaska (Eds.), *Bioeconomical Solutions and Investments in Sustainable City Development* (pp. 224–248). Hershey, PA: IGI Global. doi:10.4018/978-1-5225-7958-8.ch010

Moreira, A., & Ferreira, M. A. (2017). Strategic Challenges of the Portuguese Molds Industry: A Sectoral Innovation Perspective. In L. Carvalho (Ed.), *Handbook of Research on Entrepreneurial Development and Innovation Within Smart Cities* (pp. 534–560). Hershey, PA: IGI Global. doi:10.4018/978-1-5225-1978-2.ch023

Mujere, N., & Moyce, W. (2017). Climate Change Impacts on Surface Water Quality. In W. Ganpat & W. Isaac (Eds.), *Environmental Sustainability and Climate Change Adaptation Strategies* (pp. 322–340). Hershey, PA: IGI Global. doi:10.4018/978-1-5225-1607-1.ch012

Mundula, L., & Auci, S. (2017). Smartness, City Efficiency, and Entrepreneurship Milieu. In L. Carvalho (Ed.), *Handbook of Research on Entrepreneurial Development and Innovation Within Smart Cities* (pp. 173–198). Hershey, PA: IGI Global. doi:10.4018/978-1-5225-1978-2.ch009

Nath, R. (2019). Parametric Evaluation of Beam Deflection on Piezoelectric Material Using Implicit and Explicit Method Simulations: A Study in Energy Engineering. In J. Vargas-Hernández & J. Zdunek-Wielgołaska (Eds.), *Bioeconomical Solutions and Investments in Sustainable City Development* (pp. 65–87). Hershey, PA: IGI Global. doi:10.4018/978-1-5225-7958-8.ch004

Nayyar, A., Jain, R., Mahapatra, B., & Singh, A. (2019). Cyber Security Challenges for Smart Cities. In K. Ahuja & A. Khosla (Eds.), *Driving the Development, Management, and Sustainability of Cognitive Cities* (pp. 27–54). Hershey, PA: IGI Global. doi:10.4018/978-1-5225-8085-0.ch002

Odabasi, A., & Tiryaki, C. S. (2016). An Empirical Review of Long Term Electricity Demand Forecasts for Turkey. In U. Akkucuk (Ed.), *Handbook of Research on Waste Management Techniques for Sustainability* (pp. 227–243). Hershey, PA: IGI Global. doi:10.4018/978-1-4666-9723-2.ch012

Okay, E. (2016). Towards Smart Cities in Turkey?: Transitioning from Waste to Creative, Clean and Cheap Eco-Energy. In U. Akkucuk (Ed.), *Handbook of Research on Waste Management Techniques for Sustainability* (pp. 277–302). Hershey, PA: IGI Global. doi:10.4018/978-1-4666-9723-2.ch015

Pawlikowska-Piechotka, A., Łukasik, N., Ostrowska-Tryzno, A., & Sawicka, K. (2017). A Smart City Initiative: Urban Greens and Evaluation Method of the Sport and Recreation Potentials (SEM). In L. Carvalho (Ed.), *Handbook of Research on Entrepreneurial Development and Innovation Within Smart Cities* (pp. 561–583). Hershey, PA: IGI Global. doi:10.4018/978-1-5225-1978-2.ch024

Raisinghani, M. S., & Idemudia, E. C. (2016). Green Information Systems for Sustainability. In U. Akkucuk (Ed.), *Handbook of Research on Waste Management Techniques for Sustainability* (pp. 212–226). Hershey, PA: IGI Global. doi:10.4018/978-1-4666-9723-2.ch011

Rathee, D. S., Ahuja, K., & Hailu, T. (2019). Role of Electronics Devices for E-Health in Smart Cities. In K. Ahuja & A. Khosla (Eds.), *Driving the Development, Management, and Sustainability of Cognitive Cities* (pp. 212–233). Hershey, PA: IGI Global. doi:10.4018/978-1-5225-8085-0.ch009

Rotondo, F. (2018). The Grid Cities: Between Tradition and Innovation. In G. Carlone, N. Martinelli, & F. Rotondo (Eds.), *Designing Grid Cities for Optimized Urban Development and Planning* (pp. 109–127). Hershey, PA: IGI Global. doi:10.4018/978-1-5225-3613-0.ch007

Sánchez-Fernández, M. D., & Cardona, J. R. (2017). The Perception of the Effect of Tourism on the Local Community before the Ibiza Smart Island Project. In L. Carvalho (Ed.), *Handbook of Research on Entrepreneurial Development and Innovation Within Smart Cities* (pp. 392–416). Hershey, PA: IGI Global. doi:10.4018/978-1-5225-1978-2.ch017

Santos, B. (2017). Improving Urban Planning Information, Transparency and Participation in Public Administrations. *International Journal of E-Planning Research, 6*(4), 58–75. doi:10.4018/IJEPR.2017100104

Sardà, J. F. (2018). Cerdà/Barcelona/Eixample: 1855-2017 … A Work in Progress. In G. Carlone, N. Martinelli, & F. Rotondo (Eds.), *Designing Grid Cities for Optimized Urban Development and Planning* (pp. 19–38). Hershey, PA: IGI Global. doi:10.4018/978-1-5225-3613-0.ch002

Selvi, M. S. (2016). Physical Distribution Problems of Textile Companies in Turkey. In U. Akkucuk (Ed.), *Handbook of Research on Waste Management Techniques for Sustainability* (pp. 328–346). Hershey, PA: IGI Global. doi:10.4018/978-1-4666-9723-2.ch017

Signorile, N. (2018). Pride and Prejudice: The Murattiano-Modernism. In G. Carlone, N. Martinelli, & F. Rotondo (Eds.), *Designing Grid Cities for Optimized Urban Development and Planning* (pp. 52–77). Hershey, PA: IGI Global. doi:10.4018/978-1-5225-3613-0.ch004

Singh, G., Kapoor, R., & Khosla, A. K. (2019). Intelligent Anomaly Detection Video Surveillance Systems for Smart Cities. In K. Ahuja & A. Khosla (Eds.), *Driving the Development, Management, and Sustainability of Cognitive Cities* (pp. 163–182). Hershey, PA: IGI Global. doi:10.4018/978-1-5225-8085-0.ch007

Singh-Ackbarali, D., & Maharaj, R. (2017). Mini Livestock Ranching: Solution to Reducing the Carbon Footprint and Negative Environmental Impacts of Agriculture. In W. Ganpat & W. Isaac (Eds.), *Environmental Sustainability and Climate Change Adaptation Strategies* (pp. 188–212). Hershey, PA: IGI Global. doi:10.4018/978-1-5225-1607-1.ch007

Sood, N., Saini, I., Awasthi, T., Saini, M. K., Bhoriwal, P., & Kaur, T. (2019). Fog Removal Algorithms for Real-Time Video Footage in Smart Cities for Safe Driving. In K. Ahuja & A. Khosla (Eds.), *Driving the Development, Management, and Sustainability of Cognitive Cities* (pp. 55–86). Hershey, PA: IGI Global. doi:10.4018/978-1-5225-8085-0.ch003

Stone, R. J. (2017). Modelling the Frequency of Tropical Cyclones in the Lower Caribbean Region. In W. Ganpat & W. Isaac (Eds.), *Environmental Sustainability and Climate Change Adaptation Strategies* (pp. 341–349). Hershey, PA: IGI Global. doi:10.4018/978-1-5225-1607-1.ch013

Stratigea, A., Leka, A., & Panagiotopoulou, M. (2017). In Search of Indicators for Assessing Smart and Sustainable Cities and Communities' Performance. *International Journal of E-Planning Research, 6*(1), 43–73. doi:10.4018/IJEPR.2017010103

Touq, A. B., & Ijeh, A. (2018). Information Security and Ecosystems in Smart Cities: The Case of Dubai. *International Journal of Information Systems and Social Change, 9*(2), 28–43. doi:10.4018/IJISSC.2018040103

Üç, M., & Elitaş, C. (2016). Life Cycle Costing for Sustainability. In U. Akkucuk (Ed.), *Handbook of Research on Waste Management Techniques for Sustainability* (pp. 96–107). Hershey, PA: IGI Global. doi:10.4018/978-1-4666-9723-2.ch005

Ulker-Demirel, E., & Demirel, E. (2016). Green Marketing and Stakeholder Perceptions. In U. Akkucuk (Ed.), *Handbook of Research on Waste Management Techniques for Sustainability* (pp. 75–95). Hershey, PA: IGI Global. doi:10.4018/978-1-4666-9723-2.ch004

Vargas-Hernández, J. G., López, J. J., & Zdunek-Wielgołaska, J. A. (2019). Entrepreneurial and Institutional Analysis of Biodiesel Companies in Mexico. In J. Vargas-Hernández & J. Zdunek-Wielgołaska (Eds.), *Bioeconomical Solutions and Investments in Sustainable City Development* (pp. 89–115). Hershey, PA: IGI Global. doi:10.4018/978-1-5225-7958-8.ch005

Vázquez, D. G., & Gil, M. T. (2017). Sustainability in Smart Cities: The Case of Vitoria-Gasteiz (Spain) – A Commitment to a New Urban Paradigm. In L. Carvalho (Ed.), *Handbook of Research on Entrepreneurial Development and Innovation Within Smart Cities* (pp. 248–268). Hershey, PA: IGI Global. doi:10.4018/978-1-5225-1978-2.ch012

Velozo, R. A., & Montanha, G. K. (2017). Evaluation of a Mobile Software Development Company. In L. Carvalho (Ed.), *Handbook of Research on Entrepreneurial Development and Innovation Within Smart Cities* (pp. 514–533). Hershey, PA: IGI Global. doi:10.4018/978-1-5225-1978-2.ch022

About the Contributors

Sebastiano Patti has a PhD in Public Economics. He studied Economics at the School of Economic Science - University of Manchester (UK), where he got his MSc in Economics. He is teaching Finance at the University of Catania (I). He thought Cultural Tourism and Environmental Economics within University's courses and Academic Masters' Degrees. His research interests have led him to deepen tourism economic policies, with respect to the new tourism market trends, local development and the transition from tourism district policies to local production systems, the application of efficiency analysis tools in local public utilities and in industrial organization. He worked in the European research teams like researcher as well as research's manager within Tourism European Research Framework. Sebastiano is author of several scientific publications on tourism and environment. He is an Alumni of the Manchester University (UK).

Giampiero Trizzino is a lawyer and environmental consultant. Ph.D. expert in environmental law. President of the Legislative Commission "Environment" of the Sicilian Parliament of the XVI Legislature.

* * *

Antonino Messina He is an economic consultant, for 15 years he was President of Isea, a private research institute engaged in sustainable local territorial development. After graduating in Political Science in 1993 and completing his studies in regional economics, he worked as a consultant for various local public institutions, publishing research on sustainable tourism development and the environment.

Yuxin Huang is a master's degree student majoring in environmental engineering, Southwest Jiaotong University, Chengdu, China. She received her bachelor degree in environmental engineering at China University of Petroleum. Her research interests include environmental systems analysis, environmental risk and perception.

Huynh Viet Khai has received Ph.D. and researched as postdoctoral fellow in Kyushu University, Japan. Currently, he is a head of Department of Environmental and Resource Economics at College of Economics, Can Tho University, Vietnam. His research involves productive efficiency of agricultural production, water pollution, the demand of agricultural insurance, the solution of poverty reduction, organic production, biodiversity conservation, as well as economic valuation of non-market goods such as externality of agriculture and forest, waste management, environmental policy, the applications of contingent valuation and choice modeling methods.

Xinyue Liu is an engineer of Sichuan Environment & Engineering AppraisaI Cente. Her research interests include environmental impact assessment, environmental management and policy.

Giovanni Patriarca studied Political Sciences at the University of Camerino (Italy) and Philosophy at the Pontifical Lateran University (Vatican City State). He earned the Diploma in Islamic Studies at the Pontifical Institute for Arabic and Islamic Studies-P.I.S.A.I.. In 2008, he completed his Ph.D. in History of Economic Thought at the Pontifical University Regina Apostolorum in Rome, where he is lecturer. He was DAAD-Stipendiat at the Humboldt University in Berlin.

Kamani Sylva has spent 19 years teaching, researching and consulting in engineering management, sustainable development and related areas. She received her Bachelor's in Civil Engineering from the University of Peradeniya, Sri Lanka (1992). Then, went on to earn three Master's, one from AIT, Bangkok in Geotechnical Engineering (1995), an MBA from the Post Graduate Institute (PIM) of the University of Sri Jayawardenapura, Sri Lanka (2013) and a Master's in Sustainable Energy Engineering (SEE) offered from KTH and University of Gävle, Sweden and the Open University of Sri Lanka. She first taught at the University of Ruhuna, Faculty of Engineering (from 2000) in engineering management and sustainable development and has been teaching the same areas at the University of Peradeniya from 2014. As an accredited professional, she contributes to the GBCSL, (the Green Building Council of Sri Lanka) and to supervise undergraduate and postgraduate projects in the area of sustainable development.

Diana M. Valentini studied Philosophy (B.A. and M.A.) at the Franciscan University of Steubenville (Ohio, USA). She earned the Diploma in Integral Ecology at the Pontifical Gregorian University. She is Ph.D. student in Philosophy at the Pontifical University Regina Apostolorum in Rome (Italy) and holds a teaching position at the Marymount International in Rome.

José Vargas-Hernández has a Ph. D. in Public Administration and a Ph.D. in Organizational Economics. He has undertaken studies in Organisational Behaviour and has a Master of Business Administration, published four books and more than 200 papers in international journals and reviews (some translated to English, French, German, Portuguese, Farsi, Chinese, etc.) and more than 300 essays in national journals and reviews. He has obtained several international Awards and recognition.

Meng Yang is a master's degree student majoring in environmental engineering, Southwest Jiaotong University, Chengdu, China. She received her bachelor degree in environmental engineering at China Western Normal University. Her research interests include environmental systems analysis, environmental risk and perception.

Durmuş Çağrı Yıldırım was born in 1981. After graduating from Kocaeli University, Department of Economics in 2005, he started to study for a master's degree in Economics. In 2007, he received a master's degree in Economic Policy. In 2011, he received his PhD in Economics. While working as a doctoral student, she worked at the University of Almeria-Spain for a while. He worked as a research assistant at Kocaeli University between 2006-2012. She worked as an Assistant Professor at the Department of Banking and Finance at Recep Tayyip Erdoğan University between 2013-2015. Since April 2015, he has been working as an Associate Professor at Namık Kemal University. His current research interests are current and emerging issues such as sustainable development, energy, health, employment and Islamic economics.

Seda Yıldırım was born in 1983. She graduated from Kocaeli University, Department of Business Administration in 2006. She completed her postgraduate and doctoral education at the Department of Business Administration, Kocaeli University, Production Management and Marketing. She worked as a research assistant in Kocaeli University between 2010-2013 and as an assistant professor in Recep Tayyip Erdoğan University between 2013-2016. Since 2017, she has been working as an Associate Professor at Namık Kemal University. Her current research interests include sustainable development, green marketing, sustainable consumption, Islamic economics, marketing culture, and values. She works as an editorial board member and arbitrator in various journals. She also studies as a member of the organizing committee of various international congresses (İCOMEP, ENSCON, İSEFE).

Rui Zhao graduated from University of Hull, and held a PhD Degree in Sustainable Design and Technology. After graduation, he joined Southwest Jiaotong University, China to pursue his academic career. Currently, he holds a full time professorship in the Faculty of Geosciences and Environmental Engineering, and acts as the Head of the Department of Environmental Science and Engineering. His research interest in the field of sustainable engineering has focused on mathematical modelling and computational approaches, which is capable of providing mitigation strategies to limit environmental burden, as well as promote sustainable development. A significant proportion of his research is interdisciplinary study, whilst using system theory to identify and analyze environmental issues in order for better decision making in the area of low carbon production and consumption, green supply chain management. He has published 42 open literature publications as the first or corresponding author, including 37 SCI/SSCI indexed journal papers. In addition, he was appointed as an associate editor for journal "Energy & Environment" to handle with manuscripts relevant to energy policy and low-carbon development, and served as the reviewers for several high quality international journals, such as Journal of Cleaner Production, Journal of Environmental Management, etc.

Yuyu Zhou is a master's degree student majoring in environmental engineering, Southwest Jiaotong University, Chengdu, China. She received her bachelor degree in environmental engineering at China Western Normal University. Her research interests include environmental systems analysis, environmental risk and perception.

Index

O

P

R

S

T

U

V

W

www.ingramcontent.com/pod-product-compliance
Lightning Source LLC
LaVergne TN
LVHW061534290926
849162LV00004B/789